INDOCTRINATED

How The Conventional Education
System Perpetuates Conformity,
Mediocrity & Indistinguishability

RON MALHOTRA

KMD
BOOKS

First published in Australia in 2022
by KMD Books
Waikiki, WA 6169

A catalogue record for this
work is available from the
National Library of Australia

NATIONAL
LIBRARY
OF AUSTRALIA

National Library of Australia Catalogue-in-Publication data:

Indoctinated/Ron Malhotra

ISBN:
978-0-6454663-3-1
(Hardback)

ISBN:
978-0-6454663-4-8
(Paperback)

ISBN:
978-0-6454663-5-5
(Ebook)

THE THREE STEPS TO INDOCTRINATION

1. Repeat a message over and over again.
2. Create a strong feeling in the recipient.
3. Have the message come from people in authority.

CONTENTS

INTRODUCTION

I am known as an entrepreneur, but in my spirit, I am a teacher. Most of my waking hours are spent advising, training, consulting, speaking, writing or mentoring others, all of which are essentially forms of teaching. I feel privileged to have spent the best part of the last two decades encouraging, empowering and serving others. What I have learned over the years is that people who approach me or one of my companies are all seeking something and all value the same thing: knowledge. Whether they seek a better life, better performance, a better career or a better financial future, they know that the way to move towards their goals is through the accumulation of knowledge. But over the last two decades of interacting with thousands of educated professionals and executives, I also started noticing some predictable trends and patterns in their thinking and behaviours, and I sum up my observations here: many times, the more professional, technical or academic education these professionals had undergone, the more they tended to pre-empt situations and jump to conclusions, rather than think things through logically.

Is it possible, perhaps, that being 'educated' is not what we have always thought it is?

Is it possible that the knowledge transfer taking place through our educational institutions is inadequate? Could it be lagging through antiquated, one-dimensional teaching methods? Or is it that educational institutions have become not so much antiquated as superficial?

Is academic and professional success necessarily the be-all and end-all, an assurance of a fulfilling life and future, or should we be changing the way we think about education and what it really brings?

Historically speaking, academic and professional success has always been an assurance and a representation of a strong financial future and measure of success. It has been the promise of a confident life full of diverse and exciting experiences and something we placed high value on as the ultimate goal of what we aspire to be. I am willing to challenge that narrative right here and now as I pose the following question: as you look around your society and community, how many educated people do you see living an exciting life and lifestyle?

Or is it possible, perhaps, that an overly developed intellect can actually become a *barrier* to courage? Can it become a *barrier* to intuition? Can it become an impediment to our creative instincts and our outbox thinking faculty? Has our desire for education taken us away from our innate common sense?

All this thinking leads me to ask that, in the truest sense of the word, are people *really* educated? Or, as we advance as a culture and society, is it possible that there has been a shift in not only our thinking, but in the very definition of learning as being that of less educated and more *indoctrinated*?

This book is unlike any other book I have written; however, in these pages I will discuss several hypotheses surrounding education in an attempt to answer the question: are people with highly developed IQs *truly* educated? Are they being taught *how* to think? Or simply *what* to think?

CHAPTER ONE

Is Education Enough?

In this book, I aim to discuss modern-day indoctrination and how, in the modern-day world, it finds its roots in conventional education. But before we get to this, we need to explore the idea: is education enough?

The strength of indoctrination lies in its subtlety and repetition. It is said that repetition is the mother of all skills; yet repetition can also be misused – and when misused, repetition becomes dangerous. Indoctrination is like the gas carbon monoxide: it is colourless, odourless, imperceptible ... deadly. Indoctrination is the process of teaching a person to accept beliefs or ideologies without questioning or examining them critically. These beliefs may be religious, political, social, economic or even medical, as with the case of the COVID-19 pandemic, which we will touch on later. But before we delve into the theory of education as a system of indoctrination, let's first take a look at the role of education and how it has been important to humans, historically speaking.

After the industrial revolution and in the advent of the information age, more and more people can today be considered literate, knowledgeable and more educated than at any other time in history.

However, this does not necessarily mean they are self-aware, objective and wise.

Education should be, and has always been, considered to be the first point of call for people to imbibe societal values; it has been a point of anchor, a measure by which humans have been able to define themselves as civilised creatures higher in the food chain, as opposed to being morally and socially inept and incapable of advancement like its inferiors. For if we were unable to define ourselves as anything higher, if we were no better or aspired to be no better than anything in the animal kingdom, what would happen to us as a morally and socially inept society? We need education, and education advances us as a species, which is something that has always driven man forward since the beginning of time.

Conventional education has therefore always had its advantages; yet to the keen observer or the critical thinker it is now becoming more and more evident that conventional education also has many shortcomings, which to this day remains unacknowledged in the mainstream. Thus, there is a distinct difference between good education and bad education, which is where we now find the insidious nature of indoctrination.

THE DIFFERENCE BETWEEN EDUCATION AND LEARNING

The difference between education and learning is described perfectly in the following maxim by Japanese entrepreneur Joi Ito:

'Education is what people do to you. Learning is what you do for yourself.'

pediaa.com states that education is the process of receiving or giving systematic instruction (especially at a school), while learning is acquiring knowledge *and* skills through experience and study.[1] Mads Holmen pointed out that while education is passive, extrinsic and based on curriculum, learning is active, intrinsic and based on curiosity.[2]

On a personal note, I think one of the problems with education is that it's not being tied to the conception of its original and intended meaning. The word 'education' stems from the Latin word *ēducātiō* meaning 'a breeding, a bringing up, a rearing'. *Ēducātiō* is derived from *ēducō* meaning 'I educate, I train, I lead forth, I take out, I raise up, I erect'.

Through the etymological definition of education we may deduce that education was once upon a time seen to be a holistic process for developing the whole of an individual. Education was meant to develop an individual into a well-rounded being for themselves, their family, their community, their organisation and for their economy. Today however, we interpret education as a means of breeding or rearing, bringing up an individual to become a functional member in their workplace. Formal education focuses on moulding an individual for an active, successful career. Be the best doctor. Be the best pharmacist. Be the best engineer. Be the best pilot. Be the best accountant. Be the best lawyer. Be the best nurse.

Yet what we seem to have forgotten in the process is that learning should be a part of education. A school should be a place where people are taught to employ the totality of their intelligence. Sadly, this is not so. Conventional education primarily tests one's potential for being competent in a chosen field by how well they can *reproduce* the information received. It does not matter whether the information is understood; it does not matter whether one can apply the information; all that matters is that it is memorised and reproduced accurately.

Don't get me wrong, there is nothing bad in teaching an individual to aspire to career success. However, holistic education endeavours to groom other aspects of the individual. The classroom should be a place where a person can obtain vital skills needed for making a living, as well as creating a fulfilling life. The classroom is a microcosm of the world. Since learning comes through experience, educational systems should be structured to create these experiences for the individual to learn and grow. Unfortunately, concentrating solely on reading and passing exams makes it challenging for a student to experience anything beyond the classroom setting.

Education tells you: 'Focus on your curriculum only. If your friends distract you, cut them off. You can *only* learn from your allocated curriculum; other sources of learning will only distract you from your goals. You need to make good grades. This is the only way you can secure a bright future for yourself. Think about the multinational companies that will employ you. Think about how you will make everyone proud by passing the expectations of the conventional education system. This is what you will be judged on.'

Learning tells you: 'Focus on life. Learning comes from understanding and wisdom. Learning is about seeing the connection between science and spirituality, physics and metaphysics, medicine and health, mathematics and finance, education and awareness, intellect and emotional intelligence. Holistic education emphasises the development of not only your intellectual, but also your emotional, social, cultural, commercial, spiritual and financial capacities. This is the only way we can thrive as individuals. This is the only way our society – the world – can have a progressive today and a prosperous tomorrow.'

Through academic and professional education alone, is the individual truly free? Are they free to think outside the box? Are they free to express themselves without the fear of repercussions for speaking their mind or questioning authority? Are they free to create? Or lead? Or are they predominantly trained to comply, obey, follow instructions, systems and policies?

Often, conventional education (academic and professional) forces the individual into a prison of validations. All the person wants to do is make good grades to make their family proud, the school proud, and finally arrive at their employer, leaving them impressed. Little wonder Joi Ito said education is what people *do* to you. The individual has to soak up all of the information being transmitted by the teacher, even if it means using methods they are not comfortable with. Currently, society tends to view all education as academic; however, academic ability is not indicative of intelligence in other areas, many of which are critical to human development.

Does conventional education recognise the uniqueness of individuals and diversities of humankind? Does it acknowledge that humans don't come in standardised packages? Does it understand that each individual has a unique blend of values, strengths, passions, tendencies and zone of genius? The present rate of change in both technology and how we work means that there needs to be a significant paradigm shift in how we educate people. Human intelligence is therefore multidimensional.

One of the major shortcomings of the conventional education system is that it assumes that simply being exposed to information results in the application of information. Institutions do not acknowledge the fact that until a student deeply and regularly engages with information through self-reflection and critical analysis, the information will not convert into a belief or habit. Information alone does not cause deep transformation – insights do – and insights require the ability to question.

In the academic world, students are expected to approach what they are taught the same way. It is, in effect, a contest. The survival of the IQ driven. Those with the ability to memorise and analyse (and achieve good grades as a result), sit at the top of the food chain. Yet formal education appears to unintentionally suffocate creativity, and it does this in two ways: first, the curriculum is not flexible enough to accommodate creative processes; second, schooling takes up a big chunk of a person's time – from lessons to classwork to assignments. This is why some successful entrepreneurs like Mark Zuckerberg, for example, dropped out of college. When I typed the question 'Why did Zuckerberg drop out of university?' into Quora, the answer by Samrat Kundal captured my own thoughts. Samrat's answer could be summarised in one word: focus. Zuckerberg wanted to focus on developing Facebook[3] and this made perfect sense because the educational culture that teaches one to focus *only* on making great grades seldom allows one the room to focus on any other productive ventures.

According to Samrat, another likely reason why Zuckerberg dropped out was because he found his career with Facebook, and since college was all about learning to get a career, he saw no point in continuing with it.[4] This reason is not so far-fetched because we have already established that society has reduced education to the shallow concept of grooming one for a job, even though it should be more.

At present, many do not opt for the academic system in order to gain wisdom or high-value skills, problem-solving capabilities or to develop a performance mindset. Many take up academic education solely with the hope of memorising the chosen curriculum, making the highest grades with least resistance, to please parents and society and to get themselves (job) ready. The narrow definition of education that implies that anyone with academic capability will naturally have leadership capabilities, is fraught with risk and danger. It is not uncommon to see highly indoctrinated people with self-centred agendas being misplaced at the top of the judicial system, the medical system, the political system, the corporate system and the financial system.

For the likes of Mark Zuckerberg and Bill Gates (who dropped out of school and went on to be billionaires), this makes people question what role education and schooling play when it comes to business and financial success. And these questions may now be arising because the fraction of academically competent and professionally skilled people who are able to create innovative or disruptive ideas, or achieve financial abundance or make a significant difference on a large scale is relatively very low.

The development of society birthed education, and now education should be the training ground to teach people the values the society needs to thrive. Émile Durkheim would have disagreed with me because he argued that education could only be reformed if society was reformed – something that was argued more than a century ago. He rejected the idea of education being the force for societal transformation and healing. In Durkheim's words, education, 'Is only the image and reflection of society. It imitates and reproduces the latter … it does not create it.'[5]

If we examine this more carefully, school and university education has been reduced to a contest ground where people gather to display their intellectual prowess. Everyone is concerned about getting the best grades and then getting a good job later. Society has used education as a yardstick for measuring success – and indirectly, status. For this reason, many just want to go to school without actually imbibing the underlying values of education and how it contributes to intentional living.

It is not uncommon to come across educated individuals in the social system, the financial system, the political system, the corporate system and even in the medical system who are ethically corrupt and morally bankrupt. Yet these systems are precisely where many educated people aspire and strive to be. How many instances of unethical or immoral conduct have you been privy to? How many individuals at the top of their game understand the importance of trust, reputation and influence?

Many educated professionals may have achieved a reasonable level of accomplishments in their chosen careers, but outside of this, what is their track record?

Think in terms of health and vitality, meaningful relationships and influence, contribution and impact, financial management and wealth creation, inspiration and joy, innovation and creativity, agility and resilience, communication and connection. Reflect on how many professionals with graduate degrees you know who have the perspectives, life and lifestyle that you aspire for. Reflect on how many have holistically successful lives. This is not meant to be a dig on professionals. This is about reflecting on how we, as a society, define education in very narrow terms. Can an individual who knows how to do their job well – but does not know much about who they are, what they want and how to live authentically – be in alignment with their highest values or be considered truly educated?

I realise that this may offend many people who assume that through academic and professional education alone, they have acquired enough wisdom to be considered intelligent. But to me the hallmark of a truly educated person is one who can hold a contradictory idea and not discard it prematurely just because it may cause cognitive dissonance.

Another college dropout, Bill Gates, confessed that he has 'one big regret'. In a tweet he made on 15 May 2017, Gates wrote: 'Intelligence takes many different forms. It is not one-dimensional. And it's not as important as I used to think. I also have one big regret: When I left school, I knew little about the world's worst inequities. Took me decades to learn.'[6]

Gates' regret points to the fact that he expected the school to offer him more. *Intelligence takes many different forms. It is not one-dimensional.* But this is not what the school system teaches. We are taught to have a single, unilateral approach to learning and intelligence, affixed by standardised processes of reading, memorisation, examination performance and graduating. Somehow, we are blinded to the various inequities and inequalities plaguing humankind – what our schools ought to be teaching. Thus, we have a world filled with many educated people with little to no knowledge of philosophical or rational thought as the very essence of the earth loosens at its hems.

We can see this play out with the outbreak of COVID-19 and the controversy it has brought with it. People made rampant postulations upon postulations as to the aetiology and genuineness of the disease. Did it break out in a wet market in Wuhan? Was it created in a lab? Was it a ploy to disguise RFID chips as vaccines?

At the same time, many people accepted the government mandates and the media narrative without questioning or critically investigating the claims. When the vaccines were finally developed and released, those on the side of the government latched onto the Messianic medicines without raising questions about their safety. As long as the government, through the World Health Organization (WHO), marked the vaccines as safe, everyone assumed it was okay to receive the shots. Meanwhile, advocates of the vaccines – a group that included educated people – eagerly bought into the government narrative hook, line and sinker, without ever questioning or attempting to investigate the truth for themselves. The result? Division.

Although the proponents of conspiracy theories on the one hand – and advocates of the vaccines on the other – both antagonised each other, both groups are essentially the same. Both groups are composed of *indoctrinated* individuals who demonstrate an inability to remain objective and differentiate emotions from observations. In other words, they are made up of people who cannot think for themselves even if they were educated in the conventional sense. These recent events have indeed highlighted a major flaw in our educational system; a flaw which I aim to explore in the following chapters.

CHAPTER TWO

Learned or Just Literate?

P eople pass through conventional education systems and brand themselves as 'learned'. Is it possible perhaps that many of those whom society deems to be learned are not learned, merely literate? Literacy is the ability to read, write, speak and listen, especially in a particular language. Conventional education as we know offers literacy and a conventional road map to a given career path. As for the students, their graduation day is the ultimate celebration of the acquisition of literacy.

Interestingly, in recent times, the meaning of literacy has been broadened to include how people use literacy to function in society and think creatively.[1] I believe these attempts to redefine literacy are geared towards restoring the original intent of education. We have removed the aspect of *creative thinking* from the educational process and focused chiefly on learning to read and write in order to upgrade our market value and thereby increase our chances of landing 'well-paid jobs'.

If we can agree that being truly learned goes far beyond literacy itself, modern education may need to embrace new and different forms of learning in order to develop well-rounded and functional members of society. The total development of the individual may not only include basic literacy, academia and professional skills development, but also digital development; health development including basic nutrition; financial development including basic money management; relationship development and self-awareness; cultural awareness and spiritual development.

READING AND WRITING

Dictionaries define literacy as the ability to read and write. The *Oxford Reference* added that literacy could include basic arithmetic competence.

The definition of literacy has persisted for decades, with reading and writing as its most basic forms. Such skills are indeed necessary for the purposes of the most basic communications, and without which we would not survive. In the nineteenth century, parents considered basic schooling a necessity. The ability to read and write was the promise of a better life, preparing their children to compete favourably in society. Parents in many Third World and under-developed economies who didn't have such privileges felt that they owed this form of literacy to their children. Thus, these children learned how to read and write, but the focus was not so much on comprehension as it was the act of reading – they weren't taught to evaluate what they read or develop any analytical thought; all that mattered was that they could read the words on the page.

Like parents, colonial powers also wanted the indigenous peoples to read and write, albeit for a sinister reason. They created, in the minds of the indigenous, the desire to read and write. They would later capitalise on this desire as a weapon to control and erase the cultures of their subjects by making them read Western classics in place of indigenous narratives, usurping their culture and identity and replacing it with Western ideologies, which they quickly adopted.

Colonial powers took over lands in Africa and Asia, justifying their conquests with the *lie* that they had civilised 'barbaric' or 'savage' nations.[2] Yet their actions ultimately caused the indigenous people to lose trust and reverence for their cultures. Colonialism made colonised countries forfeit (vital parts of) their cultures and embrace the new ways offered by colonial powers. Countries like Lebanon, Tunisia, Syria, Algeria, Morocco aligned their educational policies according to French interests, while Egypt, Palestine, Jordan and Iraq reflected British policies. To impose their policies and culture on the natives, a colonial power first had to install their language.[3] This is where the definition of reading and writing as a form of literacy becomes more complex.

When we say someone is literate, do we mean they know how to read and write in English or French, or Portuguese? Is a person only literate when they know how to read and write in the language of their colonial masters? Can a person be literate in their indigenous language? Can the concepts of science, art, economics and other subjects be taught effectively in indigenous languages? Or is this definition of literacy as reading and writing presented by the West subtly and inescapably tied to colonialism?

In the days of colonialism, literacy was a double-edged sword: it promoted civilisation, yet it erased cultures. Using literacy, colonial powers sowed and sold three beliefs to their colonies. One: the indigenous cultures of their subjects were unhealthy. Two: the exotic colonial language was superior to that of the indigenous. Three: this exotic language was the *only* medium through which the indigenous people could embrace civilisation by learning the science, art and cultures of other nations.

Satish Aikant's article, *From Colonialism to Indigenism: The Loss and Recovery of Language and Literature,* points out that the British used the English language as a weapon of cultural invasion in India. Warren

Hastings, the governor-general of India from 1774 to 1785, endorsed a policy known as Orientalism, which was defined as an approach 'to assimilate the rulers into the culture of the ruled'. Indian forms of knowledge were converted into European objects and were used as instruments for colonial rule. English literary text functioned as the centre of authority that stood in for the Englishman after removing himself from colonial activities. According to Aikant, Orientalism became the tool for 'a clever indoctrination' of the Indian mind that presented a false reality and blinded the Indian to the schemes of colonialism.[4]

Aikant's submission was not peculiar to India but other countries colonised by the West also. Part of the false reality a colonial master presented to his subject was branding the subject illiterate because of their inability to read, write and express ideas in the colonial master's language. This created a hunger, a desire in the subject to do away with his indigenous language or relegate it to second place.

The subject began to consume what he read in the curriculum created by the colonial master. He allowed the colonial master to write and rewrite his stories and histories because he believed his master was superior and knew better. He read these books written about him and others without processing, without evaluating, the information for truth. He just wanted to be and become like the master. And he passed on this hunger to future generations. It got to a time when the indigenous peoples no longer required the colonial master to brand them illiterates; they branded themselves thus, and thus their social status became defined on the grounds of literacy. Being literate, therefore, translated to being considered civilised.

But civilisation, in its most basic form, is the interbreeding of cultures. If colonialism was a portal to civilisation, as the colonialists said, then what colonialism should have done was present to the colonies the technological and socioeconomic advances of the West while respecting and retaining the cultural soul of the colonies.

NUMERICAL LITERACY (NUMERACY)

There are many definitions of numerical literacy – or numeracy – and these definitions converge and intersect at the point between a person's ability to understand and use mathematics. Of all the definitions of numeracy I have come across, the one by Ball State University stands out for me. The university defines numeracy as 'the ability to analyse and understand logical arguments and statistical information commonly encountered in life, as well as the ability to express this understanding orally and in writing'.[5]

I find this definition holistic as it captures what *true* literacy should be all about. It doesn't define numeracy only in terms of understanding numbers and simple arithmetic required for transacting at the mall or calculating net profit from book sales. It is not shallow and basic like reading and writing. It is similar to the definition by Diana Coben, who states that 'to be numerate means to be competent, confident and comfortable with one's judgments on *whether* to use mathematics in a particular situation and, if so, *what* mathematics to use, *how* to do it, what *degree of accuracy* is appropriate, and what the answer means in relation to the context'.[6]

One who is *truly* literate should employ all their faculties to analyse, understand and solve problems. Maybe if students were taught to view mathematics from this premise, many wouldn't hate mathematics. A lot of students consider mathematics to be abstract, difficult and a necessary evil – a hurdle they must cross to prove their intellectual worth. Yet this notion further exposes the inadequacies of conventional education. Students do not learn because they feel subjects like mathematics would benefit them in the larger society; they simply learn to pass their exams. On the other hand, teachers fail to employ other teaching methods to make learning easy, fun and more memorable for the students.

A survey was carried out in the 2020 edition of the MathWorks

Math Modeling (M3) Challenge. This is a contest for high school juniors and seniors in the United States and sixth form students in England and Wales. These students get to work as a team to solve real-world problems similar to those faced by professional mathematicians. The challenge awards a total of $100,000 shared among different winning categories.[7] According to *Forbes*, the survey provided insights on inspiring kids to pursue higher levels in mathematics.[8]

The survey revealed that the primary reason why most students entered the M3 Challenge was that they expected it to be a fun experience. The next reason was that they received encouragement from a teacher. It was for this reason that 20% of women and a large percentage of men entered the challenge. When respondents were asked who or what influenced their interest in mathematics, two answers stood out. (1) the students being naturally good at maths. (2) a teacher. When it came to the importance of teachers, Christiana Guan pointed out that many students hate mathematics because it seemed boring and difficult to grasp. She added that if teachers could make it fun and understandable, then maths class would be enjoyable. In the survey, students also considered good teachers worthy sources of inspiration for students interested in pursuing STEM (science, technology, engineering and maths) education or careers.[9]

Christiana Guan's statement is proof that learning will never be complete if students do not enjoy the learning process. This is one of the core problems with conventional education: it is too far removed from life itself. It is incorrectly interpreted as another world, a scholarly space governed by rules not applicable to the general world. It isn't surprising then that many commencement speeches begin with the phrase, 'As you go out into the world ...'. The phrase itself connotes that students, throughout their years in school, dwell in a world excluded and separate from the real world. And when these students step into the 'real' world they inevitably struggle – because they lack the life skills they so desperately needed to learn within the structure and confines of conventional education. All they have are skills for becoming the best neurosurgeon, architect, civil engineer, biochemist, physicist, microbiologist or mathematician.

One sure way to get students to develop numeracy is by fusing numbers and literature. This fusion can even pass as a simple and literal definition of numerical literacy. Fusing numbers and literature entails relating mathematics to everyday life. Tell stories by engaging in mathematical equations at the earliest levels; make mathematics relatable in such a way that students see practical ways to apply what they've been taught, and in this way, learning will become fun. I propose that teachers should think up out-of-the-box ideas to relate their subjects to the four main quotients of human intelligence: intelligent quotient, emotional quotient, social quotient and adversity quotient. As they prepare their lessons and teaching materials, teachers should ask themselves: *How will this lesson benefit the students emotionally and socially? Can this lesson provide them with ideas required to withstand trauma?*

Other teachers and researchers have similarly proposed this idea. David Tuten, an upper school math teacher, notes that in 2002, two researchers, Maguire and O'Donoghue, put forth a broader definition of numeracy, describing it as a continuous process that takes the individual 'from the formative, through the mathematical, culminating in the integrative'. The formative deals with basic mathematical skills, computation and manipulative abilities. This progresses to the mathematical – using math in everyday life. Here, the numerate person appreciates and understands mathematical information presented in graphs, tables or percentages and applies it in different areas of their life. The mathematical then glides into the integrative, where mathematics is integrated into life's personal, emotional, social and cultural aspects.[10]

Such theories towards improving an individual's numeracy have not gone untested; on the contrary, data exists which shows that blending mathematics with literature and applying mathematics pragmatically to other aspects of life and introducing and presenting it in this way has boosted overall numeracy and love for mathematics as a whole. Karen Patten, a former civil rights attorney turned stay-at-home mom, describes how she encouraged her two sons to fall in love with mathematics through homeschooling.[11] When Karen's boys (who were seven and ten years old at the time) questioned why they should learn mathematics and memorise mathematical facts, Karen could see they were questioning its very essence and purpose; she understood their struggle and inability to understand how they would ever use or apply mathematics in the real world – a question many, if not most, students face. So, Karen decided to use literature to bring the subject to life.

Patten states that when a child can make a mathematical connection in a story, the maths becomes (more) interesting. Stories help children understand that mathematics is all around them, and they begin to connect mathematical equations to events in the outside world, applying their knowledge in real-time. According to Karen, textbooks today contain mathematical stories that are 'fun and silly' that engage students in real-life situations in real-time. Examples of such books for elementary kids include Emily Gravett's *The Rabbit Problem*, Julie Ellis' *What's Your Angle, Pythagoras?*, Kathryn Lasky's *The Librarian Who Measured The Earth*, Cindy Neuschwander's *Sir Cumference and the Fraction Faire*, Pam Calvert's *The Multiplying Menace Divides*, Lilac Mohr's *Math & Magic in Wonderland*, and Theoni Pappas' *The Adventures of Penrose The Mathematical Cat*, among others. Books for middle school include Daniel Kenney and Emily Boever's *The Math Inspectors*, Hans Magnus Enzensberger's *The Number Devil* and Wendy Lichtman's *Do The Math: Secrets, Lies, and Algebra*.[12]

Some of the greatest mathematicians in the world gleaned insight into formulas by finding the connections between numbers and other aspects of life, like nature. For example, in 1202, Leonardo Fibonacci wrote the *Liber abaci*, a work containing notations and other Hindu-Arabic arithmetic applied to practical problems like profit margin, bartering, money changing, weight conversion and interest.[13] In his work, Fibonacci used the mathematical problem of rabbits to briefly introduce what French mathematician Edouard Lucas later called the Fibonacci sequence. Fibonacci and other mathematicians in his time did not make anything out of the sequence and it was almost forgotten until nineteenth-century mathematicians studied the sequence's mathematical properties.[14] How did they do this? They discovered the sequence in nature – 'in the spirals of sunflower heads, in pinecones, in the genealogy of the male bee, in the logarithmic spiral in snail shells, in the arrangement of leaf buds on a stem and animal horns'.[15] Parmanand Singh, a contemporary Indian mathematician, would later point to the fact that the sequence also appears in Sanskrit poetic tradition[16] in his 1985 thesis titled, *The So-called Fibonacci Numbers in Ancient and Medieval India*.

This brief history of the Fibonacci sequence supports the idea that numbers and arithmetic are connected to every aspect of life – and a veritable way to improve a person's numeracy is to show them this connection. Yet the question remains: why was this knowledge lost, and why did it take Parmanand Singh to find out this is a question we should ponder on?

DIGITAL LITERACY

Master Bagh is a village in Uttar Pradesh, India. There was a time when farming was the only source of livelihood for the villagers, and those who weren't farmers migrated to bigger cities to search for jobs. But Nasim Ali rewrote this narrative.

Nasim came from a family of farmers, but he was fascinated by technology. He got a desktop PC and operated a government-accredited service centre in his village. With this move, the people of Master Bagh could explore other opportunities. Residents, like Akhilesh Kumar Yadav (who had to go to the tehsil [township] office for any documentation and stand in long queues with no guarantee of getting the work done in one visit), could now easily get all the information they needed from Nasim's centre.

Nasim began offering computer training classes certified under the National Digital Literacy Mission, increased the number of computers in the centre; while he was at it, he employed tutors and other staff and used the PC to build an ecommerce venture to connect rural artisans to consumers across India. In this simple story we see how Nasim transformed his village of Master Bagh[17], and we can see the value of digital literacy and its direct impact on once-rural lives.

Compared to other forms of literacy we have discussed, digital literacy is a relatively new concept. The term arose with the advent of computers and the development of information technology. Early users transformed the phrase 'digital literacy' to mean one's ability to read and understand information in multimedia formats. However, Paul Gilster popularised the phrase when he gave a new meaning to digital literacy in his 1997 book of the same name. For Gilster, digital literacy went beyond one's ability to use digital sources effectively; it entailed developing a special kind of mindset or thinking. 'Digital literacy is about mastering ideas, not keystrokes,' he wrote.[18]

We see a common feature across all forms of literacy from Gilster's definition; literacy entails applying information and not just collecting and storing information. It is not limited to knowing how to read and write, solve arithmetic or use a computer; it is about using what you know to birth ideas and solutions. This is why the American Library Association defined digital literacy as 'the ability to use information and communication technologies to find, evaluate, create and communicate information, requiring both cognitive and technical skills.'[19]

In the twenty-first century, where everything has gone digital, the need for digital literacy cannot be ignored. A person without the most basic understanding of digital literacy is handicapped in the modern world. Imagine the stress the villagers of Master Bagh must have endured to get their documentation done because none owned or could even use a computer? Luckily, they found a savior in Nasim. If the rate of digital literacy increases in Master Bagh, residents will no longer need Nasim. They will be capable of accessing all the information they need and be competent at carrying out documentation with their own computers or phones and internet connectivity with ease. But as stated earlier, this is only one aspect of digital literacy. And this is the only aspect most schools focus on.

Every school today (except for the ones in poor communities) has integrated digital literacy into their curriculum. These days, teachers present learning materials with PowerPoint presentations, while students use the internet to research information on topics; textbooks for the indigenous people come in electronic formats, and tuition fees are paid online; tests and exams are all conducted online and communication between teachers and parents frequently happens via email. Our rate of dependency upon the technological universe is ever increasing, and the COVID-19 pandemic of 2020 further highlighted our reliance on technology and the need for digital literacy in schools. As we isolated through the pandemic we saw the educational system seemingly change overnight; there was no longer a need for students to assemble in a classroom to learn; lectures were moved online and conducted through platforms like Zoom.

Yet, despite our giant strides towards digital literacy, there is still a deficiency. According to the World Literacy Foundation, a digitally literate student shouldn't only need to find and consume digital content; they now need to incorporate into their awareness the new challenges of cyberbullying and acquire the skills needed to stop bullies and seek to protect themselves and others from harassment. A student now needs to understand internet safety by creating strong passwords, privacy settings and complying with social media community standards.[20] This means that one who is digitally literate must also employ emotional and social intelligence. This does not apply to digital literacy alone but also to other forms of literacy.

HEALTH LITERACY

In a 2004 article titled, *Stories of Women, Words, and Well-Being: The Effect of Literacy on Women's Health,*[21] Estela Kennen, Linda Martin and Terry Davis all told stories relating literacy to health. One story was about a woman who had complained of dizziness, headaches and tiredness. It had been going on for weeks and she had not seen a doctor, but when she finally did, she went to him with a clear plastic bag containing eight bottles of medicines.

The resident doctor pulled out the bottles from the bag one by one and asked the woman, 'How many of these pills do you take?' 'One a day,' the woman replied. The doctor pulled out another bottle. 'This?' She looked at the bottle. 'One a day.' The doctor then held out all the bottles and asked the same question. After she was done, the doctor put three of the bottles together and said to her patient, 'You see these three? They contain the same medicine. They are for your blood pressure. This little bottle has forty-milligram pills, the other two have ten milligrams, but they are all the same.' The woman was silent as she digested this information. The doctor continued. 'See these two other bottles? They are for your cholesterol. You were taking too many medicines, and this is the likely reason for your dizziness.'

Kennen, Martin and Davis didn't state whether this story was fictional or not, but whichever it is, the story mirrors the reality of many people. Health illiteracy is a serious problem. Kennen, Martin and Davis continued to share more real stories in the article of women who couldn't read and comprehend their doctors' health directions and advice. But this article was slightly faulty: it tied health literacy to one's ability to read and write; the inference here being that once a person can read and write, they are most likely to be health literate. But this is largely untrue, because the ability to read and write does not directly translate to health literacy – it only boosts a person's *capacity* for health literacy. Avanthika Panchapakesan, in an article for the World Literacy Foundation, states that health literacy is 'measured as the degree to which an individual has the skills to comprehend and make informed choices based on the information given regarding their health'.[22] (This definition may include protecting our physical and emotional health through physical and emotional literacy.) Physical literacy is the motivation, confidence, physical competence and understanding a person has to engage in a lifelong commitment to physical activity,[23] while Steiner defines emotional literacy as 'intelligence with a heart: [making] our emotions work for us and others around us instead of against us'.[24] Later in this book, we will see the critical roles emotional literacy and intelligence play in restoring education's purpose.

A person may know how to read and write yet be unable to comprehend and make informed choices regarding their health. A lot of learned people read the warning on a cigarette pack yet continue to be chain-smokers. They are informed about the merits of a balanced diet but their diet is anything but balanced. They are aware of the negative effects of stress but do not have the skills to manage life's stressors. Is it possible perhaps that merely having intellectual exposure to a concept doesn't necessarily translate into an understanding of that concept?

These educated, learned people clearly know the information – they've read it, absorbed it, shown proof of their understanding of the dangers – yet they still decide to make the wrong choice towards their health. Why? Is there any difference between an individual who is informed and knowledgeable about their choices yet makes the wrong choice, versus the one who doesn't know and makes the wrong choice? As far as health goals are concerned, these two categories of people would still arrive at the same devastating outcome and negatively impact their health.

As I come to understand it, health literacy isn't limited to making informed choices concerning one's physical and mental health; it also involves showing concern for the health of others. It entails asking yourself, *How would my actions impact the health of another?* In Bonus Chapter Two we read about the 2017 study carried out in Karachi, Pakistan. In this study, the two forms of health illiteracy manifested itself in the 'uneducated' participants. The uneducated couldn't make informed decisions about their health with regards to HIV/AIDS. They believed the infection could be transmitted via the water, and because of this belief, they would risk engaging in unprotected sex because HIV/AIDS is waterborne. Second, they discriminated against infected people – and were completely unconcerned about how their discrimination affected those infected's (mental) health.

Ironically, there are educated folks out there who are also unconcerned about the health and wellbeing of others. These days, there seems to be unending news about domestic violence, sexual abuse, emotional abuse, cyberbullying and other vices that leave devastating and long-lasting consequences on the victims. So while we label these societal ills as threats to overall health, so too should we see poor health choices as a threat and clear demonstration of *gross* health illiteracy.

FINANCIAL LITERACY

Ruga Ignatova, Bulgarian businesswoman. The woman who called herself the 'Cryptoqueen'. She was popular between 2014 and 2017 when she floated a fake cryptocurrency called OneCoin. She scammed the world, proclaiming that her OneCoin would rival Bitcoin and would 'kill' it – and the world believed her. From Bulgaria to the United Kingdom, Finland to Sweden, Norway to Latvia, Hungary to Italy, Croatia to India, Germany to Thailand, Belize to Nigeria, nearly $4 billion was 'invested' in Ruga's scam[25] between 2014 and 2017. Then, one day in 2017, Ignatova disappeared without a trace – and the world has never seen or heard from her since.

Ruga, it can be said, is a proven fox, ingenious in her craftiness. But the one question that crossed my mind when I read about her was, *How could one woman deceive the whole world so easily?* The answer is simple: financial illiteracy.

Investopedia states that financial literacy is the foundation of one's relationship with money and should be seen as a lifetime journey of learning to understand and effectively use financial skills such as personal financial management, budgeting and investing.[26] To add to this definition, financial literacy also involves *gathering financial knowledge* to make sound and informed financial decisions.

The emphasis here, I think, is on gathering financial knowledge, yet this is where many people, both educated and uneducated, inevitably fail. If we use this as our yardstick, we could safely say that many people out there are indeed financially illiterate. The financially literate say 'knowledge first, money later' while the financially illiterate reverse this to say: 'money now, knowledge later'. This was indeed the case with Ruga's victims.

Ignatova first floated her coin in 2014, and by 2016 it had started to gain in popularity. By 2016, Bitcoin and blockchain technology was already six to seven years old, meaning that there was no scarcity of information about the cryptocurrency industry. Yet people invested their life savings without carrying out the proper research, trusting only hearsay and popular opinion. If they had investigated, they would have discovered that OneCoin, aka 'Bitcoin Killer', was not built on any blockchain. Every cryptocurrency is built on a technology known as blockchain. Blockchain technology is the platform on which all cryptocurrency transactions are carried out. Therefore, a cryptocurrency can't exist if it is not on a blockchain. (It's like a web designer saying, 'I created a website but it is not on the internet.' Senseless and hard to imagine, right?) This is basic knowledge, yet thousands of people were ignorant. And Ruga milked their ignorance.

In Bonus Chapter Two I mention that Uganda had fallen victim to over eighteen Ponzi and pyramid schemes and lost over $1 billion to these scams. I attribute this to financial illiteracy – because educated folks, even the Ugandan president, couldn't tell fake investments from genuine ones.[27]

Like with health education, one may think there is *always* a direct correlation between reading/writing and financial literacy. But this is not the case. Some wealthy people are 'illiterates' by societal standards, where even brilliant folks, seemingly successful in other areas of life, fall victim to financial scams because they simply do not understand money and business management.

In a LinkedIn article, *The Illiterate Billionaire*,[28] Laurel Bloomfield shares the story of a billionaire she met on a plane as she journeyed from the east to the west coast. The man told Laurel that he couldn't read till he was twenty-one and had only learned to read after making his first million. Coming from an underprivileged background, he'd picked certain vices. When he finally went to school, he was considered undisciplined and unteachable, so the school sent him home. His mother tried to find a school that would accept him, but her efforts yielded no fruits. He went on to start a trucking company at sixteen and by the time he was twenty-one, the company had blossomed into a national freight company. Despite being illiterate, this man understood the importance of education, and he paid for a reading education program to teach him to read. At the time he was recounting his story to Laurel, his reading proficiency was not top-notch and he confided to Laurel that he still needed to hire lawyers to read complicated stuff for him.

Despite not knowing how to read, this man was able to build a billion-dollar business. His inability to read or write didn't affect his business acumen, and this goes for other wealthy people who similarly have little to no education. John D Rockefeller only attended high school until he was sixteen before learning bookkeeping and going on to seek employment. At sixteen, Henry Ford left his family farm and relocated to Detroit to become an apprentice in a machine shop. Amancio Ortega left school at fourteen and began running errands for local shops. Richard Branson struggled with dyslexia and dropped out of school at sixteen. Joe Lewis left school at fifteen and started in his father's catering business.[29]

There is more to financial education than knowing how to read and write. It is a soup of logic, emotions, instincts, awareness and timing. But how many academics and professionals recognise this?

MEDIA LITERACY

The evening of 4 August 2011 was like every other evening in Tottenham, North London, until two gunshots exploded through the peaceful town. The disorder and chaos that followed would continue on for days afterwards and would never be forgotten in UK's history.

That evening around 6:15pm, twenty-nine-year-old Mark Duggan, a black British civilian, was shot and killed by the police. Specialist firearm officers and officers in charge of gun crimes had been carrying out an operation in African and Caribbean neighbourhoods in the UK[30] and Duggan happened to be nearby in a minicab. The officers forced the vehicle to pull over, and when the vehicle came to a stop, Duggan got out. The officer open fired on him – twice – first in the arm, then in the chest. The officer claimed he'd seen a gun in Duggan's possession, and feeling his life was being threatened, had acted in self-defence.[31]

The shooting of Mark Duggan led to a peaceful protest in Tottenham. However, the London riots (known as the 2011 England riots) were not caused by the shooting but by something that *ought* to be less dangerous than a gun: the media.

The peaceful protest escalated when newspapers reported the incident without fact-checking. They had falsely reported that Duggan was a drug dealer, a thug determined to avenge his cousin's death. They reported he'd been armed when the police stopped him. All of this was proven to be false, biased and misleading reporting based on wrong information gleaned from the police. Duggan's family flatly denied the claims, stating that he'd had no prior criminal record.[32] The report infuriated the protesters; and what began as a peaceful protest soon became a full-blown riot across all of England. For six days straight, England saw looting and arson across its cities and towns – from London metropolitan to the West Midlands, Greater Manchester to Merseyside, Leicester to Cambridge. Five people died and more than three thousand people were arrested, and all this happened because the media was not meticulous or accurate in their reporting of an incident they knew to be as sensitive and racially charged as a white cop killing a black man.

Media literacy, as we can see, is as important as any other form of literacy because it is a vital component of any society. It can be used to save and to malign, to influence and dictate trends and the way information is given and received. Because of the inherent power it holds, media literacy cannot be ignored, and being media literate means one can evaluate the credibility of both the information received and the information source, be able to correctly distinguish between appeals to emotion and logic and use critical thinking capabilities to analyse the truth through the breakdown of information ascertained through various sources.[33]

While this attempts to define what it means to be a media literate person it is not foolproof because it assumes an enormous duty of literacy to fall *only* on the information consumer, whilst excusing the producer. This is probably due to the *erroneous* idea and assumption that the producer is already media literate. Yet as we know, media houses, both in print and broadcast media, are just as guilty of media illiteracy as the elderly man in a remote village who obtains his news from a bench outside his house on a portable transistor radio; one cannot assume the media houses have greater credibility as the producer, since in processing the information, the producer could prove to be just as ill-informed or illiterate as the man on the bench.

Suppose a journalist or a media house cannot accurately evaluate the credibility of information, separate emotions from logic or analyse *and* tell the truth? In this case, we can (and should) unapologetically question and challenge the media literacy of such journalists or media houses, irrespective of their backgrounds, education or years of experience. Unfortunately, journalism these days leans toward sensationalism rather than truth and appropriateness which instantly shakes their level of credibility; as such, one cannot therefore begin to raise the bar on media literacy in consumers without first improving the literacy of producers and raising literacy standards across the board. Every media house wants to dish out eye-catching headlines, and this is the nature of the business – but is there enough truth in the story beyond the headlines?

Words are powerful and can easily stir up any human emotion from fear to happiness to apathy. If we were to make a checklist of qualities belonging to a media-literate person, the first quality would undoubtedly be this: the ability to show resistance toward actors who deliberately want to use the media to manipulate and malign, plus the ability to tell the *truth* at all times, at all costs.

There is no shortage of information in our current world, and information can be accessed easily in the information age we are living in; however, we must also come to understand that what comes with greater access is higher levels of corruption in the information we receive. In fact, it's all around us. This brings to mind a story I stumbled upon on a platform called NEDA – National Eating Disorders Association. On NEDA's blog, Gisselli Rodriguez shared her story[34] of how she believed she was programmed to define feminine beauty as 'small waist, long legs, voluminous hair, big breasts'. As a child, Rodriguez was, like most young girls, exposed to 'Barbie, Victoria's Secret advertisements and novellas', all various avenues of marketing aimed at her target audience, all of which further cemented these beliefs when it came to concept of the self and self-image. Rodriguez internalised and imbibed the messages of mainstream media and over time became dissatisfied with her body when the images perpetuated in the media did not match up in real life.

Rodriguez documented the experience, stating that as a result of constant and relentless marketing aimed at young girls in her age bracket, she developed an unhealthy relationship with herself and her body before she even reached high school. Like most teenagers her age, Rodriguez prayed and hoped to be magically gifted with these 'ideal' features of a beautiful woman, yet the image staring back at her in the mirror of a girl who was short with frizzy medium-coarse hair and small breasts, came to be features she learned to despise. The slow and gradual descent into self-hatred was only exacerbated by the women she envied on TV – women with large breasts and the girls at school who emulated them. Dissatisfied with her self-image, Rodriguez found herself watching reality shows that promoted plastic surgery, and she started to believe that altering one's body was the norm.

Soon she was hounding her mother for breast implants when she turned eighteen, despite the fact that her family faced financial struggles. At one point, Rodriguez poignantly wrote that, 'Somehow, my unhappiness with my body felt more important than my family's fundamental survival needs. That is how powerful the media is to the vulnerable consumer.'

Had Rodriguez learned about media literacy in college she would have been able to remove herself from social stereotypes by understanding how power structures maintain such stereotypes by over-representing an image as a way of reinforcing social values. Through this understanding, and through greater media literacy, Rodriguez could have critically and effectively analysed the intent of the content creator's messages and saved her from much heartache and dissociation/disconnection from the self.

We cannot take anything away from the inspiration and education this story provides; however, we cannot help but notice the fact that Rodriguez's salvation from low self-esteem came through a unidirectional flow of media literacy. She was able to know that the media gave a false representation of beauty. Still, many other young girls like her were constantly fed these lies by the media and lacked the opportunity to be taught the truth. So, what's their fate? Leaving the consumer to search for the truth themselves is only a temporary solution to a persistent problem; the permanent solution lies in dealing with the problem at the root – cutting the flow of misinformation, misrepresentations and falsehoods off at its source.

More often than not, most media houses do not tell the truth, and even if they do, we cannot and should not trust their objectivity. Most consumers know this too, so they seek to source and provide information by and for themselves, and social media gives them the perfect platform for this. Unfortunately, however, the advent of social media has created a new system of validation, a new measure of self-worth: engagements. As a result, there is an incessant desire to be heard and seen at all costs, which has led to the corruption of social media by the same virus of inauthenticity backed by sensationalism. In order to garner followers, likes, comments and reposts, many deliberately put up *false* versions of their stories, the stories of others and/or the stories of society until we cannot even rely on social media to correct the mistakes of traditional media. We are essentially trapped in a loop of misinformation, feeding off itself and perpetuating the lie.

This is not to say that there are no social and traditional media platforms that are not bound to truth and appropriateness; but they are merely edible crops trying to survive in a field of weeds. False narratives thrive in the media because many people are drawn to feel-good lies rather than inconvenient truths. One example that comes to mind was the story of three MIT scholars who conducted a study and discovered that false news spreads faster than true stories on Twitter. (And in case one many think that this spread was technologically manipulated through the use of bots – the study proved that humans, not bots, were responsible for the spread.) In fact, what the scholars discovered was that false news has a 70% greater chance of being retweeted than true stories. False stories can reach 1,500 people six times faster than the time it takes for true stories to reach the same number of people. And in terms of Twitter's cascades or unbroken retweet chains, false news gets a cascade depth of ten – which is about twenty times faster than true stories,[35] the results of which show that our journey towards media literacy is still significantly far off.

CULTURAL LITERACY

Cultural literacy may be quite unpopular but its influence on a person's literacy level in society cannot be overlooked. Cultural literacy was a concept first developed in 1983 by Eric Donald Hirsch Jr, an American educator, academic literary critic and professor emeritus of education and humanities at the University of Virginia. Although not the central idea of his work, Hirsch subtly presents cultural literacy as a solution to linguistic and/or media illiteracy. He accurately notes that people cannot learn to read and write without first possessing 'culturally assumed knowledge' that influences people's communication.[36] The same goes for the media. In his work titled *Cultural Literacy*, Hirsch writes: 'A newspaper writer must also assume a "common reader" but for a much bigger part of the culture, perhaps for the literary culture as a whole … Acculturation into a national literate culture might be defined as learning what a newspaper's "common reader" in a literate culture could be expected to know. This would include knowledge of certain values (whether or not one accepted them), and knowledge of such things as (for example) the First Amendment, Grant and Lee, and DNA.'[37]

It is this marriage of culture and literacy/education which is integral in erasing indoctrination and reinforcing the true purposes of education. But before this can happen, we will need to broaden Hirsch's concept to include knowing and recognising the dynamism of culture. Tethering linguistic and media literacy *rigidly* to cultural knowledge is risky if people do not first understand that culture isn't static. Individuals who don't understand this dynamism would likely not bring in their cognitive faculties to analyse the information as long as it aligns with their cultural beliefs. Let's use food, a common cultural marker of many people, as an example. An American would probably not understand why an African eats bushmeat. Let's say he reads an opinion piece or watches a documentary on Africans eating bushmeat … we can assume his first reaction might probably be, 'Gross! This is unhealthy both to the human body and the environment.' The African, on the other hand, would not understand why he shouldn't eat bushmeat. If he reads the newspaper or watches a documentary of Americans protecting wild animals, the African would be like, 'What are these people doing? Why let go of the food?' The

African mind needs to receive a reorientation to understand that not all cultural practices are healthy for him and the environment.

Therefore, linking linguistic and media literacy to cultural literacy is too simplistic. I just used an example of food, which is not particularly harmful. But what about other cultural practices that harm the inhabitants and upholders of the culture, or even those outside the culture? What about cultures buried knee-deep in patriarchy, cultures that practice female genital mutilation, cultures that uphold child marriages and many other cultures that devastate the human mind and body?

Western Sydney University noted that culture is often described as an iceberg. We easily see and experience many aspects of culture above the water: arts, behaviours, clothing, celebrations, food and language. The ones below the water are the aspects those within the culture know and understand without thinking or questioning. These include values, customs, roles, status, rules, thought patterns, beliefs, perceptions and traditions. They are influenced by history and assumptions and have a real impact on people's lives.[38] The rigidity in cultural beliefs lies in these cultural aspects below the water. These are the aspects cultural literacy should focus on. Suppose cultural literacy could be the cure for the various pathologies that plague our society. If this were indeed the case, then the owners of these cultures should learn to understand that values, perceptions, traditions, beliefs and other invisible aspects of culture are not set in stone. They can be questioned. They can be modified. And they can be erased.

*

Imagine a person who embodies all these types of literacy in their truest form. Such a person could easily pass off as the perfect human because they would be able to use their cognitive faculties to process information in all facets of life and arrive at sound judgments. If every student left school equipped with greater forms of literacy they would perform as more well-rounded, functional members of society. Unfortunately, this does not happen because it is an ugly truth and one that we have to come to terms with – and that is that conventional educational systems fall short.

CHAPTER THREE
How Conventional Educational Systems Fall Short

'Academic and professional education makes
you more prone to groupthink than independent
thinking.'
– Ron Malhotra

'It's easier to land a man on Mars than it is to
change the school system.'
– Elon Musk

A 2019 article by the World Bank begins with a shocking opening paragraph that reads: 'THE NAME OF THE DOG IS PUPPY.' On the surface this seems like a simple sentence; but did you know that three out of four third-grade students cannot understand it in Kenya, Tanzania and Uganda? In rural India, nearly three-quarters of third graders cannot solve a two-digit subtraction problem such as forty-six minus seventeen – and by grade five more than half still cannot do so.[1]

Isn't it ironic that students cannot understand simple statements or solve basic arithmetic in a structure built for learning? Why does a pupil wake up in the morning, have breakfast, pick up their backpack and head to school, if not to learn? To what purpose is the stress?

One may suggest that it is the kids' fault, that they are dull and too slow to learn. This could be true, and if this be the case, then it only further exposes the school's flaws. It is like a hospital saying it cannot cure more than half of its patients because they respond too slowly to treatment. 75% of patients cannot respond to treatment slowly – if patients are not getting well, it may mean that the medical practitioners are not getting it right. Similarly, if 75% of pupils perform poorly, then academically speaking, could it be possible that the narrow scope of education that academia promotes is simply not stimulating enough to students?

Conventional educational systems are inadequate in many ways; yet to wrestle with these inadequacies, we must first accurately diagnose the problem if we are to find the solution. Conventional education has several defects, and I pinpoint five of them here. They are (1) intellectual classism, (2) wrong beliefs, (3) assumptions, (4) impatience and (5) the confinement and rigidity of time and ideas.

INTELLECTUAL CLASSISM

What is most often discussed when it comes to education is classism: the discrimination of students based on their socioeconomic status. But there is a another, lesser kind of classism that we need to shine a light on, and I call this *intellectual classism*.

Intellectual classism is best described as a situation that develops wherein the student finds themself discriminated against because of their academic performance. Teachers often favour the 'bright' students, while students who are not academically sound are often labelled stubborn, truants and never-do-wells. This brings to mind a story[2] I came across in *The Guardian* about a state school in London called St Olave's Grammar School.

St Olave's is a leading state school situated in Orpington, Greater London. The 450-year-old institution boasts of a couple of achievements like being the *Sunday Times* State Secondary School of the Year in 2009 and the *Evening Standard* School of the Year in 2015. St Olave's is the alma mater of John Harvard, the first benefactor of Harvard University, and between 2010 and 2017, more than two hundred St Olave's students occupied places at the most esteemed Oxford University.

Due to its prestige, securing a placement at St Olave's is intense competition. It is said that every year the school receives over 1,100 applications for the 128 available slots in year seven. Applicants and parents alike have seen the academic excellence St Olave's produces and want to be part of it. Any wonder, because in 2017 the school celebrated an incredible feat: 90% of the students who took the GCSE had A*/A grades in mathematics and english, while 96% of sixth form students achieved A*/B grades at their A-level exams. Incredible results from an institution prized for its academic success. But there is another side to this story.

Critics put forth claims (with substantial and mounting evidence against the school) that St Olave's could only record such high performance levels because it had selectively weeded out the academically weak students in year twelve. Let me make this clearer: year thirteen is the final A-level year, and what St Olave's did was deliberately and *unlawfully* withdraw any year twelve or sixth form students who did not get top grades in their AS (Advanced Subsidiary) and equivalent internal examination. The school further allowed only certain students to continue after making them sign a contract that stated if they failed to get the minimum B grade, the school had the right to deny them entry to sit the A-level examinations.[3]

As expected, many parents were upset and horrified. But the school didn't care, neither did it care about the emotional wellbeing of the students. Parents and teachers criticised the school for being 'an exam factory' that focused solely on producing results at the expense of students' welfare. The excommunicated students were then forced to look for alternative schools in order to complete their A-levels at a time when finding new schools was a struggle – being newly dislocated, coupled with the fact that the students had to forgo valuable friendships.[4]

The school offered no counselling, neither did they invite students' parents in to discuss onward educational planning; in a most cruel fashion they simply dropped the bombshell on the affected students, serving notifications that they had been withdrawn.[5] St Olave's is just one example of an institution that embodies and fosters intellectual classism in schools and the news only made headlines because the school took the most extreme measures of termination of its students. Underperforming students in other, similar schools may not find themselves withdrawn in the same manner, yet it is common to hear reports of their being discriminated against and treated as lesser students, lesser beings.

A teacher at St Olave's admits that it's hard to witness the stress students undergo in order to keep up with the school's standards of academic excellence. The teacher went on to explain how weaker students are treated as collateral damage in pursuit of the school's objective: maintaining their position on the league table. Students who did not make top grades were not worth talking about[6] – and in this case, did not deserve a place in the school. The weaker students became branded and didn't have it any easier at subsequent institutions, since other schools had readily adopted St Olave's method.[7]

Sadly, this classism we see being bred in the educational system has spilled over into the larger society. Some courses are now more revered than others, while the more esteemed courses (e.g. medicine, engineering, law) are associated with 'intelligent' students. At St Olave's, the headmaster 'advised' a student to continue his studies in another school, noting that he would not be allowed to pursue an A-level program if indeed the student insisted on staying. Instead, he would be offered a General National Vocational Qualification (GNVQ) in health and social care because it corresponded to the student's ability.[8] This may sound more like sound academic counsel, but the underlying principle is still the same: vocational training is reserved and recommended to underperforming students. (To wit: the headmaster may likely have been surprised if ever an intelligent student had opted for vocational training over higher institutions of learning.)

There is no doubt that intellectual classism is detrimental to the emotional wellbeing of both performing and underperforming students. While underperforming students are left to battle self-esteem issues and lack of confidence (because they have been taught to equate academic excellence with life success), performing students also face the pressure of falling short of expectations. It is a huge burden for young minds to carry that may force them to focus solely on academic performance at the expense of neglecting other important developmental areas critical to their growth.

WRONG BELIEFS

As education evolved through time, certain ideas transformed into beliefs, which were passed down as truths. Recall that in the previous chapter we learned that beliefs are aspects of culture below the water's surface, aspects that are often not analysed or questioned. We have held onto these beliefs without considering their validity. Before I expound on these beliefs it is important to note that these beliefs or ideas are in no way valid. If they were, then our educational systems wouldn't be so deeply flawed. (And then, there would be no need for me to write this book.)

Belief 1: The duty of learning lies with the student

I would like to call this first belief 'The Employer Mindset'. When an employer puts out a call for applications whilst stating that prospective employees should have a minimum qualification, the employer is passing an indirect message to the employee that translates as: 'The only way I can trust the value you will bring to the company is through your qualification. It assures me that you are also equipped for the role, so don't expect me to provide further training for you. Do your job. How you do it is totally up to you.'

Conventional schools expect the student to come to school with a degree of intelligence and knowledge. Therefore, learning is often seen as not as much a collaborative effort between teacher and student as it is to provide classroom instruction. How the student processes and comprehends this instruction is left totally up to the student, but this preconceived set of standards actually makes it harder for the student to learn and does not factor in the individual or individual learning styles.

Rote instruction and learning does not understand the finer intricacies of teaching: a teacher is not just a teacher but a coach, like a soccer coach. And the best coaches – for example, Jürgen Klopp – are those who understand that they play a huge role in the lives of their players and that learning is a collaborative effort, a process of engaging over subject matter and creating meaning from it.

A lesson from Klopp

It is 22 July 2020 and Anfield Stadium glows in red phosphorescence. Colourful bands emanating from the stage lights slice through the air. Liverpool players, gold medals dangling from their necks, dance and jump as they await the arrival of their captain, Jordan Henderson, to grace the stage and accept his medal – and the coveted trophy. Jordan drapes the medal around his neck, and trophy in hand, approaches his teammates, lifting the trophy above his head. The stage erupts with jubilation. The sky is a shower of pyrotechnics as the sounds of fireworks and the song of champions fills the arena. Liverpool are crowned the champions of England after thirty years.

A few metres from the stage, a bespectacled, middle-aged man stands on the pitch. A Liverpool scarf hangs from his neck like a soft medal. He waves at the players, blows them kisses, the wide smile on his face radiating joy and fulfillment. He has done what no other coach could in the last three decades, and he knows that when the story is told of how Liverpool broke a thirty-year curse, one name – his name – would always be foremost in people's minds: Jürgen Klopp.

Klopp leading the Liverpool team to victory was not a stroke of luck but a deliberate process of hardwork, teamwork, and most importantly, *relationships*. Building a strong relationship between himself and the players was the secret ingredient Klopp brought to the game and something other coaches hadn't been able to tap into for thirty years. Rafael Benítez, the team's coach from 2005 to 2010, surely did his best and guided the team to win a couple of trophies including the UEFA Champions League – yet, despite being loved by the fans he had a poor relationship with players like Steven Gerrard, Javier Mascherano and Fernando Torres.[9,10] Similarly, Brendan Rodgers who coached the team from 2010 to 2015, also had strained relationships with some players because he wanted them to play according to what *he* wanted, rather than tapping into their individual, unique talents.[11]

But Klopp was different. Players and fans saw him as a father figure, and Klopp understood that to harness the excellent qualities inherent in each player he needed to be much more than a coach or manager. He needed to create a bond. Unlike the cases of Benitez and Rodgers, where players had to leave the club on account of a sour relationship, Klopp's relationship with the players attracted players from other clubs to the team.[12]

Klopp's knack for discipline did not affect the connection he had built with the team either. He fought to give the team well-deserved breaks and supported players under pressure through motivational words at press conferences or by resisting external influences and the temptation to quickly transfer an underperforming player.[13] Such attributes fostered unity and an incredible performance by the team because the players, and even Klopp himself, knew that they were his sole priority. In a podcast interview, Klopp reportedly said: 'It's important to know who you are working with, and it's important to know why somebody is determined and motivated …'[14]

I wish to emphasise the most striking points gleaned from Klopp's statement here. His words provide us with a guide for every teacher in the art of effective teaching. Klopp works with full-grown men who can provide intrinsic motivation for themselves. All they need to do is remember they love the game and want to excel in it. It may not be out of place to suggest that this might be the thought of many coaches; that is why they focus only on the tactical and technical aspects of the game. But Klopp realised he needed to think differently around these players; he had to understand his own impact on a player's ability to perform and work on building individual relationships with each of them, understanding that their performance was tied to the totality of the player as a human being. Klopp knew that the players' personal lives could directly affect their performance too, so he created an avenue for them to share their lives with him. If this method can work for adult men and make them successful, just imagine having a similar impact on young, impressionable students who need direction in life.

As a teacher, one must desist from the belief that a student's personal or private life cannot interfere with learning. Students do not drop their emotional baggage (or whatever poses a barrier to learning) at the door before entering a classroom; they lock it up in their hearts. But this baggage can weigh heavily on the learning process and adversely block the impartation and uptake of knowledge. The teacher's job therefore is to recognise the presence of such invisible burdens and find creative, productive ways to take them off the student. And this can only be done effectively when there is a bond, the formation of trust and a relationship.

Just like Klopp also said, a person's normal life can affect their performance. The student's life outside the four walls of the classroom naturally influences their life in the classroom. So, if the student is having a hard time learning, the cognitively aware teacher is able to consider the student's learning style to ensure that full comprehension is achieved. Learning is not the sole duty of the student; it is a collaborative process between teacher and student. The teacher has a responsibility to *know* the student, yet many teachers today do not know anything beyond their students' names and other superficial information in their biodata. This is not the ideal. The teacher should get to know the student's fears, likes, dislikes, desires, dreams, goals, family and other key areas of the student's life. This way, the teacher can more accurately pinpoint the source of potential learning challenges.

For the teacher to do this, the learning process must be *conversational*. A lot of conversation – dialogue – can occur in and outside the classroom. Students are willing to open the door to their hearts when they see a teacher who is ready to *communicate*, not one who simply dishes out instructions and orders. Our present educational structure is based on information/knowledge being handed down, not exchanged. The student is coerced into *memorising* information based on the teacher's terms, however with this approach, learning becomes partial and involuntary at best. Academic teachers must realise that the end point of learning should be doing what makes the student better, not what makes the teacher better – and let teacher satisfaction come from the student's success. On a typical school day, should a teacher be fulfilled because they ticked off the necessary items on their to-do list – teach, assign tests, mark scripts – or should their fulfillment be a *by-product* of facilitating learning that improves perspectives, builds awareness and feeds the students' ambitions?

Teachers often fail to develop a connection with their students and the few who do are only attracted to intelligent students. The teacher-student bond then formed becomes a reward for winning – for being (among) the best in class. What if the teacher partnered with a student to help the latter's learning process, regardless of whether the person is a straight-A student or an all-F student? As we see through Klopp's teaching philosophy, his relationship with his players is *constant* whether they lose or win a match. In the same vein, and to apply this logic further, we need to let the student's performance not define the student but see their learning as merely part of the whole.

I think it's important to note here that making learning a collaborative and communicative process for students' benefit should not make the teacher dishonest. By this, I mean that teachers should be careful not to trap themselves into telling lies in order to encourage students. Do not obscure a student's weaknesses simply because you do not want them to feel discouraged. This would be counterproductive in the long run. Working *with* the student should be a truthful, direct and honest process and equal exchange. Let the student know their weaknesses and let them know where their strengths lie so that those strengths can be chiselled, sculpted and leveraged. With this approach, the student is much more likely to develop an appetite for courageous and convicted action, something that is the hallmark of many a successful entrepreneur.

Belief 2: A school is a strict training ground (learning cannot be engaging)

Schools often function as strict training grounds – a place where students have to primarily do one thing: study. In conventional education, engagement is alien. Even when students get to have fun or play it is referred to as an 'extracurricular' activity. I find this term and the meaning it conveys incredibly faulty.

Indeed, school is a preparatory ground for higher learning, but its activities are not meant to be aggressive and rigid. This is the reason a lot of students see schooling as a necessary evil. Maybe it is also why Winston Churchill said, 'Personally, I'm always ready to learn, although I do not always like being taught.' Learning institutions are fraught with hectic processes and activities which inevitably results in the learning becoming a more taxing endeavour they wish to escape.

The brief periods students get to socialise and interact with their peers are called 'extracurricular' activities. The prefix 'extra' here means 'outside of'. This implies that socialisation within the school is an activity that is outside of – and removed from – the learning process. Is this potentially an erroneous idea?

A school is a universe for learning. As humans, the universe we find ourselves in has biotic and abiotic components that function to make living possible and worthwhile. Students and teachers need to expel the belief that students pause their cognitive faculties when participating in extracurricular activities, because the truth is a lot can be learned from enjoying team participation as a method for developing leadership acumen amongst students.

A school also shouldn't be a sanctuary with rigid rules and precepts that result in students developing antipathy towards learning. Every aspect of a school should be redesigned to provide a flexible and engaging learning experience. In her article for *The Atlantic* titled 'In Defense of Play', American professor Alison Gopnik notes that play is an 'elaborate detour' to being smarter, more focused and more empathic. She further states that play has a pattern of repetition and variation, and that it is the 'very silliness of play, the random weirdness of it all [is what] makes it so effective'.[16]

However, based on this recommendation, there is a tendency for teachers (and parents) to consider play effective only if it achieves the goal of learning. According to Gopnik, play is often treated as a 'disguised form of work, something that only has value because it eventually leads to some practical end – physical health or moral uplift'.[17] If this is the case in schools, then the aim of making learning engaging would be defeated. I think the current challenge with conventional education began when learning became considered effective only when a child showed they were excelling academically. We cannot repeat the same mistake if we actually want to reorient our beliefs.

This does not mean that play doesn't have or lead to practical benefits – it does. But as Gopnik recommends, teachers should not aim for these benefits, nor should they teach students to aim for the same. Both teachers and students should bear in mind that play has a fundamental paradox: 'in order to be able to reach a variety of new goals, in the long run, you have to turn away from goal-seeking in the short run actively'.[18]

Making learning spontaneous and engaging is not just a personal recommendation; it is a method with effective outcomes proven by science. It has been shown that using humour and emotional impact, even in a statistics class, strengthens the student-teacher relationship and reduces boredom; it makes the course more interesting and helps students recall the subject matter. It provides amusement, brings back attention, lightens the mood, reduces monotony and increases motivation.[19,20]

Schools could also borrow a leaf from companies that have designed their spaces to promote optimal engagement at work. For instance, to get people to use the stairs instead of the escalator, Volkswagen converted a flight of stairs next to the escalator in the Odenplan subway in Stockholm to a working piano through 'The Fun Theory' initiative. They discovered that the number of people who chose to use the stairs (or piano) instead of the escalator increased by 66%.[21]

Other companies like Twitter hold rooftop meetings, while the staff and management of Facebook work in open office spaces; meanwhile, Google famously introduced internal office 'fun slides' as an alternative and playful mode of movement inside the workplace, raising the bar on job perks and changing the face, culture and definition of employee satisfaction. These unconventional workspaces have been found to increase productivity and creativity.[22,23]

Imagine if we had a school system where classes are held in open spaces under nature's watchful gaze. Imagine a classroom where students would be allowed to design and personalise their desks. Imagine a classroom designed in such a way that every corner of the class reminds the student that learning is fun and necessary. By making subtle yet important changes to the learning environs such as the brief examples I give here, we could systematically and fundamentally change the whole learning experience for the better, indeed, the face of learning.

One of the issues of conventional education is that it conforms to a lot of traditions. (Little wonder it is called 'conventional' education.) The educational system is boxed into rigid requirements which we see easily extends to and impacts the students (who, by no fault of their own, find themselves in a *paradoxical* educational set-up that boxes their creativity). The current educational system needs to modernise itself, be flexible in its approach if we are to solve this problem. Let's leave out the tradition and stick to education. Education and learning is a holistic, ongoing process and it is therefore of paramount importance that we begin to change our thinking on this, and acknowledge that learning does not start and stop in the classroom.

Belief 3: Academics is the main medium for education

You have probably not heard of Marcus Hutchins, but he is a celebrity, a star, a Messiah in the hacking and programming universe. In

2017, he single-handedly stopped the worst malware attack the world had ever seen – and literally saved the internet.[24] But we only know of Hutchins' heroics because he defied both parents and teachers who wanted him to dump the computer for a more productive enterprise: academic education.

Hutchins' parents and teachers obviously had good intentions but they displayed these intentions the wrong way. Hutchins was a child whose love for computers was evident as early as a young burgeoning six-year-old; and his thirteenth birthday would be the only time his parents ever nurtured this interest by getting him the components he needed to build his own computer. They were conventional parents who pandered to the dictates of conventional education that sold the conventional belief that books were the only gateway to knowledge. Teaming up with his teachers, his parents then tried to get Hutchins to abandon programming altogether and concentrate only on academics. This remarkably backfired, and as a result, Hutchins would become more determined than ever; it strengthened his love for the computer, diminished his interest in education and set him on an irreversible path into the programming universe.

Now imagine if Hutchins' parents and teachers had understood what we now know, that learning is not restricted to academics alone. His parents could have played a more integral role in honing Hutchins' talent. And if Hutchins knew that his parents and teachers supported his skill set, he probably wouldn't have seen the need to skip classes. They had a duty to guide and channel their son's skill appropriately, and yet they failed at this. What's more, their attempts to shield him from the computer gave him all the more reason to rebel and steer himself further adrift from academics than if they had left him alone to focus on his talents. Sadly, this rebellion led Hutchins into the dark world of cybercrime, although thankfully, he eventually managed to retrace his steps to morality's path.[25]

If there is any information we can glean from Hutchins' story, it is that parents and teachers need to do away with the belief that academics is the only portal to knowledge.

When parents and teachers see students taking a keen interest and developing skills in technology, music, creative writing, arts and so on, they should seek ways to marry these skills with the students' academic activities. For instance, a maths teacher could teach maths concepts using the tune of the students' favourite songs, and a chemistry teacher could create stories out of atoms and molecules. There is always a way to unite students' interests with their schoolwork because they are not mutually exclusive. One should not always give way to the other. This unification is, I believe, a veritable step towards boosting students' overall creativity and intellectual prowess. Unfortunately, this unification still does not exist and remains wishful thinking on my part, mainly because learning in a conventional system is based on certain costly assumptions.

ASSUMPTIONS

Before I speak at any event I ask questions about my audience. Who are they? Why are they coming to the event? What are their likely expectations from the event and my speech? I must ask myself these questions to ensure that what I'll say resonates with their experiences. I don't make any assumptions about their lives or backgrounds, even though it may seem like the ethos of my speech gives me this privilege.

Opting for assumptions would make me prepare my speech faster; yet I know if I did this, I wouldn't be able to impact my audience in the way I desire. My speech wouldn't bring anything new to the table because it would be full of generic ideas that have already been documented throughout history. If I try to avoid the ease and speed of assumptions just to leave a mark on people I do not know and probably would never meet after the event, then why should a teacher take this path to influence students left in their care for a year or more?

Conventional schools are founded and managed based on several assumptions. The university or college lecturer assumes that the high school journey has equipped the student with a certain level of knowledge and intelligence. The high school teacher assumes that the student arrives with a solid background from middle school. The middle school teacher assumes the elementary school did its job. The elementary school teacher assumes the parents have played their role well as the child is prepared for and introduced into the school system. And the student is the victim and the one sandwiched in a long trail of assumptions and expectations and buying into a narrative they have not chosen for themselves. If we take a step back to look at things here, we can clearly see the domino effect playing out as one incorrect assumption leads to another and another in the chain until it snowballs into a system that is beyond our control.

Another major assumption that holds true in conventional schools is that every student has the same learning capacity – and when a student shows that their capacity falls below expectation, they are seen as liabilities. Like, why waste time on few dull students when having intelligent students makes teaching easy? This wrong assumption, coupled with students' inability to meet academic expectations, is the beginning of intellectual classism.

Teachers make these assumptions because they ignore the fact that learning is a progressive process. Assumptions release and free one of the 'burden' of details and the tailored/personalised learning approach a teacher would otherwise have to carry out to effectively educate students. With 'assumptions', teaching then becomes a 'tick-the-box' activity, which it is not meant to be and which steers the whole goal of education away from being for the individual – and towards groupthink.

Education is not a process to be rushed. A teacher's duty is to seek productive and innovative methods to impart knowledge to every student, whether academically sound or dull. But this is not the case in many schools. Teaching is often fast paced and rushed. Teachers are not patient enough to ensure that the students learn. They forget or intentionally ignore the fact that students learn at different paces. This impatience in the teaching and learning process is another way in which conventional education falls short.

IMPATIENCE

Inventions are often not achieved the first time around, right off the bat. Inventors need to work and rework components so they can function perfectly. Musicians rehearse to create awesome compositions. Authors take years to birth eternal stories. Yet for some strange reason, when it comes to education, students are not afforded the luxury of patience in the learning process.

Students are expected to learn *and* pass every subject taught. Conventional education is a system that judges intelligence based on how well and how fast students can reproduce what they're 'taught'. To meet this requirement, the students engage in the most inappropriate method of learning: learning by rote. The *Merriam-Webster Dictionary* gives the most precise definition of rote learning, defining it as the use of memory, usually with little intelligence, mechanical or unthinking routine, or repetition.[26] Rote *suppresses* an individual's intelligence. It is a mirage of knowledge that creates a false sense of academic valiance. But we cannot blame students for subscribing to this limited style of learning because the fact remains that they belong to an impatient system, a system that cannot (and does not) wait for them to grow and fully form at their own pace and in their own way.

One may argue that underperforming students are given a chance to try again by repeating a class/grade. Allowing a student to repeat a class would be great – if only the repeating student were not made to feel like a dullard and a failure. Conventional education doesn't use repeating a class – known as grade retention – to groom the student further or afford them a second chance; rather, grade retention is a tool for intellectual classism. Where a student is failing, the institution will retain the student, then label them academic weaklings for not rising up to meet set standardised measures of learning. Teachers and progressive students do not see the retained students as works in progress; rather, they see them as folks biding their time in a system that is not for them. The result here is that the retained student will struggle with issues of self-esteem which ultimately leads to developing apathy and/or antipathy towards schooling in general.

Laura McGuinn states that grade retention offers no help or advantage to a child's learning. Instead, it leads to low self-esteem and other emotional and social difficulties. She further states that the American Academy of Pediatrics opined that children become most successful when they advance with their peers while the reasons behind their poor performance are addressed.[27] If schools could stop associating failure to grade retention, maybe grade retention wouldn't be so frowned upon.

However, McGuinn does provide us with a suitable alternative to grade retention. She suggests that schools could adopt multi-age grouping; that is, mixing children from two or more grade levels in the same classroom. In this way, the child still learns amongst their friends despite their curriculum being different. Not only does this improve the child's intellectual wellbeing, it develops them socially and emotionally as well.[28] Multi-age grouping also encourages mentoring amongst students and across age and ability levels, where younger and academically weaker students can learn from older, more academically sound students. Overall, this promising system of learning would groom students more in developing much-needed social and leadership skills whilst reinforcing other skills such as collaboration and teamwork, heightening their overall achievements.[29]

Multi-age grouping also allows the teacher to identify the student's unique academic needs, and to guide the student towards meeting these needs. With multi-age grouping, learning is gradual, holistic and tailored to students' needs. Schools that have adopted this learning approach have discovered that it gives teachers the chance to meet learners where they are at and assess each student at an appropriate level. It also encourages students to strengthen and share a communal bond by learning and contributing as a cohesive unit.[30]

It is important to note here that, compared to conventional methods of retention, multi-age grouping *also* focuses on the social and emotional wellbeing of the student. This is because education should always be seen as a holistic process. Sadly, conventional education focuses only on the intellectual wellbeing of the individual and dampens other faculties like emotional intelligence and spiritual awareness.

Academic education is generally based on the premise that intellect is always more reliable than intuition. Individuals with highly developed intuitive capabilities are those who recognise the power of intuition and use it in combination with their intellect to make superior decisions. Those with highly developed intuitive senses likewise understand the limitations of data and logic and are able to acknowledge the power of imagination and epiphanies. Multi-age grouping addresses the need for a more holistic style of learning that encompasses the whole of the individual to include non-academic skills such as intuition as well as social and emotional components, far from straight academia.

THE CONFINEMENT AND RIGIDITY OF TIME AND IDEAS

The conventional educational system is confined to a fixed time. Students are expected to complete a session within a year, irrespective of their learning capacity. This is, I believe, a major reason behind the resulting impatience defining conventional institutions. The learning process in modern-day institutions is so hurried and harried primarily so that students can move on to the next level in a 365-day cycle. In some cases, students have a window of just eight to ten months of learning. And it doesn't end there. Each subject is allocated a particular number of hours in the week, so for the majority of students, education is a constant race against time.

In learning, time should be our friend, not our enemy. Unfortunately, conventional education does not recognise the critical nature of time as it applies to learning, nor does it make a case for it. And when students do not catch up within the allocated time, they are labelled unintelligent or less intelligent through standardised measures and are expected to repeat the level. We have seen this process play out as the norm in modern education today, but is this really healthy – and is this actually ideal for the student?

The 2009 award-winning Bollywood movie *3 Idiots* perfectly reflects the dangers of conventional education. In the movie, a student, Joy Lobo, commits suicide after failing to meet the project deadline. Acts of suicide as a result of school pressure are not only fictional; sadly, this is the reality of many students in today's world. In January 2018, Patrick Turner, a student of Newport Harbor High School, California, committed suicide. By day he looked happy and successful around his friends, but his parents, teachers and school peers could never have known how he was being crushed by the weight of academic expectations and pressure of being in a highly competitive high school that expected – nay, demanded – academic excellence. Excerpts from Taylor's suicide notes were telling: one read, 'One slip-up makes a kid feel like the smallest person in the world. You are looked at as a loser if you don't go to college or if you get a certain GPA or test score. All anyone talks about is how great they are or how great their kid is ... It's all about how great I am. It's never about the other kid. The kid who maybe does not play a sport, have (*sic*) a 4.0 GPA, but displays great character ... So much pressure is placed on the students to do well that I couldn't do it anymore.'[31]

Sadly, in system fuelled by haste and expectation, teachers gradually lose their feelings of commitment to their job – and in some cases, their humanity – as output and results become the goal. They give students worksheets on topics not yet taught and expect them to understand the topics before exam time. Patrick Turner made a point of this in another one of his suicide notes. He wrote: 'A handful of the problems I have had this year are: teachers giving us worksheets, then not teaching while the whole class messes around, having a teacher tell me that there will be something on the final that we have not learned (and will not learn), having things on prior tests that we have either not learned or barely gone over at all, and a mean teacher who made every day I had with this teacher something I dreaded to. I especially want to emphasise the rudeness this teacher showed to us students. This teacher was beyond strict.'[32]

Once again, the current system is one that does not regard the emotional, physical, spiritual and mental wellbeing of individuals entrusted to their care. Schools are meant to refine individuals and put them out into society as well-rounded and functional people – but the system fails in their duty of care towards the individual to the point where students detest the system so much they will seek any means of escape – including death.

Shining a light upon the inflexibility of time in schools is not a problem without a solution. Online or remote learning proves that learning *can* be self-paced because students can take control of their own learning and have access to course resources to study at their own pace and time. This results in more successful learning as the student is able to digest the information without having to hurry for the next lecture. So why are schools slow in offering students the opportunity for self-paced learning? Research carried out by Jasmine Paul and Felicia Jefferson to determine student performance in an online versus face-to-face environmental science course over a seven-year period showed no significant differences in students' performance with respect to modality, gender or class rank. Although there are other factors to consider, researchers suggest that, since there's no significant difference, it makes sense for conventional schools to make the shift to online learning a gradual process. If this is done, they will capture a larger audience and increase cost efficiencies and school revenue.[33] I agree.

Conventional education not only confines the student to a time frame, it confines them to a set of ideas and sets forth the expectation that without education, they cannot be more. It makes the student believe that their entire life should be tethered to academics and to relegate other talents to the background because they don't want to be distracted from their studies. Yet, more often than not, what we see here is that when these students graduate, they do not return to these talents; instead, they become fixated with employment prospects and ferry their résumé from one office to another in search of jobs. The educational system strips the student of any creativity they may have once had and replaces it with academia-related goals.

When a group of researchers investigated the people's perception in Somaliland towards education, they discovered that both educated and uneducated parents shared a desire for their children to go to school. A primary reason for this was because they felt academic education would give their children an upper hand in society. One of the residents, a woman with two sons – one educated, the other uneducated – believed that the child who had been school educated would be more successful in the future, and thus be able to help her out financially. Yet there is an irony to this mother's belief, because as at the time of this research, the educated son did not have a job, while the uneducated son did all sorts of casual work (the reason he left school in the first place) to cater for his mother. According to the woman, the educated son had at one time been a teacher but no longer had a regular job. 'Sometimes he teaches, but there is not enough work and payment for him, so he is usually idle and lives on Allah's mercy,' she explained. She admitted that the uneducated son was her means of financial support, but she still looked forward to when the educated son would 'earn more and do a respectable job' and support her more in the future.[34]

This woman's educated son reflects how the conventional education system serves to confine and limit the individual more than the uneducated child, who moves (and hustles) around to fend for himself and his mother, while the educated son sits idly at home waiting for 'the right opportunity' – unable (or unwilling) to make any attempt to employ his creativity. The educated child sees hustling and being resourceful like his brother as something that is beneath him, his education affording him the subtle attitude of entitlement. Instead, he sits, waiting for his résumé to pave the way for him, sold on the idea that his financial wellbeing is tied to his certificate(s). This is not unique to an educated student from Somaliland; it is the reality of a lot of people who pass through conventional educational systems and are bred to believe they are somehow superior beings whilst ironically having been stifled throughout the process.

The shortcomings of conventional education would lead an inquisitive mind to question why the system still exists in its current form without having undergone any significant changes or modifications in recent times. The answer is simple: society believes that conventional education *still* plays a major role in preserving culture and promoting civilisation, and that it should evolve *only* along these lines. Is it perhaps time, therefore, to consider the possibility that conventional education promotes *closed-minded indoctrination* that does not acknowledge the shortcomings of the system and does not seek alternatives whilst being too quick to dismiss alternatives when they are presented?

Skill development helps us understand the tasks that we can do. Personal development helps us to understand the person that we are, or are becoming. And spiritual development helps us understand and see all the potential we have, the light that shines within us. The conventional education system is supposedly designed to focus on the first. What we need to start realising is that academic education is not an antidote to indoctrination. In fact, many times it is the source of it.

CHAPTER FOUR
The History of Education

I t is difficult to pinpoint an exact time in history as the beginning of education. This is because as human societies evolved there arose the need to *preserve* knowledge by transmitting it from one generation to another. To examine education's journey down through the annals of history, it is imperative to explore different societies of past eras – from the prehistoric all the way to the modern era.

EDUCATION IN THE PREHISTORIC AND PRIMITIVE ERAS

In prehistoric times, education was basically cultural transmission. This is because the primitive person was static and absolute, and as such, they equated their culture to the totality of their universe – a culture they sought to preserve through transmission and without any need for deviation or dilution.[1] Therefore, primitive education focused solely on guiding the young to grow into good members of their tribe, where adults served as teachers and taught their young the ways of society through instruction and demonstration. The young also learned by observation, *imitation* and participation. Being a hunter-gatherer society, education was simply practical. The young were taught how to hunt and gather, manipulate tools, fish, cultivate crops and build a shelter. They participated in games, initiation ceremonies and other communal activities.[2]

Learning during prehistoric and primitive times took place without constraints and continued throughout life.[3] This corroborates with the unique quality of the primitive human as stated in *Britannica* as: The primitive human has 'a relatively fixed sense of cultural continuity and timelessness'.[4]

EDUCATION IN THE EARLIEST CIVILISATIONS OF MESOPOTAMIA

Primitive societies later evolved into civilised ones. Mesopotamic societies were the first to embrace civilisation, followed by Egyptian and Chinese societies. People in these early civilised societies enjoyed surplus food and economic stability due to the rise in agriculture and trade. Farming and hunting no longer became the only professions; there developed an array of different professions, including masonry, music and tailoring.[5]

Mesopotamia was the cradle of education. Key subjects taught included reading, writing, religion, law and medicine. Early Mesopotamia had one striking quality: being a highly religious society, there were as many temples as there were schools. Thus, education served a double function: schools were used to expand civilisation, while the temples were used to preserve an integral aspect of their culture – religion. It was pertinent to preserve the religiosity of Mesopotamic culture because they believed that by keeping the gods happy it would balance out the world. In daily life therefore, they were taught to say prayers, bury the dead properly and respect the gods in the work they did.[6]

EDUCATION IN THE EARLIEST CIVILISATIONS OF EGYPT

A similar event played out in ancient Egypt. Judith Cochran, in her book titled *Education in Egypt,* was quick to note that Egypt's civilisation revolved around the Nile; the river irrigated their farms and also served as a transportation channel for produce to get to the market. Thus, their way of life needed to be preserved through handed-down knowledge. 'And this knowledge, passed from father to son, enabled Egyptians to be secure and thrive in a country which stood as an agricultural and commercial centre for thousands of years.'[7]

It was not long before civilisation exploded in Egypt and skills like writing, geometry, human and veterinary medicine, surveying and accounting became commonplace. As it was in Mesopotamia, education in Egypt took place in temples. Cochran notes that education and religion were similarly inseparable in ancient Egypt.

Thus, it was the exclusive duty of the priests to preserve and control culture and education. The priests were seen as powerful intellectual bulwarks who guarded against cultural diversity, rigid in their approach and severe in their discipline. They employed learning methods like drills and memorisation to achieve: (1) uniformity in cultural transmission and (2) strict compliance with the conventional thought pattern.[8] (We can assert that this defensive approach against cultural dynamism and diversity led to the first and fundamental flaw of education: indoctrination – which we will explore later in greater depth.)

In formal schools, priests taught the subjects of science, medicine, mathematics and geometry, while vocational skills like architecture, engineering and sculpture were taught informally – and most likely in workshops. There were two types of formal schools for people from privileged backgrounds, and these were led by government officials and priests who supervised the schools. The first school was for scribes, while the second was dedicated for the *curates*, or priests-in-training. For the former, pupils were enrolled in the writing school at the age of five and learnt how to read and write until their late teens. In their early teenage years (between thirteen and fourteen), they began to receive practical training in the offices for which they were being prepared. The *curates*, on the other hand, were enrolled into the temple college at seventeen, with the duration of their training dependent on the requirements for the priestly office for which they were being groomed.[9]

EDUCATION IN THE EARLIEST CIVILISATIONS OF NORTH CHINA

In the book *Education as Cultivation in Chinese Culture*, Shihkuan Hsu highlights that in China, education was not limited to obtaining knowledge and skills for a profession, but also as a means of cultivating an individual to imbibe the revered virtues of justice, wisdom and trust. These beliefs didn't just appear in modern-day China; they were founded and carefully cultivated over three thousand years ago in the Zhou Dynasty.[10, 11]

Around 1100 BC, the Duke of Zhou established the Rites of Zhou to teach people the common rituals and ways of being. He did this to educate defeated rebels and unite the different kingdoms that separated China. For the Chinese, education was an essential blend of knowledge acquisition and character building. Confucius, who was regarded as the sage of teachers, was instrumental to the development of Chinese education. Confucius believed that education was progressive – starting with an individual's cultivation of character and virtue – and graduating to the individual's family and finally expanding to the governance of his people and country. According to Qian 'the meaning of education [in ancient China] is not for the delivery of knowledge, nor for the training of profession. It is not even for children, youth or people younger than middle-aged only. It is for all the people in the society and even for all humankind'.[12]

In China, education was seen as a tool used to cultivate a sense of moral sensitivity and duty in the individual towards people and the state. Little wonder their curriculum consists of human relations, rituals and music. Students learned from bamboo books. They learned moral and ritual practices through oral transmission and by example. Since education was regarded as a developmental process emanating from within, rigid rote learning (as practiced in Egypt) was strongly condemned. Unfortunately, this same method of rigid learning, once condemned, now characterises much of modern Chinese education today.[13]

EDUCATION IN THE CLASSICAL ERA

The classical era refers to the civilisations of ancient Greece and Rome. These civilisations played an important role in the history of many aspects of human development, including politics, public speaking, literature and music. But in this discourse, we will concentrate on the historical aspects of education in ancient Greece and Rome, plus ancient India and Israel.

EDUCATION IN ANCIENT INDIA

As we move through the history of education, it is interesting to note the similarities between cultures steeped in religion. Just as in Mesopotamia and Egypt, a strong marriage existed between religion and education in India. In fact, author A S Altekar writes that, to understand the educational theories in India, one had to study the various rituals connected to the student's life. Chief among these rituals were *Vidyarambha Sanskara* (performed at the beginning of primary education) and *Upanayana Sanskara* (performed every time the student meets a new teacher).[14]

The social strata in ancient India had four classes, or *varnas*. These classes were the Brahmans, intellectuals who became priests and men of learning; the Kshatriyas, the nobles and soldiers; the Vaishyas, farmers and traders; and the Shudra, who were artisans and labourers.

These distinct classes were all connected by religion and formed the bedrock of Indian education.[15]

One main feature of education in India was the study of Vedic literature – a collection of hymns composed in archaic Sanskrit recited or chanted during rituals as praises to several gods. As the tenets of religion were handed down from generation to generation, other vital subjects like philosophy, law, morality and government were passed across as well.[16]

In his book, *Education in Ancient India*, author Harmut Scharfe notes that the social caste system in India was developed to create a stable administrative atmosphere, where life was regulated by the union of customary laws and the instructions of the Brahmans. It was the duty of the members of the three upper classes – especially the Brahmans – to hand down the sacred texts and customs of the state.[17]

Teaching was done orally,[18] and the instruction method depended on the nature of the subject taught. Students used *memorisation* to learn the particular Veda of their school, with emphasis on correct pronunciation. *Comprehension* was used in the study of law, logic, rituals and prosody. Teachers employed *parables* in personal spiritual teachings, such as the conclusion of Vedas. While *catechism* was used in higher learning, the teacher discourses at length on topics asked by the pupils.[19]

EDUCATION IN ANCIENT ISRAEL

For the Hebrew child, education started at home. Mothers taught their daughters and the very young, while fathers imbued morals, religion and handcrafts in their sons. Education in the classroom was considered an extension of the home. Writing, which they borrowed from the Phoenicians, was an integral part of Jewish education, and they used it to write letters, draw up contracts, keep records and prepare orders.[20]

In this chapter we have seen a strong association between education and religion in different ancient societies – and it was no different in ancient Israel. Jewish synagogues were not only houses of prayer, but schools. There's an aspect of the synagogue called *bet ha-safer*, meaning 'house of the book' and another called *bet ha-midrash*, meaning 'house of instruction'. These houses correspond roughly to elementary and advanced levels of education, respectively.

In the 1998 book, *Education in Ancient Israel: Across the Deadening Silence*, James L Crenshaw illuminates what life was like for the Hebrews, where education became so much more than memorising information and taking tests. They searched for the plan and presence of God through patient observation and engaging in listening communication with Wisdom, and the feminine incarnation of the Divine.[21]

According to contemporary ideas, there was a little fault with the Jewish educational structure: only boys attended schools, girls were taught at home.[22]

EDUCATION IN ANCIENT GREECE

Education in ancient Greece has a complex, yet interesting, history. Greece produced some of the greatest philosophers and thinkers the world had ever seen – from Aristotle to Socrates to Plato to Pythagoras to Democritus. Unlike other ancient cultures where religion influenced education, for the Greeks, it was to philosophy, poetry and politics where they sought life's answers.

Ancient Greek society was aristocratic and militaristic. It was common for the son of a nobleman to either entrust himself or be entrusted to an older man he admired, and to seek out counsel and education through the example of such a senior. Asides from wise counsels and their examples, dance, poetry and instrumental music helped the Greeks develop a cultivated civilisation and a strong educational foundation. The formation of education then evolved, along with the political transformations of a society that valued collective devotion to the community.[23]

The key objective of education in ancient Greece was to impart physical and strength training, which was thought to be essential for developing an individual's appearance, potential, endurance for war and health. But this didn't diminish their dedication to learning subjects such as biology, chemistry, rhetoric/oratory, geometry, astronomy and meteorology. Students were known to memorise and mock performances of epic poems like Homer's *Odyssey* and *The Iliad*. Generally, education in ancient Greece prepared the student to contribute their quota as a good citizen. However, there were seen to be some differences in their approach to education when it came to individual city-states.[24] And Greek education (and civilisation) cannot be properly discoursed without highlighting the influence of their two principal city-states: Sparta and Athens.

The Spartans were strictly militaristic. This brings to mind a scene in the 2006 movie, *300*, where King Leonidas asked his three hundred Spartan warriors what their profession was and their only response was a battle cry, signifying that they were soldiers – unlike the large Arcadian army, which consisted of a potter, a sculptor, a blacksmith and men with no military training in rather ad hoc fashion.

Military and civic education dominated the curriculum of the Spartans. They believed that the citizen-soldier must be ready to fight – and die, if it came to that – for his country. Thus, education, which was entirely controlled by the state, became the exclusive preserve of men – and not just men, but specifically warriors. Children trained from age seven to twenty. However, the education of young females was reduced to grooming them for motherhood.[25]

A young man of Sparta who trained for the military would be alienated from his family and kept in a garrison with other youths.

They were lightly clothed, slept on bare floors, were poorly fed and encouraged to steal to supplement their rations. It was a rigorous discipline intended to toughen up even the weakest man. The Spartan youth was taught to obey superior orders blindly.[26] They were taught that deception, lying and stealing were all virtues as long as they were directed at a foreigner. They were encouraged to distrust foreigners and use the principles of Machiavellianism in their dealings with them.[27]

Athens, however, sat in stark contrast to Sparta. Although they encouraged citizens to defend their country when necessary, Athens became the first city-state in Greece to reject education leaning towards military training. According to Mark Griffith, they were open-minded and promoted cultural experimentation of Athenian liberalism as against Sparta's totalitarian system, which was designed to produce brave but blindly conformist citizens. Athens became home to the arts, free expression and all kinds of exploration, which finally led to its housing the very first universities. The city-state became the centre of operations for big names like Socrates, Isocrates, Plato and Aristotle, who would go on to make their mark as great leaders and philosophers of their times. Perikles described Athens as 'the education for all of Greece'.[28]

Athenian schools became privately run and citizens were free to choose whatever education befitted their children.[29] Children were taught literacy by writing masters known as *grammatistes*, who taught them letters and numbers. Advanced forms of literacy – such as the study of poets, playwrights and historians – were taught by instructors known as *grammatikos*. Boys were also taught physical and military activities in the wrestling school. Education in Athens became a truly holistic affair; teachers didn't just educate the *body*, they educated the *mind* too. Morality was valued and taught because the Athenians believed in the ideal of *kalos k'agathos* – the 'wise and good' man. Teachers oversaw the formation of a child's character and conduct alongside tracking the child's progress in the subjects taught.[30]

As Athens developed more politically, a new need began to emerge. The Greek man, no longer interested in athletics and elegant, leisurely pursuits, sought to assert himself as a political creature, and this gave rise to a group of people called the Sophists, who strived to meet this need. Sophists were professional educators focused on providing realistic direction and education entirely for political participation. However, the issue with their teachings was that they neither sought nor transmitted the *truth* pertaining to humans or their existence; it was offered strictly as an art for political success, a point of view that would prevail at all times and by all means. Hence, they taught their students two key disciplines: the dialectical argument – the art of logical argument, and rhetorical argument – the art of persuasive speaking.[31] This idea the Sophists' had diluted, to a great extent, the significance of education. It was a corrupt idea injected like a virus into the gene of education and persisted through generations. Little wonder Socrates kicked up a fuss against it.

Socrates staunchly opposed the pedagogy of the Sophists. He was of the view that the supreme ideal of man and of education was not in the search for efficiency and power – but in the disinterested search for the absolute and for virtue; for knowledge and understanding.[32]

Later, two great educators, Plato and Isocrates, arrived on the scene to (re)organise the structure of Greek education. Plato, a then-pupil of Socrates, founded a school called The Academy where he taught and prepared a band of scholars to be leaders. He believed that a good government could only come from an educated society where 'kings are philosophers and philosophers are kings'. In his literary dialogues, Plato revealed that the ultimate educational quest should be the search for the good – the ultimate idea that binds together all earthly existence.[33] This is a stance I agree with. Education needs to enable the individual to see, understand and connect the dots of human existence, ethics and morality, and this connection should begin with the individual, using education as a tool to unite the tripartite, or the three parts that make up a human being: the body, the soul and the spirit. The Bible tells us in 1 Thessalonians 5:23 that we were all created with three parts – a spirit, a soul and a body:

'And the God of peace Himself sanctify you wholly, and may your spirit and soul and body be preserved complete, without blame, at the coming of our Lord Jesus Christ.'

Similarly, note 5 on 1 Thessalonians 5:23 acknowledges [that] *'This word strongly indicates that man is of three parts: spirit, soul and body. The spirit as our inmost part is the inner organ, possessing God-consciousness, that we may contact God (John 4:24; Rom. 1:9)'.*

Indeed, it is important – nay, critical – that, in terms of speaking about and addressing educational needs and development, we acknowledge and address the three parts of man, for 'in the spirit, God as the Spirit dwells; in the soul, our self dwells; and in the body, the physical senses dwell'.

Based on this statement, one aspect cannot – and should not – ever be neglected over another, given that all three must exist inexhaustibly and eternally as part of the tripartite; therefore, were one to dismiss one over another and so on, this could only be viewed as a miscarriage of justice. Yet the modern-day educational system does just this, and the many examples we now see globally of poor leadership in the modern world are of high consequence to the fact that business and political educational institutions under-emphasise the importance of character and trust building, which is such a critical part of moral, ethical or religious duty. But, I digress.

Returning to Plato's view on education, one can appreciate his deep, holistic perspectives about education and his desire for education to influence the totality of a person, and not just be a showcase of scholarly prowess and institutionalised achievements. This was why Plato vehemently argued that the world consists of the *visible* – perceived with the senses – and the *invisible* – the intelligible aspect of the world that only the mind can comprehend. He further divided the visible realm into two: the realm of appearances and the realm of beliefs. He noted that human experiences are only visible appearances that give birth to opinions and beliefs – and this is the world so many people are stuck in today; the visible world of opinion, a world many find difficult to leave in order to cross over into the realm of the intelligible.[34] This particular concept of Plato's is what is most integral here, and what in fact birthed the idea for this book – and is something I wish to explore in more detail. In fact, one of the aims of this book is to challenge you to stretch yourself mentally speaking, enough to will yourself to cross over into a new way of thinking. To make you see and question things in a new light, and to break free of the traditional and somewhat indoctrinated ways of thinking we were born into. But more on this later.

Speaking of education, Plato took his pupils through a rigorous fifteen-year study of dialectics and mathematical reasoning in order to attain an understanding of genuine reality composed of the good, the true and the beautiful. Recall that Athens was a highly political society, so Plato believed that only those who survived his training were fit for state offices and capable of maintaining and dispensing justice.[35] Yet, despite the nobility of Plato's educational approach, he too did not escape his fair share of criticism or rivalry.

Isocrates had a more pragmatic counter-approach, which was to cultivate wisdom not in some abstract manner, but on the practical basis of providing common-sense solutions to life's problems. His pupils received more literary lessons than scientific ones and they studied music, gymnastics, Homeric classics and rhetoric. His program consisted of five to six years of theory, analysis and imitation of great classics, and practical exercises.[36]

Plato's and Isocrates' views on education may not have been parallel, but they intersected at some points. First, they both opposed the Sophists' ideas. Second, both men did not entirely reject the central ideas of the other. Plato recognised the importance of literature and rhetoric, while Isocrates promoted elementary mathematics and philosophy – the former as a form of mental training and the latter to broaden the mind to question the essentials of life.[37] Together, the ideas of these two men provided a framework for educational development.

EDUCATION IN ANCIENT ROME

Since this is a discourse on education, we could quip that the Romans took a leaf from the educational book of the Greeks. However, as education evolved in Rome, it clearly took on its own unique and distinct form that set them apart from Greek philosophers.

Unlike Greece (where education was strictly the preserve of the noble), education in Rome also became suitable for rural, traditional people. It instilled in the youth a total, unflinching respect for the customs of their forebears and became a model based upon three key aspects: (1) the practical aspect, which involved instruction in farm management, including overseeing the work of slaves and advising tenant farmers, (2) the legal aspect, which was formal and technical and required citizens to study it dutifully and (3) the moral aspect, which, as we have seen earlier, inculcated the rural virtues of respect, good management of one's inheritance and a sense of frugality.[38]

The Romans wanted the individual to be one of concrete character. To be Roman was to be pious, courageous and prudent by imitating the old Romans who embodied these virtues.[39] This is why family played a key role in education. Children received instruction in reading and writing at home before they were old enough to be enrolled in elementary schools. Quintilian, the teacher of rhetoric and a leading teacher in Rome, encouraged children's early, purposeful training. Of this, he wrote: 'Though the knowledge absorbed in these years may be little, yet the child will be learning something more advanced during that year, in which they would otherwise have been occupied with something more elementary. Such progress each successive year increases the total, and the time gained during childhood is a clear profit to the period of youth … Let us not waste therefore the earliest years.'[40]

If Quintilian were here today, I am sure he would have frowned upon how societies now gauge a person's worth through academic brilliance; how they have eroded the fundamental concepts of education and reduced it to a *simple* input-output process. For Quintilian believed education should be an enjoyable process of inculcating knowledge into the child. At no point should the child find education distasteful. In fact, Quintilian stated: 'I am not however so unacquainted with differences of age as to think that we should urge those of tender years severely, or exact a full complement of work from them; for it will be necessary, above all things, to take care lest the child should conceive a dislike to the application which he cannot yet love, and continue to dread the bitterness which he has once tasted, even beyond the years of infancy. Let his instruction be an amusement to him; let him be questioned and praised, and let him never feel pleased that he does not know a thing; and sometimes, if he is unwilling to learn, let another be taught before him, of whom he may be envious. Let him strive for victory now and then, and generally suppose that he gains it; and let his powers be called forth by rewards, such as that age prizes.'[41]

Imitation was a strong approach to learning in Rome. This was why Quintilian stated that it was important that the child be surrounded by a proper choice of associates – parents, mentors, teachers and companions. Further, he advised that the child be placed among educated people who thought well, spoke correctly and were well articulated.[42]

EDUCATION DOWN THE LINE

After education began to develop in ancient civilisations it started to spread to other parts of the world, and with its spread came its evolution. For example, in the seventeenth century, education was chiefly religious and rationalistic, but by the turn of the eighteenth century, it had become secular and progressive. It was also in the eighteenth century when teaching in one's mother tongue became of paramount importance, because prior to this all teaching had been delivered in Latin. Also, the sciences were introduced into the curriculum, and it was at this time when questions about the pedagogical methods of teaching arose.[43]

The nineteenth century would see an explosion of commercial activity and rivalry, increased national wealth, and new socioeconomic and intellectual structures that erased the aristocratic cultures of the old. This same century saw major technological innovations like the steam engine and the factory system that led to industrialisation, urbanisation and mass labour. These socioeconomic and technological transformations challenged schools to broaden their curricula to meet the changing face of society. Education was now expected to promote literacy, mental discipline and morals, and prepare the individual for citizenship, employment and personal development. However, these new teaching methods still leaned heavily towards memorisation and discipline.[44]

Schools began to witness a huge influx of students; thus, individual recitation methods had to give way to group methods. The influx created a series of problems which included teacher shortage, and which the monitorial or Lancastrian system tried to solve. In the monitorial system, teachers could engage older pupils to teach certain lessons to younger pupils in groups; and to cope with bulging classroom sizes, schools adopted the practice of dividing pupils into classes according to age. These were the first changes to educational practice that began in Germany in the eighteenth century.[45]

Fast-forward to the twentieth century; the emergence of two world wars would irrevocably change the world. Both wars weakened European imperialism and eradicated colonialism, and this was closely followed by the emergence of new independent countries in Africa and Asia – forcing the international community to think in other directions in order to cater to the needs and powers of these countries. Thus, education became not only an instrument for national development but the springboard to scaling national and cultural walls. Schools, especially secondary and tertiary institutions, sprung up everywhere in an attempt to eradicate illiteracy. Between 1950 and 1970, the number of universities doubled, tripled even – a growth surge driven not only by the requirements of modern technology but by the increasing demand for workers and high-level professionals.[46]

The global educational structure continues to metamorphose in the twenty-first century, and we witness continuous improvement as our educational systems become ever more flexible. From time to time, there have been demands for school curricula to undergo updates – demands which have sparked debates and given rise to headlines like 'Schools should teach all religions' – archive, 1976 – *The Guardian,* 21 May 2020. Other equally dramatic and challenging headlines read: 'Public schools shouldn't preach. But they should teach kids about religion' – *The Washington Post,* 8 September 2015. 'Does Australia's sex education curriculum need to include more on sex positivity, LGBTQI+ relationships, and intimacy?' – *ABC News,* 26 January 2021. 'High schools must teach LGBTQ-inclusive sex education in England' – *NBC News,* 8 September 2020. 'China proposes teaching masculinity to boys as the state is alarmed by changing gender roles' – *NBC News,* 5 March 2021. 'All teachers must "improve racial literacy" in order to teach children to be anti-racist' – *Metro,* 17 Jun3 2020. 'Michigan teacher resigns after proposal to teach more on Black Lives Matter is denied' – *Detroit Free Press,* 26 February 2021.

The world of education and educational debate continues to meet with new issues as new and different problems arise; and as the world continues to change through the face of social challenges and reconstructions, so too do our educational institutions which sit smack front and centre as representations of societal change.

I think a good and pertinent question here to reflect on is whether or not the current academic education system is still producing the independent thinkers, the difference-makers, the visionary leaders, investors and entrepreneurs society needs ... or is it/are we primarily producing workers (blue-collar for factories and white-collar for corporations) – who are more comfortable following instructions to work for other institutional structures, such as capitalists, investors and entrepreneurs?

CHAPTER FIVE
The Abundance-Scarcity Paradox

S adly, conventional schools evolved through history only to stuff students with so much knowledge without teaching them *how* and *why* they should use it. The conventional educational system focuses on intellect alone and relegates social and emotional faculties. This is the key reason for what I call the abundance-scarcity paradox.

We live in a thriving information economy. There is no shortage of information on any subject. Not only is there an abundance of information, there is also relative ease of access. With the click of a button, our eyes glued to a screen, we enter into a world of boundless information and drink from the wells of online knowledge. Yet, despite having access to such a wide array of information, the world as we know it continues to be deprived of and lack wisdom. Wisdom is truly the end point of knowledge; it is the application of knowledge. But it has become a scarce resource in our world since ancient times when wisdom was aplenty and it was commonplace for wise old men to impart their knowledge and hand it down through the generations. Thus, we now live in a paradoxical new age – we enjoy the boom of access to seemingly unlimited knowledge, yet suffer from wisdom bankruptcy. Access to information is always useful when we know what we don't know. But, what about what we don't know that we don't know? Well, this requires us to have a keen awareness and a thirst for wisdom, or to put it another way: curiosity. Yet, how often today do we see students demonstrate academic curiosity beyond areas that fall outside of their curriculums?

WHAT IS KNOWLEDGE?

The *Merriam-Webster Dictionary* defines knowledge as 'the fact or condition of knowing something with familiarity gained through experience or association'. It also defines it as 'acquaintance with or understanding of a science, art or technique'.[1] Knowledge deals with being in constant physical or mental contact with a person, animal or concept. Knowledge is vast and abstract, thus it has been partitioned into several types to give us a comprehensive understanding of what it actually is.

The online academy, Udemy, lists six types of knowledge. They are *a priori*, *a posteriori*, explicit knowledge, tacit knowledge, propositional knowledge and non-propositional knowledge.[2]

- **A priori:** Literally, *a priori* means 'from before'. If a person knows something without having prior experience, that person is said to have *a priori* knowledge. It is also known as reasoning. You don't need to have the experience to know that astronauts can't go to the sun. It is knowledge deduced from reasoning.

- **A posteriori:** In contrast to *a priori*, *a posteriori* literally means 'from what comes after'. Here, a person gains knowledge through experience. Philosophers believe that this knowledge is gained through the five senses and is a mix of experience, logic and reflection. The person has the experience, then uses logic and reflection to interpret and understand this knowledge. Philosophers also refer to *a posteriori* knowledge as empirical knowledge – knowledge based on observation.[3] If you've been scalded by fire, the experience imparts immediate, firsthand knowledge to you that fire is hot. From that experience, and applying it to future situations, you can now logically infer that a volcano would be hot as well.

• *Explicit knowledge:* This is the knowledge gained from documented sources that can be articulated, documented, stored, accessed and transmitted. Examples of explicit knowledge include encyclopedias, research reports, dictionaries, recipes, manuals, databases, etc. Explicit knowledge is the most basic form of knowledge and does not require the individual to have to stretch their cognitive capacities in order to learn. All they need is access to the source.

• *Tacit knowledge:* Unlike explicit knowledge that can be documented and accurately transmitted, tacit knowledge is difficult to articulate, store. A person with tacit knowledge knows a thing and gets results from this knowledge but cannot accurately tell or transmit *how* he got there. Talent, instinct *and* experience therefore play a huge role in acquiring tacit knowledge. Take, for example, Warren Buffet, often called the Oracle of Omaha. Buffet got his nickname because his predictions and comments about the stock market were incredibly accurate. Now, I'm sure Buffet was not the only one who made accurate comments about the market, but there was one distinguishing factor that even Buffet himself couldn't explain: he might only have been able to tell you the next movement of the market, but could not explain how he knew this movement. Similarly, Lionel Messi could write a textbook on football but be unable to explain his playing style and magnificent dribbles. A protégé of Buffet or Messi may only come to understand the unique quality of his mentor through personal experience and practise. But by constantly watching and relating with his mentor, the protégé may discover that he too can make these accurate predictions or amazing dribbles (though similarly be unable to explain how). Udemy notes that tacit knowledge can only be transmitted through 'consistent and extensive relationships or contact'.[4] Chris Drew gives another interesting example of tacit knowledge. He points out that emotionally intelligent people are sometimes 'just that way'; yet they may not be able to communicate to other people how to network, make friends easily, and make people feel welcomed and comforted.[5]

• *Propositional knowledge:* Simply put, this is when a person knows that a proposition is true. Everyone knows that Messi is a footballer, Michael Jackson is a musician and Mark Zuckerberg founded Facebook. It is not a deep form of knowledge, but rather common knowledge and shared knowledge. Udemy points out that a person may read and memorise a textbook or pamphlet of computer programming. The person may even recite all the steps on how to program a computer, yet that person does not have the slightest idea of how programming works.[6] According to Chris Drew, teachers in the twentieth century relied on propositional knowledge. Students learnt through passive learning; they were responsible for reading and internalising the content. However, they did not have the opportunity to apply it in the real world.[7] Sadly, students in the twenty-first century suffer a similar fate. Propositional knowledge is the knowledge *of* something.[8] But this is not enough. Knowing is good, but knowing *how* to do it is better – and that's where non-propositional knowledge comes in.

• *Non-propositional knowledge:* This is knowing *how* to do something. It is also called procedural knowledge – knowledge that can be used.[9] It is knowledge gained by doing, by experience. It is expertise. A person becomes an expert by constantly doing a thing. With constant work, they can develop their own procedures which can be patented. Non-propositional knowledge is a precursor to creativity. Udemy states that in today's world, experience (non-propositional) 'eclipses' education (propositional). 'Sure, education is great, but experience is what defines what a person is capable of accomplishing. So someone who "knows" how to write code is not nearly as valuable as someone who "writes" or "has written" code.'[10] Examples of (patented) non-propositional knowledge include KFC's secret recipe, Google algorithms and *The New York Times* bestseller list.

Personally speaking, I do not think non-propositional knowledge is enough to reshape the intellectual capacities of individuals. Propositional knowledge is good; non-propositional knowledge is better; but *wisdom* is best.

WHAT IS WISDOM?

For a quality so deep, enriching and fulfilling, wisdom has a very simple definition. It is simply the application of knowledge. If you want to get more complex, wisdom is knowing when to rely on instinct, when to use intellect and when to trust intuition. Can a person who has only been taught to develop their intellect understand *how* to tap into their instinct and listen to their intuition?

A person can only be said to be wise when they are able to use and apply the knowledge they have. Wisdom requires the *intentional integration* of one's conscious as well as superconscious faculties – sense, imagination, memory, intuition and intellect – to process knowledge.

To fully understand wisdom, we need to ask a vital question: why wisdom? What is the role of wisdom in the world? The answer to this question will lead us into the second section of this book; that is, an exposition on the importance of education to the individual and society at large. We have seen that education gives us the power to dream, provides skills for living and refines the individual, enlightening the mind as a whole – but if education does all these things, then it begs the question: why is the world in such a sorry state? Conflicts abound in many countries. Political instability continues to exist in almost every nation. Economic downturns still pepper society's way to financial growth and maturity. Environmental degradation is ongoing and unresolved, and social inequalities and injustices continue to exist at every turn. We now see evidence of the misuse of media to malign us, and online wars are sprouting as a direct result of our intolerance to divergent views. The list is endless.

One would expect that with such a thriving knowledge economy, our world would be a better place. To the contrary, it now seems that, despite our increase in academic and professional knowledge, we still need to question whether wisdom truly exists in the world. Knowledge certainly abounds. Yet what we continue lacking is wisdom. The French have a peculiar, yet telling, phrase that crops up when they want to say they miss someone. The most basic way to say 'I miss you' in French is: '*Tu me manques.*' Interestingly, you may notice here that the pronouns are reversed; this is because the French often reverse them from the English order. Yet, when this is literally translated back into English, the phrase means 'you are lacking to me'. I have marvelled for a long time at this construction, because when the French feel they are 'missing' something, they see it as a personal lacking, a shortcoming. Similarly, when they see in themselves a shortage of knowledge or wisdom, they correctly perceive this as a personal lacking, something they are pragmatically aware they need to seek to fill. Only through wisdom can a person apply knowledge so that the essence of humanity can be preserved, and this, I think, is the goal of wisdom: preserving humanity. Humanity keeps diminishing before our eyes, and now the reason is clear: in order to restore ourselves to wisdom, we must first seek to fill the spaces in which we find ourselves *lacking*.

Epicurious and his wise words resonate in me now:

'Let no-one be slow to seek wisdom when he is young, nor weary in the search for it when he has grown old; for no age is too early or too late for the health of the soul.'

To diagnose the problem further, we can use a pictorial representation to show the relationship between information, knowledge and wisdom.

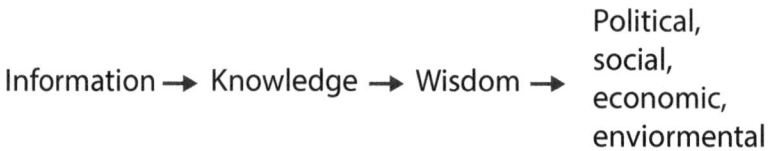

Information → Knowledge → Wisdom → Political, social, economic, enviormental

Figure A: The Ideal Transition from Knowledge to Wisdom

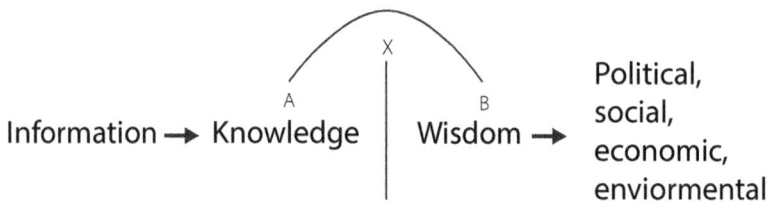

Information → Knowledge | Wisdom → Political, social, economic, enviormental

Figure B: The Barrier to Wisdom

Figure A shows the simple process that takes place or should take place in an individual. A person processes information to knowledge, knowledge is the process toward wisdom and wisdom is required for the world's greater good.

Figure B shows an anomaly in this process. The process flows well from information to knowledge, but meets X's barrier from knowledge to wisdom. This means that there is an accumulation and abundance of knowledge that is not converted to wisdom. Therefore, the world is starved of wisdom and every form of prosperity – social, economic, political and environmental.

Notice that this barrier, factor X, occurs at point *b*; however, it is implanted at point *a*. In other words, factor X is planted into the individual at the point where he receives the information that would normally be processed into knowledge. This seed sown does not manifest until the individual is meant to convert what they know into wisdom for themselves, the people around them and the world at large. And this seed – factor X – is the barrier to wisdom in what is known as indoctrination.

Here's another way to look at it:

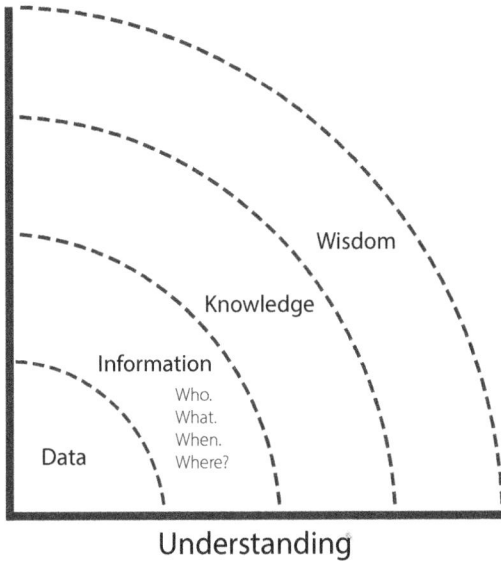

Wisdom

Knowledge

Information

Who.
What.
When.
Where?

Data

Understanding

What percentage of educated people do we know who are inspired and living lives of meaning, purpose and fulfillment, making a positive difference in the world?

CHAPTER SIX

The Gaping Holes and Blind Spots

The abundance-scarcity paradox creates a gaping hole, a deep human need that cannot be satisfied. We can deduce that it is the origin of the various pathologies that plague the world. This deduction is simple: wisdom is the application of knowledge, the full and intentional integration of human faculties. Therefore, without wisdom, nothing – in any sphere of life – works. It is like having a sick patient in a hospital, where the doctor refuses to apply his medical knowledge to treat the patient. The knowledge is there, but the illness lingers because there is no application of knowledge to counteract it.

This gaping hole (created by the scarcity of wisdom) has led to what I like to call blind spots, and these exist in three key areas of human existence: socially, financially and religiously/spiritually.

SOCIAL BLIND SPOTS

Humans are complex social beings, yet our social connections are integral to our existence. This is why blind spots in our social lives can be dangerous. Indoctrination serves to blind us to our own humanity and numbs our feelings. Over the years we have seen the successful indoctrination of members of the military, police force and other armed services to the point where there was a complete refusal and inability to acknowledge the moral and ethical considerations inherent in their duties whilst simultaneously defaulting to, and adopting new, mantras such as 'I'm *just* following orders' or 'I'm *just* doing my job'. This type of thinking demonstrates a lack of independent or autonomous evaluation devoid of moral or ethical understanding, preferring instead to sign up to this kind of postmodern 'groupthink' mentality that requires no effort or period for individual analysis. A similar sentiment can often be witnessed in corporations, whereby an individual will demonstrate their lack of curiosity and enthusiasm or out-of-the-box style of thinking by reverting to the words 'it's not my job' as though some kind of standardised response that results in disengagement and complete lack of accountability. These blind spots manifest in so many ways that if I were to write them all down it would need to be called *An Encyclopedia of Social Blind Spots Fuelled by Indoctrination*. In the interests of time and reader satisfaction I shall refrain from listing them all here; suffice to say, I will highlight just some of the key manifestations I believe are continually plaguing our society today. These include racism, crime, political malpractices, sexism, child abuse and terrorism.

RACISM

It is surprising to see racism continue to thrive in a world where the well-worn cliché 'variety is the spice of life' is as old as time. Classifying human worth based on skin colour is one of the most absurd, and may I say, deranged pathologies of humankind, and I often think about racism and ponder its origins.

Speaking of racism, the discourses of Elizabeth Culotta and Jennifer Kubota both provide suitable psychological and biological explanations to this end. Culotta accurately notes that in order to protect their tribe, humans divide the world into an 'us' vs. 'them'. As humans evolved, group life enabled them to adapt quickly to the environment (such as, the next person could lend you whatever you need for survival – from water to bow and arrow, etc). Now, if another group were to compete for these resources necessary for survival, we would immediately see our survival instincts emerge as we viewed the competing group as the enemy.[1]

According to Culotta, two schools of thought provide possible explanations for hatred and hostility towards the competing group. The first posits that people feel more loved within their group. They are more peaceful, cordial and honest within the confines of their group structure than they are outside the group. And because they are favoured and treated more nicely within their group, there lies a natural tendency to be hostile towards outsiders in order to protect the group's interest. The second school of thought argues that the reverse is the case, theorising that hostilities arising from competing interests between groups fosters an 'in-group love' because it is a well-known fact that united and cooperative groups are more likely to win.[2]

From a biological viewpoint, Kubota and other researchers suggest that the part of the brain known as the amygdala is associated with the formation of racial beliefs and the attitudes that originate from such held beliefs. The amygdala is also associated with fear conditioning – which is important to note because a clear correlation exists between fear and subsequent racial responses. Kubota's work also points to other areas of the brain which are believed to play key roles in racial responses. For example, the fusiform face area (FFA) is implicated in facial recognition – and this area is more active when individuals view faces from the same race. In fact, individuals tend to recognise faces from the same race faster and more accurately than they do with faces from a *different* race.[3]

Culotta and Kubota's work share a common theme: that the

human mind is programmed to seek and recognise differences, and this need to be different could go a long way towards explaining just how racial beliefs and attitudes are formed. In-group love amplifies out-group hate – and hostility towards the out-group highlights the need for in-group love – because both groups recognise that they are different. And at the biological level, the amygdala or FFA becomes more or less activated when a face signals 'difference'.

The human mind therefore creates a bed of difference upon which hate, more often than not, is planted. We are hardwired to look for what makes us different from others – from skin colour to language, religion to wealth, gender to ideologies. This is not entirely a bad thing; the problem lies in what we do with these differences. As Eric Knowles, a psychology professor, said: 'An us-them mentality is unfortunately a really basic part of our biology; but how we define those groups, and the tendency to draw divisions along racial lines, is social, not biological.'[4] And indoctrination plays a huge role in our tendency to create the divisions and behaviours that follow.

Indoctrination and the origins of racism

Human beings began to conceptualise race with the formation of the United States and the evolution of the words 'white' and 'slave'. While early Europeans were recorded using words such as 'race', 'white' and 'slave' in the 1500s, such words were not considered connotations for segregation at the time, and it was not until they found their way into the diction of North Americans. The meanings of these words evolved with the needs of a developing America.[5]

Before the sixteenth century, 'race' referred to kins and the connection they shared. The current definition of race (which categorises people based on physical attributes), is a social construct invented between the seventeenth and eighteenth centuries. The seventeenth century was the age of European Enlightenment. Change would come about as philosophers began to shape society through secular reasoning, rationality and science instead of religion. These new perspectives birthed the belief that 'white' people were inherently smarter, more capable and embodied humanity's essence more than 'non-whites'. This belief and categorisation became the first signs of indoctrination, as well as the justification for colonisation and slavery.[6]

Seventeenth-century American philosophers knew that, whether white or non-white, every human being was made up of blood and bones. This knowledge ought to have made them treat everyone equally – but this was not the case. The need for distinction and hierarchy created a new line of thought that divided human beings along racial lines. This thought spread like wildfire – burning and engraving falsehoods into the minds of the American people. So instead of becoming a model for equal treatment, segregation and bullying became the order of the day.

The white people saw black people as inferior beings with no rights. To them, they were nothing more than slaves and property to be utilised according to benefit. Yet, despite their disdain for black people, they kept buying black slaves because they had advanced skills in farming, carpentry, bricklaying, metal and leatherwork. The white people knew that the development of their society depended on 'black' labour.[7] And that is where the irony lies: the white people first claimed they were smarter and more capable, yet they relied on the creativity *and* ability of black people to advance their society. This simple truth should have been sufficient grounds to steer their minds away from racism and other forms of segregation, but it did not – because indoctrination obscures the truth.

The obscurement of truth was the strategy used by Hitler to promote racial discrimination through Nazism. In my book, *How To Speak Like The World's Top Public Speakers*,[8] I discuss how Adolf Hitler used public speaking as a tool for indoctrination and propagating

Nazism. He sold false narratives to the Germans – told them that they shouldn't regard Jews as humans, and that the only way to restore German glory and virtue was to exterminate them. According to Benjamin Carter (who I mention in the book), Hitler got the support of the Germans because he was able to get them to reject a 'rational, factual world'. In other words, he used his propaganda to block the transition of knowledge into wisdom – and six million Jews died in the process.

Regarding racism, (mis)leading people towards developing a superiority complex is not the only barricade to wisdom; indoctrinated fear serves as significant a barrier. White people in America discriminated against blacks not because they thought them to be inferior, but because they simultaneously feared black prosperity. Jeffery Robinson, the deputy legal director of the American Civil Liberties Union, attributed this fear as the root cause of the Tulsa massacre in 1921. In the twentieth century, the Greenwood neighbourhood in Tulsa was home to wealthy black and Native Americans. The whites resented the black community for their prosperity and used this to level an allegation of sexual assault on a young black man. The black community protested and tried to prevent the lynching of one of its members. Sadly, this escalated to a gunfight between the black and white communities that left about three hundred people – mostly blacks – dead and ten thousand people homeless.[9]

Fear was again one of the fundamental catalysts of apartheid in South Africa. The whites were in the minority and feared losing their jobs and culture if the blacks weren't suppressed.[10] Just as in the US, white South Africans made laws that segregated blacks: blacks weren't allowed into the cities. Blacks were prohibited from taking skilled and semi-skilled jobs. Yet, all the while, the whites needed and relied on the skilled labour of blacks to run their factories.[11]

From these brief accounts, we can see that the history of racism across different societies is rooted in the same ideologies: superiority and fear. To the rational mind, racism makes no sense. The whites claimed superiority, yet they needed and relied upon black people for their society to thrive. They claimed superiority over the blacks, yet the potential prosperity of the black community also threatened them. How can you fear that which is beneath you, and that which you already assert power over?

Racism shoots itself in the foot time and again, and its irony is not lost on the fact that it showcases the values of cooperation, the strength of variety and the progress a society ultimately denies itself through segregation. What racism reveals is that we all need one another, that no one human being can ever be inferior or superior, and that at the end of the day we are all humans capable of making unique contributions to the world.

To the rational mind, racism makes no sense. However, in the presence of indoctrination, rationality dissolves into nothingness. In modern society, racism is not as overt as it used to be – but it is still relatively easy to indoctrinate people into a discriminating and segregational mindset. Even today we can see recent examples of discrimination playing out in the form of medical apartheid being openly promoted and flouted by western world governments under the umbrella/s of medical safety; the concept of dividing a society into two groups of the vaccinated and unvaccinated was quickly and readily adopted by many indoctrinated minds with surprising ease and very little resistance; they were encouraged to further separate, isolate and ostracise any member of society who even wanted to ask questions about the efficacy of the recent COVID-19 vaccines as a matter of natural curiosity. Such people were quickly labelled 'anti-vax' as opposed to being 'cautious', 'sensible' or 'vaccine-hesitant'. How can you identify the indoctrination in this instance? Quite easily: through the lack of nuance demonstrated by the proponents of the discrimination between those who willingly got vaccinated versus those who didn't.

CRIME

The following exposition on slavery brings to mind a name: John Wilkes Booth, the man who assassinated Abraham Lincoln. Booth was a young, excellent actor and a member of a distinguished acting family in the nineteenth century. Apart from his theatrical prowess and fame, Booth was an egocentric advocate of slavery and was boldly vocal about this, plus his hate for Abraham Lincoln. He recruited other advocates and they conspired to abduct Lincoln, but after many failed attempts to capture the president, Booth finally found and seized his opportunity at Ford's Theatre, where Lincoln happened to be at a comedy performance. He shot Lincoln at the back of the head and escaped.[12]

At the core of this, and every crime, is a belief. A belief powerful enough to suppress the voice of conscience in a person and pay no mind to the laws of the society. At the core of every crime is a belief, **an indoctrination.**

Crime is a complex aspect of human nature, and origins cut across social and psychological lines. Despite its complexity, one fact remains true: indoctrination sits at the core of its origin. Crime is one way through which indoctrination interferes with the human condition. A person most likely becomes a criminal because through indoctrinating thought processes they arrive at a somewhat skewed and tainted outlook on life.

Analysing the different forms of crime in the world would be beyond the scope of this book; instead I've chosen to look at three serious offenses categorised as felonies in all parts of the world. They are murder, rape and burglary/robbery.

Murder

Dr Peter Morrall, a mental health and behavioural science expert, condensed the motives for murder into four groups: lust (e.g. a thrill killer or a murderer driven by lust would kill a rival competing for their object of desire); love (e.g. euthanasia or the 'mercy killing' of a loved one with an incurable disease); loathing (e.g. hate directed to a person – an abusive person killing their partner; a group – LGBTQ community or a religious group; or a nation – the Nazis killing the Jews); and loot (e.g. murdering someone for financial gain).[13]

With the crime of murder, there are two important points to note. First, for me, love as a motive for murder simply does not count. As with euthanasia, the 'murderer' bears no ill will towards the 'victim'. Euthanasia is even legal in some countries. So, in the context of crime, I wouldn't touch on murder as being motivated by love.

Second, as Morrall points out, not everyone driven by lust, loathing and loot turns out to be murderers. This means that the motives for murder are multidimensional; yet these motives all share a common denominator, and one that Morrall couldn't pinpoint – but I can. Individuals who kill because of lust, loathing, loot or any other cruel motive, have one thing in common: they've been *re-engineered* to undervalue human life.

Nobody is born a murderer. In fact, the word 'child' is synonymous with innocence. If, given in our purest birth form we are innocent beings, then our descent into becoming murderous or engaging or entering into a murderous state could be a direct result of environmental influence; that is, they have either been in an environment where life seems worthless, or they have learned to see murder as a means to an end. Murderers learn to place their desires (e.g. money, sexual satisfaction) or emotions (e.g. hate) over a person's life. This is how child soldiers and terrorists become hardened killers. Ann O'Neill wrote in a CNN story titled 'Stolen kids turned into terrifying killers':

'The journey from boy or girl to killing machine follows a horrifying route of indoctrination, including being forced to execute friends and family.'[14]

In 2016, twelve-year-old Nasir, a child soldier trained by ISIS to be a suicide bomber in Syria, narrated his experience to CNN. Nasir said the ISIS commanders would lead the young soldiers to hide in tunnels during air strikes. They would tell them that the Americans – the unbelievers – were trying to kill them, while convincing them that they – the ISIS commanders – were trying to save the boys because they loved them. The commanders told the young soldiers they loved them more than their parents and would care for them even better than their parents did, effectively brainwashing young recruits into believing that their parents were unbelievers and that their first duty was to kill them.[15]

Once the mind learns to enthrone desires over human life, murder becomes easy – inevitable, even. Education can play a vital role in pre-serving the sanctity of life, but its shortcomings have made this quite impossible. People have lost faith in conventional education because it has failed to give them the much-needed skills and philosophies required to navigate life. Instead, they are exposed and brainwashed by a society of unscrupulous people at the helm. People who answer to the gods of ambition, without assuming any social, moral or ethical responsibilities, and people who, in many cases, would do anything to satisfy these desires. The level of cooperation at the political, cor-porate and pharmaceutical industry level may be a testament to that fact.

Rape

Lust does not generally push people to commit murder; rather it drives them to force a victim to have sexual relations with them. Both men and women can be guilty of rape in different ways; however, for the sake of argument here we will assume the position of the more common scenario, that of men raping women.

A man rapes a woman because of one reason alone: he believes that he has power over her and her body. This belief arises from a societal indoctrination popularly known as patriarchy. By its definition alone, patriarchy begins in the home. It is a structure that gives a man – or more aptly put, the father figure – sole control of the family. Merriam-Webster defines patriarchy as a 'social organisation marked by the supremacy of the father in the clan or family, the legal dependence of wives and children, and the reckoning of descent and inheritance in the male line'.[16] This birthed a culture deeply rooted in sexism, with rape as an offshoot of sexism.

At the core, a rapist believes that his power as a man extends to the woman's body, so he objectifies the female form, viewing her as merely a tool for his pleasure. He *may* request to have sexual intercourse, but he doesn't expect her to decline his request. He also doesn't respect her decision to say no. And if she does, he ignores her right to refuse by then forcing himself on her.

Rape passes a subtle message to the victim, which is that 'society has given me right over your body. You have no right or power to reject me or any other man'. And the situation is further compounded by the fact that, in blaming the victim, the culprit continues to retain this power even after the act.

Rape cases become all the more sinister when the sexual predator is in a position of power and influence. This position reinforces his overall power as it mutes the victim's voice. If the victim once had the power to say no, she now loses that power because the predator's position also tethers the victim to a place of fear. And fear becomes the tiny voice in the victim's head that reminds her of what she might lose if she says no. The predator then leverages his voice to suppress the victim's voice and will even further. We see a perfect example of this in 2017 with the emergence of the #MeToo movement.

Harvey Weinstein wielded so much power and influence in Hollywood as a dominant figurehead, owning the film companies Miramax and The Weinstein Company, which produced top-grossing movies like *Django Unchained,* catapulting many actors to fame and fortune. It was easy then for Weinstein to wield such power and influence over his victims for sex. In 2017, the #MeToo movement spread like wildfire as over eighty brave women finally came forth to share stories of how Weinstein sexually assaulted and abused them. One actress claimed that Weinstein had forced her to sleep with him if she wanted the role in a movie. According to her statement, Weinstein had bragged about being the reason behind the success of another actress who had won an Oscar.[17] Weinstein denied these accusations, claiming that the encounters with these women were only ever consensual.

As far as rape cases go, it is always the word of the victim against the predator. However, given the circumstances, the accusations against Weinstein are not far-fetched. There have been countless cases of influential men using their positions to objectify and sexually abuse women. Rape is not just about vile men; it is about men who have been raised wrongly. As with murder, it is about men who enthrone their desires above a woman's will because they feel they have the power to do so. But the even greater underlying issue here is about indoctrinated men who have assumed an incorrect belief system.

Burglary/Robbery

This is the hardcore truth: thieves feel entitled. Apart from kleptomania, every other reason for stealing cannot be justified and most likely stems from indoctrination. Thieves have the erroneous thought that the only way to partake in the equitable distribution of wealth is to forcefully transfer it from the haves to the have-nots. Many people who engage in corruption are also indoctrinated with the same belief. However, when it comes to stealing, engaging in corruption or robbery, the fault does not lie with the culprit alone. Society must assume a huge chunk of the responsibility because it remains the major agent of indoctrination. Societal conditioning cultivated over time exposes people to certain behaviours which predisposes them to stealing. This conditioning manifests in two forms: first is the despising of wealthy individuals, while the second – which is like the first – is the segregation of people based on socioeconomic status. As a result, people steal because of necessity/poverty, greed, jealousy, low self-esteem, peer pressure, feeling socially excluded or having a desire to prove their independence.

We have been conditioned to define success *primarily* by income standards. There is hardly any acknowledgement of the fact that career success (with high income) – and which lacks meaning, inspiration, purpose, meaningful relationships and a stable mental state – is not really success at all. You only have to look around to see the indoctrination of students and professionals who strive for career and income success with little to no awareness about who they are, what they want, what makes them come alive and what difference they wish to make. Most people are so goal-oriented and success-oriented they listen only to their heads because they have lost the heart and soul connection. And this isn't even the worst part. Even those who are career and income motivated do not understand that income has a poor correlation to a financially secure future. Many have been so brainwashed as they pursue income and fancy job descriptions that they fail to realise that the skill of making money in the first place is not the same skill required to keep or grow money. Due to heavy indoctrination practices (which are noticeably devoid of financial education), people have little to no awareness of the need to plan for their financial future, or how longevity trends (living longer in retirement) impact inflation and their standard of living when their income stops at retirement. I think many educated professionals are in for a rude awakening. Imagine facing a huge drop in living standards after thirty to forty years in the workforce? How can this happen? The simple fact is that heavy indoctrination blinds us to the bigger picture and has the ability to make us more microscopic than macroscopic when it comes to understanding our life vision. Any individual who strives to achieve greatness or fulfillment needs to also understand that academia gives us only a fraction of what is required to be a holistically successful human.

Uruguay's former president, José Alberto 'Pepe' Mujica, who led the country from 2010 to 2015, is regarded as the poorest president in history because of his austere lifestyle. Of Mujica's house, the BBC wrote in a 2012 article: 'Laundry is strung outside the house. The water comes from a well in a yard overgrown with weeds. Only two police officers and Manuela, a three-legged dog, keep watch outside.' They continue to assert that he 'shunned the luxurious house the Uruguayan state provides for its leaders and opted to stay at his wife's farmhouse off a dirt road outside the capital, Montevideo'. As president, Mujica donated about 90% of his $12,000 salary to charity and lived on $775 monthly.[18] It is for this reason he was considered the poorest president in the world. But *was* Mujica really poor as a president? We will delve into two expositions to answer this question – that is, an account of Uruguay under Mujica's leadership, plus a comparative look at Mujica and other presidents.

It is said that under Mujica's leadership, the country enjoyed financial prosperity, having a consistent GDP and per capita GDP growth.[19] His leadership saw a tenfold decline in poverty rate, a 75% growth in the economy and a 50% increase in public spending. The wealth gap in Uruguay was bridged, social spending increased and schoolchildren had free laptops.[20] Mujica was described as a socially progressive leader, as he respected and protected the rights and choices of pro-choice individuals and those of different sexual orientations. So, with these qualities in mind (which earned him great respect and trust amongst his countrymen), would we say Mujica was an inspiring president? Whilst most of us can safely agree that Mujica was an inspirational leader, how many young graduates would wish to follow his life model, or are even aware of him?

Furthermore, the description, 'the poorest president in the world', does not stand alone; the description was in context to other presidents which makes the claim inappropriate. Many leaders live lavish lifestyles in today's world, while the electorates that voted them in to *serve* remain impoverished. For example, Burundi, with a GDP per capita $263.67,[21] is the poorest country in the world. Yet, when its former president, late Pierre Nkurunziza, was about to leave office, the parliament voted to pay him $530,000 and give him a luxury villa after he handed over his position.[22] This same president plunged the country into a constitutional crisis after successfully running for a third term. According to the BBC, his rule was characterised by 'human rights abuses, including executions, arbitrary arrests, torture and sexual violence'.[23]

In a world that sidelines humanity and glorifies wealth without meaning or contribution, Nkurunziza would most likely be revered more than Mujica. The latter was consistently described as poor even though he led a prosperous nation and had the choice to enrich himself with the nation's wealth. Yet Mujica's simple way of living was a deliberate choice: he would rather have a prosperous nation than have a nation impoverished at his expense. He had the option of living in the presidential, one-hundred-year-old palace, but he chose his humble farmhouse where he parked his twenty-five-year-old blue Volkswagen Beetle in a dusty garage. Mujica once described his austere lifestyle as a way of fighting for his personal freedom. 'If you complicate your life too much in the material sense, a big part of your time goes to tending that. That's why we still live today as we did forty years ago, in the same neighbourhood, with the same people and the same things. You don't stop being a common man just because you are president.'[24]

This is not to say that being wealthy is bad or that a wealthy person cannot be a good leader; but glorifying wealth and defining an individual only through financial standards is also problematic. Mujica is mostly remembered as the poorest president that ever lived, rather than by his prosperous and effective leadership. 'The poorest president' tag did not just describe his eccentricity, it became the basis for unfair comparison of Mujica against his presidential counterparts.

This description and consequent comparison might have pushed Mujica into stealing public funds had he had no moral grit. But Mujica was wise and understood contentment and the place of luxury in the grand scheme of things. His life is an example that some people steal not because they are discontent with their present financial status, but because they want to live up to the standard of a world that glorifies wealth and classes people according to their financial status. They do this to measure up to societal perceptions.

Psychologists Federica Durante and Susan T Fiske released a disturbing finding. They discovered that preschoolers classify people based on wealth, and by the tender age of six, are already capable of perceiving a rich person as 'smarter' and more hardworking. Between the ages of four and six, children are already choosing their friends through subtle wealth cues as they gravitate towards the 'competent' and 'popular' kids. (White kids go even further to associate race with social status.) By the time they reach middle school, children are also already keenly aware of their social status; an awareness founded on wealth and status consequently births negative stereotypes towards poor people, while leaving out the middle-class and the rich.[25] This has caused some kids to resort to stealing their parents' money or the toys of other kids so as to *belong* to the cool kids.

Society has normalised classism. It is a social inequality that does not garner attention and social media traction like discourses on racism, sexual orientation and gender equality. Yet, classism continues to eat at and erode the fabric of society.

We can therefore conclusively trace all financial crimes to an indoctrinated society, one where socioeconomic inequalities thrive and wealth is glorified without meaning or real contribution. And let's not stop at just financial crimes; it is important to consider that politically corrupt systems similarly pervade the world.

POLITICAL MALPRACTICES

One aspect of any society where indoctrination manifests strongly is politics. When indoctrination permeates the political arena it becomes like a bug-infested house – hard to control, harder still to get rid of. Unfortunately, the world is currently going the wrong way when it comes to seeking solutions, and here's why: the world thinks that the political structure of many nations, including the United States, is broken. But Katherine M Gehl, speaking in reference to the US political system, says that it is not broken, it is fixed.[26] I agree with her.

In her 2020 TED Talk, Gehl rightly notes that healthy competition motivates businesses to do better to keep customers happy, and this general set-up becomes a win-win situation for companies and customers alike. Yet when it comes to politics, this is simply not the case. For Gehl, when the Democrats and Republicans keep doing well, the customers (the electorates) are still unhappy. Unlike entrepreneurship, politics is win-lose game.[27]

Gehl's Ted Talk centres around the concept that this win-lose scenario is intentional. According to Gehl, politics is not broken. It is fixed. 'It's doing exactly what it's designed to do. It's just not designed to serve us, the citizens, the public interest. Most of the rules in politics are designed and continuously fine-tuned by and for the benefit of private gain-seeking organisations. That's the two parties, a textbook duopoly, and the surrounding companies in the business of politics. *And they're all doing great. Even as the American public has never been more dissatisfied.*'

Politics could only go against the people it was designed to serve because it has wielded the tools of indoctrination. Recall that indoctrination is the barrier that stands between knowledge and its right, effective application – wisdom. Gehl does not blame the politicians, rather she blames the system. And she's right. However, we must understand that systems do not just arise out of nowhere. For example, in the human body, cells make up tissues, tissues make up organs and organs make up systems. Similarly, a simple, unchecked misnomer that persists over time would eventually be recognised as a system; a body of rules *set in stone*. This is the simple mechanism and basis for indoctrination. And we are all prisoners of it – both the villains *and* the victims.

Most political systems, if not all, are designed to exist as a duopoly where two parties with differing ideologies compete for power. Political systems are not designed to cater to the needs of the people because politics is a battle of ideologies. A battle of and for control. Hence, politicians become ideologically fluid to achieve their political ambitions. Take Donald Trump for example. In Jonathan Rauch's article in *The Atlantic* titled 'How American Politics Went Insane', Rauch states that although Trump belonged to the Republican party, he was never a Republican. '... Since 1987 Donald Trump has been a Republican, then an Independent, then a Democrat, then a Republican, then an "I do not wish to enrol in a party", then a Republican; he has donated to both parties; he has shown loyalty to and affinity for neither.'[28]

Elections do not bring in people who are ready to do the bidding of the people; rather, it brings in political actors who are there to foster political ideologies and fulfill their private political ambitions. An average political party indoctrinates its members to believe they will only hold offices if they serve the party's interests over the people. Gehl accurately notes that if a member of Congress were to vote on a bipartisan bill, the question that would be most important to such a member would be, 'Will I win my next party primary if I vote for this bill?' Of course, the answer is almost always no; however, it is rare to see the interests of the people and the interest of the party intersect in this way.

Political indoctrination also extends to the electorates. Firstly, the system must indoctrinate the general public to believe that the single **most popular** choice is the right choice. Secondly, the electorates learn to indoctrinate to polarise themselves, like the politicians, into political ideologies. However, unlike the politicians, the electorates are not ideologically fluid. On the contrary, we seem to find that most times, electorates remain rigid with their beliefs – and this benefits no-one more than the politicians.

As long as the electorates remain ideologically divided, the parties are able to retain their power. If, for example, a highly populated state is a blue state, the Democrats remain confident in their ability to triumph in that state; if it is a red state, the Republicans are confident of their continued success. This is why parties work hard to maintain the status quo in the constituencies where they are sure to triumph.

Yet this style of indoctrination takes the electorates' focus away from their socioeconomic needs and directs it only to the party ideologies and philosophies. People no longer cast their votes based on confidence and faith in the candidate to perform; rather, they cast their votes based on how left- or right-winged the candidate is. They continue to chant slogans as they blur the lines between ideologies and their national needs; and they teach others to do the same. Ask a person why they support a particular candidate and the answer likely hovers around the candidate's level of conservatism or liberalism. Electorates no longer ask the simple question: who is capable of meeting our collective needs?

In India, the political system is further flawed. People do not just vote based on ideologies, but on caste and religion. Casting votes based on caste and religious sentiment is deeply flawed, because a politician is then more likely to institute progressive reforms based on ideology rather than their caste or religion. For instance, José Mujica, whom we looked at earlier, is an atheist[29] and his policies were more inclined to the left. Barack Obama is a Christian[30] and his policies leaned to the left, too. Clearly, religion plays a lesser role in governance than ideological inclinations. However, unfortunately in many countries like India, religion is a major influence over voters' decisions. And no cultural component of any society blinds more than religious indoctrination.

In the 2019 Lok Sabha election in India, 29% of the 539 winners have at some point been guilty of serious crimes including murder, attempted murder, rape and kidnapping. Since 2009, this figure recorded an increase of 109% of Members of Parliament (MPs) guilty of serious crimes. Such MPs are detrimental to their constituencies as they reduce economic growth and increase poverty. This being the case, how then do these MPs get elected? The answer is simple: the electorates – who are poorly informed and have no background knowledge about the records of these politicians – vote solely along the lines of caste and religion.[31]

It is worthy to note that this voting direction has a strong correlation with literacy. Non-literates and those educated up to school-level were more likely to vote a candidate because of their caste and religion.[32] But this is not to say that literacy solves the problem. After all, the United States has a literacy rate of 99%, yet they face a 'broken' political system. The real problem is not illiteracy, but indoctrination. With politics, many Indians are indoctrinated along caste and religion, while many Americans are indoctrinated along ideological lines. Same problem, different manifestations. Indoctrinated people often cast their votes because of long-held societal norms. Didn't some people refuse to vote for Hillary Clinton simply because she's a woman?

SEXISM

The 2016 US presidential election was a particularly interesting time historically because Hillary Clinton became the first woman and female candidate to get the backing of a major political party in America. While this historic feat was celebrated all over the world, Hillary's candidacy reflected a chronic societal ill: sexism.

Amidst the celebration and support Hillary received, several questions remained paramount: how did the world get to a point where we jubilate over a woman's achievements? How come we still see a woman's achievement as a rare feat? The answers to these questions are the same and tied to indoctrination. Jubilating and celebrating a woman's achievements is a strong indicator that we are still freeing ourselves from indoctrination's hold. But how did this form of indoctrination come to be? How did we arrive at this point?

Our societies were not always male-dominated and steeped in patriarchy. As hunter-gatherers, there were no gender roles, and both men and women moved around hunting what they could find, gathering what they could for their survival. A man could move to live with his in-laws or a woman could do the same, or the couple could completely move away from their families. Patriarchy and patrilocal residence only became a thing as societies became agricultural because farming called upon the basic need for physical strength, and this tipped the balance in favour of the male species.

Describing this in detail, Anil Ananthaswamy and Kate Douglas write: 'With the advent of agriculture and homesteading, people began settling down. They acquired resources to defend, and power shifted to the physically stronger males. Fathers, sons, uncles and grandfathers began living near each other, property was passed down the male line and female autonomy was eroded. As a result, the argument goes, patriarchy emerged.'[33] The emergence of patriarchy could be excused in early societies because these societies were structured according to physical strength. Males in general were physically stronger. They tilled the soil, hunted, went to wars and provided for the family, while the women stayed and cared for the home and the children. By virtue of physical strength, men assumed leadership roles in the home – and extended it outside the home. Men began to lead everywhere – schools, religious houses, meetings, everywhere – and this soon became the norm.

This norm began to suppress women, their strength, their voices, and women became second-class citizens who felt they had to obey the dictates of men whether they were favourable or not. Women were relegated to duties like cooking and weaving, and we see an example of this in the first book of Homer's *The Odyssey*. In one scene, Telemachus, Penelope's adolescent son, tells her: 'You should go back upstairs and take care of your work, spinning and weaving, and have the maids do theirs. Speaking is for men, for all men, but for me especially, since I am master of this house.'

This scene, far from being a figment of Homer's imagination, was the reality of women in Homer's time. Ancient Greek and Roman societies were deeply steeped in patriarchy, and such societies *perpetually* made women silent and invisible. The classicist Mary Beard, author of the book *Women & Power*, in an interview with the *Los Angeles Times* in 2017, makes an interesting observation regarding the 'persistence of female disempowerment'. Beard writes, 'There's a basic rule of thumb that the more a culture oppresses women, or oppresses anyone, the more culturally preoccupied they are with that.'[34] In simpler terms, the oppressor never wants the freedom of the oppressed so he preoccupies himself with the thought of what would happen if the oppressed were ever to become free.

The institution of patriarchy birthed gender stereotypes handed down from one generation to the next. We see this manifest itself in 'manly' and 'ladylike' behaviours, masculine and feminine colours, hobbies for men and hobbies for women, toys for boys and toys for girls, duties for men and duties for women, jobs for men and jobs for women. And it created a snowball effect:

- A man should not cry.
- A lady should be prim and proper.
- Blue is for boys.
- Pink is for girls.
- Men should drive.
- Women should knit.
- Boys should have cars.
- Girls should have dolls.
- Men should work and provide.
- Women should clean and cook.
- Men are doctors.
- Women are nurses.

The list goes on and on. The indoctrination of gender stereotypes has become so normalised that we are immune to the subtle nature of it. The funny thing about stereotypes is that we swallow them hook, line and sinker without ever knowing how they came about. For example, when it comes to the stereotypical colour designations of blue and pink, many do not know that in the twentieth century, pink was for boys while blue for girls. Pink was seen as a more decidedly strong colour, while blue was seen as dainty and prettier.[35] Who would have thought that pink (which many men avoid because it is today considered a 'girly' colour) was once considered the strongest hue?

This is just one reason why stereotypes cannot be trusted. Stereotypes indeed tend to change when they no longer satisfy the narrative. It is only when stereotypes consistently support a narrative that they become passed down as norms. Pink was for boys and blue for girls; that was the norm until parents started dressing their kids as miniature versions of themselves. Then the colour switch happened almost overnight, and it has remained so ever since. Even when parents tried to favour unisex clothes and colours because they felt dressing girls in feminine clothing limited their opportunities for success, the trend did not last long before the gender polarity returned.[36]

Gender stereotypes manifest not only in mundane affairs like clothes and colours, but also in deep and serious issues such as leadership positions. As previously stated, the institution of patriarchy served to silence women's voices. There seemed to be an unwritten rule that women were not born leaders, thus they were relegated to the background. There is probably much truth to the old saying that *behind* every successful man is a woman. Women were at best support systems as society did not allow them into the spotlight. In one example, Lucretia Mott and Elizabeth Cady Stanton were denied participation in the World Anti-Slavery Congress in 1840 because – you guessed right – *they were women*.[37] What's wrong with being a woman? Nothing. Then why have women been marginalised for so long? The answer is clear: society brainwashed everyone to do so.

I am not suggesting that it is only males who are indoctrinated on this issue. There are many women who expect men to be the ones to make the first move, ask women out on a date, pay for dinner, be the main breadwinner and so on. Ayanna Charelle, an online influencer, recently wrote a post that gained in popularity amongst her largely female base of followers. Her post reads: 'My nails/feet are $90. Eyebrows are $12. Rent is $1674. Utilities is $180. Other needs average at $590. If you're in a relationship with me ... YOU'RE PAYING FOR ALL OF IT. Period! ME AND MY BILLS ARE A PACKAGE DEAL!! Pay up or leave me tf alone.'

One of the hallmarks of indoctrination is a fixed and closed view (usually unexamined or reinforced through personal biases) that is acquired through culture, media, religion or education.

Under mass indoctrination, people can become radically intolerant of opposing views. If someone challenges this worldview, the group under the spell of indoctrination will exhibit contempt or even aggression because they feel that their way of life is being threatened. At the same time, they are radically enamoured by anyone (especially those in a position of authority) who will reinforce their inner narrative. Genuine curiosity about an alternative or opposing perspective, however, is not an ingredient of an indoctrinated mind. This may explain why even today (in 2021) the majority of students continue to spend an enormous amount of time and resources acquiring tertiary education promoted by institutions themselves (a by-product of the industrial age), instead of developing or seeking out knowledge that is highly valued in the digital/social era.

Prior to the institutionalisation of education and work through universities and corporations, circumstances forced our forefathers to practice creativity and ingenuity to make a living, no matter what their occupation was.

How many students or professionals do you know who are aching to improve their skills in the areas of communication, persuasion, personal branding, money management, investing, marketing, negotiation, critical thinking, decision-making, content writing, consultative selling – or any other skills that are deemed to be highly valuable, desirable and lucrative in the social age? If we look at this objectively you will agree that most people seem to be making their career choices by looking in the rear-view mirror, blindly and unconsciously following the actions of the majority.

Indoctrination limits us from asking questions – the right questions. And even if we eventually do arrive at these questions, the weight of lies and inaccuracies over centuries that have clouded our minds makes it difficult for one to see or truly accept the truth, because truth will appear to us as this new and radical and foreign thing – and so we fight it. Humans are scared to change. We would rather remain in the prison of indoctrination even if it comes at a cost or dilutes our advancement.

RELIGIOUS BLIND SPOTS

Religion is a subset of the culture or social life of a people. Humans have always felt the desire to connect to a world beyond this one. I postulate here that this desire stems from three main reasons.

We can find the first reason in Brandon Ambrosino's interesting and profoundly true statement. He states that our religions exist because of our increased capacity for sociality.[40] From this statement, we can infer that since nature abhors a vacuum, our natural human instinct is to create the desire for a new connection, a fresh experience. As humans we feel that there is a world beyond this corporeal space and we want a taste of that world.

Secondly, I believe that the world's magnificence is a match that ignites human desire for the metaphysical. The galaxies, oceans, trees, birds, reptiles, mammals and all the beautiful intricacies of and in nature that have been explained and unexplained by science all point to the fact that, for many of us, there must be a grand architect that we cannot feel or fathom, a powerful being we want to know and connect with.

Because of this hunger for spiritual connection, people began to venerate what they conceptualised as God. Then they invented rituals as a means of worshipping and communicating with their god. They heard or claimed to hear the voice of this god who taught them what life was all about and how to relate with Him and other human beings. They went further to document these messages as tenets for their beliefs. As they propagated their beliefs and got other people to identify with it, these documents evolved to become holy writs – spiritual constitutions – that guided the lives of the new believers.

Many of these beliefs have evolved into organised religions today and hold on dearly to one goal: to transition into the metaphysical through death and have a real and eternal connection with their deity; a connection never to be interrupted by any corporeal element. This goal forms the third reason why I think it is that humans desire to connect with the supernatural. For most people believe that what they do on earth either grants or denies them access to the afterlife. Hence, they do all it takes to please their deity so as to gain entry into eternal bliss. This is, of course, the beginning of religious indoctrination.

Don't get me wrong. Personally, I believe religion is good and can be a wonderful source of teaching us the values of wisdom, connection, courage, faith and love. However, it is also a known fact that religious indoctrination produces the worst forms of suppression, atrocities and control. Indoctrinated people do not mind pleasing their religious leaders at the same time as committing indecent, immoral or unethical acts on others. It is also a well-known fact that the human mind can be made to rationalise any belief. An indoctrinated mind will go to great lengths to rationalise their own belief, even though they have not examined that belief and quickly dismiss any narrative prematurely that opposes or challenges it.

In a world where we ought to coexist and work towards our collective good, we see many people put up barriers of segregation simply because of religion. Many describe others outside their religion as 'infidels' or 'unbelievers'. They interact and relate with opposing religious beliefs with a long pole, never entertaining the possibility that nuances exist in every complex situation.

Earlier, we saw that in India, religion was one of the major influences of electorates' choices. The electorates do not care about the competency of the individual – as long as the person prays to the same deity, he is seen as worthy of leadership. Between November 2019 and March 2020, Pew Research Center carried out a survey on the religions in India. The majority of the almost thirty thousand respondents practicing different faiths – Hindus, Muslims, Christians, Sikhs, Buddhists, Jains – said that they were '*very* free to practice their faiths'.[41] They also perceived religious tolerance as an integral part of their lives as a nation. Describing this, the Pew Research Center writes: 'Across the major religious groups, most people say it is very important to respect all religions to be "truly Indian". And tolerance is a religious as well as civic value: Indians are united in the view that respecting *other* religions is a very important part of what it means to be a member of their own religious community.'[42]

It's not enough that these religions respect one another; they also share some common beliefs. (1) About 77% of Hindus *and* Muslims in India believe in karma. (2) 32% of Christians and 81% of Hindus believe that the Ganges River has the power to purify. It is important to note that this – the purifying power of the Ganges River – is a central belief in Hinduism. (3) In Northern India, 12% of Hindus, 10% of Sikhs and 37% of Muslims identify with a mystical tradition associated with Islam called Sufism. (4) All religions in India teach their faithful to respect elders.[43]

This survey sounds pleasant and hopeful as it paints India as a nation united amid religious diversity. But reading further into the report, it may seem that we were too quick to describe India as religiously tolerant. The faithful of these religions see themselves as different from one another, even if they are all Indians dwelling on the same land. For example, the Hindus see themselves as different from Muslims, and the Muslims feel the same way too.

Furthermore, members of these religious groups do not approve of inter-religious marriages. Two-thirds of Hindus in India said they would prevent Hindu women and men from marrying into other religions. 80% of Muslims state that it is important to prevent Muslim women from intermarrying with other religions, while 76% shared the same opinion with respect to Muslim men. This religious wedge in India is not only seen in marriage but also in friendships. Most Hindu respondents revealed that most, if not all, of their close friends were Hindus. One may want to excuse this as inevitable since the majority of the Indian population are Hindus; however, a similar phenomenon is seen among Sikhs and Jains, who make up approximately 2.3% of the entire population of India. Despite their small number, Sikhs and Jains still manage a close circle of friends with whom they share the same religion. The survey also revealed a very disturbing fact: some Indians stay in neighbourhoods where only people from their religion reside. Many say they would even keep people of certain religions out of their neighbourhoods or villages. Up to 45% of Hindus said they would be unwilling to share neighbourhoods with people of one or more of these religions – Islam, Christianity, Sikhism, Buddhism or Jainism. 61% of Jains didn't want a Muslim, Christian, Hindu, Sikh or Buddhist neighbour. Also, 36% of Hindus and 51% of Jains categorically stated that they didn't want a Muslim neighbor.[44]

Is religious tolerance in India a farce? Is it a house built on sand? And the wind, when it comes, would it reduce the proverbial house to rubble? What we have in India and in many other nations are people who just coexist because they have to. No actual bond of unity exists. Isn't it ridiculous, then, that some people say they wouldn't allow someone from a different religion into their neighbourhood?

Why would someone not want to associate with another because of their faith? I bet you know the answer by now.

Many religions teach – or rather, indoctrinate – their followers to see people from other religions as outcasts. Unbelievers. Infidels. This indoctrination often does not come from the founder of the faith; rather the followers develop it over time. As Culotta says, the need to protect our group creates an 'us' vs. 'them' mentality. Some religious faithful believe that associating with other religions may contaminate their purity or steer them off track. Many believe that it is they who serve the one true God and that theirs is the one and only true religion. It is this belief that has led to faulty human relationships, resulted in horrific acts of terrorism, and skewed the relegation of cognitive faculties.

Oncologist and writer, Jalal Baig, in a 2016 opinion piece for *The Washington Post*, writes that a patient of his refused him from treating her because he was a Muslim. The patient had just watched a Fox News broadcast of a bomb attack at an airport and train station in Brussels. About her reaction after seeing the clip, Baig writes: 'The sounds of my patient's voice rose, eclipsing the thump of her heartbeat that I was painstakingly trying to hear. She sounded distressed, anguished even, about the loss of innocent lives on the TV screen. "These foreign people only come here to kill and ruin things," she said. Then she said, "Donald Trump is right: America should ban all Muslims from immigrating." And then perhaps she noticed the subtle change in my facial expression. "I'm sorry, but your people and people who look like you make me uncomfortable," she said. She refused to let me treat her.'[45]

Baig's article was melancholic, the hurt behind his words palpable. He blamed Trump for his patient's actions and the Islamophobia that pervaded the United States. This patient may not have been affiliated to any religion, but through the news she had listened to and

heard consistently, she had developed an antipathy towards Muslims
– without even understanding how her decision could directly affect
her health. Religious indoctrination need not necessarily come from
a religious cleric; it can come from anyone. All it takes is to plant *and*
water a thought. In Trump's case, he planted a thought and the terrorists wasted no time in watering it.

Many Muslims have condemned terrorists who kill innocent
people in the name of Allah. However, their condemnation, while
commendable, does not erase the fact that Trump promoted propaganda against Muslims, simply because *certain* Islamic sects gave him
the opportunity to do so.

In 1986, Osama Bin Laden founded Al-Qaeda. The group started
as a logistical network to support Muslims during the Afghan War
against the Soviet Union. But the group would soon morph into
something far more dangerous; like a malignant tumour, their logistical network turned into a militant organisation. One would expect
that when the Soviet Union withdrew from Afghanistan in 1989, the
group would either disband or provide social support to Muslims.
But none of these things happened; instead, the Al-Qaeda began to
oppose what they considered corrupt Islamic governments and foreign presence (particularly, the US) in Islamic lands.[46]

They quickly merged with other militant groups and trained tens
of thousands of Muslim militant recruits from countries around the
world. And then they began to strike. In 1998: The destruction of
US embassies in Kenya and Tanzania. In 2000: A suicide bomber
blew up the US warship *Cole* in Yemen. In 2001: The unforgettable
destruction of the World Trade Center and The Pentagon, and a plane
crash in Pennsylvania – all due to Al-Qaeda militants hijacking four
domestic flights.[47, 48] The reason for these attacks? To oppose Western
capitalism and *ungodliness* in the world.[49]

This is the message they have passed to all members of the free world, and which they continue to promise to act upon as they terror-ise in the name of ridding the world of evil and ungodliness. They also anticipate a great reward in the afterlife. This may not be consistent with the true tenets of Islam, but as long as these fanatics perpetrate evil in the name of Islam, people like Baig's patient will continue to feel uneasy in the presence of a Muslim. With Baig's story, we see two types of indoctrination: on the one hand, religious terrorists act as agents of religious cleansing because they have been indoctrinated to see others as ungodly; on the other hand, Trump's soft and subtle indoctrinations were an attempt to breed a developing phobia and disdain for *all* Muslims instead of aiming to unite the collective as a strong leader, president and ambassador for world peace. Trump had a fiduciary responsibility as a president to help people understand and distinguish the religious faithful from religious fanatics, not create further chaos and discord.

For indoctrination to be effective it needs the indoctrinated person to relegate their thinking faculties. We see evidence of this as it plays out particularly in religious indoctrination. Many religious followers imbibe every doctrine hook, line and sinker. Take, for example, what happened in Mumbai, India, in 2012. Water trickled down a statue of Jesus Christ at the Church of Our Lady of Velankanni in Mumbai. This was declared a rare phenomenon – a miracle. The locals collected it as holy water and began to promote the church as a pilgrimage site. But when author Sanal Edamaruku came on the scene, he made a discovery that deflated the excitement of all. And the church that was once venerated as a holy ground became a building for Christians once again. What did Sanal Edamuruku do? He discovered that the water was neither holy water, nor a supernatural phenomenon; it was but a simple leakage from a faulty sewage system which trickled to the feet of the statue through capillary action.[50]

That is how indoctrination works. It fixates only on what you know, keeps your attention fixed predominantly on what you believe and restrains you from thinking beyond your present knowledge. The locals in Mumbai have already stuffed their minds with the supernatural. They faithfully read their Bibles, probably even travelled to Israel to behold phenomenons peculiar to their faith. So, when they saw water dripping from a statue, none saw anything extraordinary in it, and no-one felt the need to investigate the cause. They just automatically labelled the water as holy and venerated the statue and the church. What's more interesting is that after Sanal's discovery, the church accused him of blasphemy and charged him with offences punishable by three years in prison. According to Sanal, the Catholic archbishop of Bombay said they'd drop the charges if only he apologised for his 'offence'. Sanal disagreed. He also received death threats and had to seek exile in Finland.[51]

The events surrounding the weeping crucifix in Mumbai perfectly explain the representation of indoctrination. Sanal presented valid information to the church and its locals. Because of him, they *knew* where the water was coming from, and they knew sewage water was dangerous to human health. The next thing they should have done was to apply wisdom. They had to fix the leakage and discard any 'holy' water they had collected, but because of indoctrination, they did not do this; instead, they charged Sanal to court. We can never underestimate how far the indoctrinated mind will go in terms of resistance, but we can see here that an indoctrinated person can become so indoctrinated, so ingrained in their belief, that they will make illogical decisions – even in the face of the most logical evidence.

FINANCIAL BLIND SPOTS

One may wonder if humans could be financially indoctrinated. It may seem bizarre to suggest the concept of indoctrination and finances side by side, but the fact is our financial behaviours mostly stem from how we've been wired to view money. Some of the indoctrinations or misconceptions we have about money, wealth and finances include:

Financial indoctrination 1: The way to become financially successful is to get a degree and a job

This is a misconception shared by many people. Having a degree is important; but the fact remains that a degree is still just a means to an end and not an end in itself. People should understand that it is not the certificate itself that brings you wealth, but the ability of the individual to use the knowledge they've obtained from college and translate this into monetary value. Your degree only provides you with the knowledge and platform through which you can then create wealth. If this is true, how can some people struggle when they have a degree from a quality institution, while others can be successful without a college degree or in a field unrelated to their degree? Simple – because a college education doesn't guarantee success. Success begins from a mindset, and having this mindset (plus other driving factors), are skills which colleges don't teach. The mindset of obtaining a degree and getting a job is one of the oldest indoctrinations people readily adopt without thinking; yet nowhere does it acknowledge that simply making money is an assurance of keeping money or growing money. Growing money is also called wealth creation, and hundreds of millions of professionals are predominantly focused on making money in the 'now', but have not been trained on how and why to create wealth for their future. How big of a problem is this? Imagine hundreds of millions of retired professionals having to rely on their families or governments (most of which face huge deficit and have a deteriorating social security system) to sustain themselves at retirement. Most people are sadly blind to the realities of financial indoctrination, where hardly any emphasis is placed on proper money management and wealth creation in the conventional education curriculums and where very little, if any, real instruction exists.

Financial indoctrination 2: People and systems working for you (business)

This can be the zenith of financial independence and legacy. Being at the peak of your business is where money not only works for you but for people and systems as well. At this stage, you move from being an employee to being an actual business owner. Not everyone needs to be a business owner; however, there is a marked difference separating the typical employee mindset from an entrepreneurial mindset. Employees exhibiting an entrepreneurial mindset are more likely to embrace risk, have a bigger vision and seek out diversified experience.

Working for money cannot result in financial independence without having a plan for Point 1 or Point 2, or both, and only results in living from pay cheque to pay cheque (something most professionals do not recognise). If they did, they would not settle for titles and incomes, but proactively aim for executive positions, profit share, equity or even being a part of an emerging startup. Have we become indoctrinated enough by the current systems in place to be blinded by shiny incomes and fancy job titles? I'll let you be the judge.

Financial indoctrination 3: It takes money or financial capital to make wealth

Having money is just the preamble. Being able to utilise and channel your money into profitable ventures makes for financial independence. Aside from money, what do you have?

- **Do you have financial skills?** These are the skills required to uphold financial practices and maintain financial stability within a business, some of which are: education and training, interpersonal skills, ability to communicate, problem-solving skills, management experience, etc. This helps not only to build a business but to sustain it as well.

- **Do you have a mindset that values high achievement and**

productivity? The difference between a wealth creator and a person stuck in financial struggle begins with their mentality. A person inhabiting a wealth mindset understands the need to spend less on their lifestyle, make wise investments and look for ways to improve financial standing with minimal risk. Conversely, a poor mindset believes the pursuit of wealth is wrong, that being wealthy is largely a matter of luck and that it is generally difficult to maintain one's integrity and still become wealthy. Deeply hidden beliefs can therefore reveal the level to which the person has become indoctrinated. Many people who value academic and professional education but lack business or financial education have no plans for securing their financial future. They become okay with the status quo because they get by every day. But what happens when push comes to shove – what will they have to show for their years of labour? Unfortunately, too many people find this out the hard way, whether through premature redundancies, industry downturns, disability or injury. They were so preoccupied with day-to-day living, too busy making a living and focused on making ends meet that they had nothing to fall back on – they forgot to make a life. Indoctrination is a blinder; it always prevents you from seeing the bigger picture.

Millions of successful entrepreneurs become financially successful through bootstrapping, not raising capital. Millions of investors become financially successful through prudent investing, risk management and allowing long-term compounding to take its course. Many build their empires and legacies from scratch. There must be times when, as entrepreneurs, they feel like quitting, regret decisions made, yet the one thing they all do understand is that good things don't come easy. Their experiences show that having prior access to capital or money is not necessarily a prerequisite for creating wealth. Yet so many people continue to assume that this is the case. Indoctrination perpetuates unexamined assumptions.

Financial indoctrination 4: You need to buy the right investment to become wealthy

Wealthy people don't stop at mere savings; they make investments. However, this is not the only requirement for wealth creation. To create wealth, one needs:

- **The right plan:** Aside from random investments, it seems many educated people have no plan or strategy for their financial future. Could this perhaps be one of the shortcomings of conventional education, that so many educated professionals invest more time in a holiday or the purchase of a washing machine than in planning their financial future or the future of their family? How can the conventional education system not train and prepare hundreds of millions of graduates to understand that a person training to do a job to make money is only half-trained if they don't know what to *do* with that money? The wealthy person spends considerably more time planning their finances than the average middle-class individual, proof that wealth creation is a deliberate and planned action that requires commitment, discipline and patience. Such qualities are missing/or noticeably absent from the portfolios of most degree holders. After all, isn't securing a better financial future the whole point of pursuing a degree? How can so many totally miss the point here? Does indoctrination also make one myopic?

- **Ability to understand and mitigate risk:** Risk management requires an understanding of second order consequence, meaning it is not what will happen soon after one makes a decision, but what actually happens after the decision is made. Yet the conventional education system perpetuates first-order thinking. As a consequence, most graduates and professionals choose short-term security over long-term freedom (job over entrepreneurship/equity), income over wealth, job titles over purpose and impact. It appears that indoctrination results in perpetuating short-term thinking over long-term consequences.

*

The way to solve any problem, I believe, is to shed light on it. Just as doctors canvas patients during a diagnosis, questioning serves to broaden our perspective. It exposes the root of the problem, makes room for the explorative and expository. Our current social, religious and financial blind spots are roadblocks from our being able to shine a light on truth, yet they exist because indoctrination serves as an opaque barrier, simplifying and standardising things that should never have been standardised to begin with.

Conventional educational systems ought to be agents of change that encourage us to break down barriers and guide students towards truth, yet sadly, today, the opposite is true; the current systems in place in conventional education only serve to promote indoctrination, limiting one's ability to think outside the box.

CHAPTER SEVEN

Indoctrination: Education's Imperceptible Aberration

The Cambridge Dictionary defines indoctrination as the process of repeating an idea or belief to someone until they accept it without criticism or question.[1] Personally, this is the best definition of indoctrination I have found to date. It sums up the entire process from the indoctrinator to the one who is indoctrinated.

It is important to understand that this process sometimes is not obvious. Political and religious indoctrinations are most times obvious, but the indoctrination within the conventional educational system is far more subtle, imperceptible and insidious – and an aberration from the true purpose of education. Schools should not be agents of indoctrination; rather they should inculcate knowledge and teach students how to utilise this knowledge for the greater good of humankind.

Indoctrination in conventional schools is subtle, yet if we study the nuances of the current system, we are able to uncover the more subtle methods through which indoctrination happens. I have narrowed these findings to ten key methods of indoctrination, which, like any other form of indoctrination, serves to cause more harm than good, despite having become normalised in schools all over the world. In the practice of indoctrination:

1. Conformity is promoted.
2. Collaboration is discouraged (labelled cheating).
3. Individual expression is discouraged.
4. Intellect (memory recall) is prioritised over creative imagination.
5. Fear of failure is common in pupils at exams.
6. Risk-taking is rarely discussed or encouraged.
7. Punishment is allocated for questioning and standing up to authority (disruption is discouraged).
8. Emotional dependence is perpetuated.
9. Self-education, identification with self-passion, values and purpose is non-existent.
10. Pandering and approval-seeking behaviours are encouraged.

CONFORMITY IS PROMOTED

'The higher the level of education, the more sensitive people are to mass formations.' – Dr Mattias Desmet (Professor of Clinical Psychology, Ghent University)

'The way I see it, conformism (or sheepism) is one of the most harmful forms of ignorance. Not only does it affect those who succumb to it, it also affects the entire human race on a core level of reality. Without the creative brave ones who consistently challenge the status quo, we would never expand as a species, or grow and experience anything new.' – Gordana Biernat

'Here's to the crazy ones, the misfits, the rebels, the troublemakers, the round pegs in the square holes … the ones who see things differently – they're not fond of rules, and they have no respect for the status quo. You can quote them, disagree with them, glorify or vilify them, but the only thing you can't do is ignore them because they change things. They push the human race forward, and while some may see them as the crazy ones, we see genius, because the people who are crazy enough to think that they can change the world, are the ones who do.'
– Steve Jobs

As social animals, humans easily develop and form herd mentality. We are more likely to pick up a habit because others possess the same habit. This predisposition to conform to the majority conversely makes us *uneasy* when we see an individual daring to deviate from the norm. Conventional schools are guilty of perpetuating such behaviours. They make no allowance for difference. Teachers aim to groom every student in the same way because difference and uniqueness translates as rebellion. Thus, many students lose themselves in this grooming process and unwittingly sacrifice their essence on the altar of societal validation.

For example, many teachers still see being left-handed as an abnormality. Sarah Harris, in an article in *The Daily Mail*, explains that teachers go to 'extraordinary lengths to force left-handed children to use their right, from tying their preferred arm to assigning fellow pupils to sit with them and make sure they did not do what came naturally.' She further reveals that 'children are still being "penalised" for being left-handed because many teachers are unable to spot the signs that they are struggling with their writing and do not know how to help them effectively'.[2]

I am of the opinion here that it is not so much about teachers not being able to spot the signs and help effectively as it is about them already having closed their minds to difference and uniqueness. They have translated that because, statistically speaking, '90% of the world's population are right-handed' to mean that everybody should be right-handed; therefore, the remaining 10% should be expected to conform. I know this is probably an extreme example, but it cannot be denied that conformity is almost always duly rewarded in the education system.

Schools normalise a culture of conformity and it manifests in myriad ways, from little things like changing a child's preferred hand to bigger, more significant things like grooming all students to learn at the same pace and in the same way. Two possible results stem from this perpetual culture of conformity: (1) The individual becomes a shadow of themselves as they come to live a life not theirs; or (2) The individual, unable to conform, finds people with similar uniqueness and forms a clique or cult.

The second result is, I believe, the reason we are now seeing a rise in activism globally, as a lot of activists break free of societal expectations to reassert their individual rights.

Schools need to make a better effort at celebrating and teaching students uniqueness and variety. As long as a person's uniqueness and choices are not detrimental to the individual or humanity in general, pushing conformity and conformist narratives today does more harm than good.

COLLABORATION IS DISCOURAGED

There is a thin line between cheating and collaboration. Teachers often classify both as the same. When students work together on a project or assignment and come up with a solution together, this is collaboration. However, when one student works entirely on a project alone to arrive at a solution, and where the rest copy from that student, this is cheating.

Teachers should be able to tell the difference and act accordingly. Academically weak students tend to cheat when they are not guided properly. Already students are victims of intellectual classism, wrong beliefs, assumptions, impatience and the rigidity of time and ideas in the system. So, they cheat to please a system that judges and measures their intelligence by grades.

Weak students rely on the intelligent ones to carry out projects because they have resigned themselves to a certain fate. They have learned to see themselves as failures, and as such, they do not try to contribute. Instead, they pass the bulk of the work to the students conferred upon as the bright ones and copy from them since they want to pass, graduate and leave the school.

The status quo here *has* to change. If collaboration is not actively encouraged, schools will continue to raise docile, compliant and agreeable workers instead of innovators with disruptive entrepreneurial spirits. The only way to do this is to recognise the students' strengths and weaknesses, then give class projects where every student within a group can contribute to the project's overall success. Students should then be graded by their strengths and how significant their individual contributions are to the group. No student should ever feel left out. Also, teachers should encourage the students to complement one another, where the weaknesses of one are supplemented by the strengths of another, and vice versa.

If schools could integrate new and more collaborative learning styles, the so-called weak students would look forward to participating in teamwork and no longer feel marginalised. They would be celebrated as individuals contributing to the whole, rather than signalling to their failure/s that only ever results in a reluctance to participate.

INDIVIDUAL EXPRESSION IS DISCOURAGED

'The litmus test for determining if you're potentially being indoctrinated is when your sense of self-expression or speech is continually silenced.'
– Ron Malhotra

This follows my previous point: students are not allowed to express themselves individually. They are taught en masse at the same time, expected to learn at the same pace and expected to all graduate at the same time. Too much focus is placed on moving forward or progressing with their class, which is not entirely bad – but shouldn't there also be allowances made for individual expression? It is a well-known fact that the most accomplished members of society aren't necessarily those who have skills, but those who have skills *and* prominence. Prominence is achieved through visibility and a personal brand. However, most professionals seem to be more comfortable fitting in than standing out. They spend years or decades acquiring the necessary educational certificates and degrees but spend virtually no time building their networks, their influence, their personal brand or their ability to lead. Indoctrination pressures people and leads them into conformity, not towards individual expression. This is, I think, why the majority of professionals are uncomfortable about building their own personal brands in their industry or marketplace.

I recently stumbled on an excerpt of *The Soul-Crushing Student Essay* written by Scott Korb.[3] Korb's essay perfectly mirrors my ideas on individual expression and self-expression. I wouldn't want to dilute the profundity and truth behind Korb's ideas by paraphrasing his words; therefore I partially include the excerpt of Korb's article below, verbatim. To read the article in its entirety, search *"The Soul-Crushing Student Essay,"* written by Scott Korb.

'But my experience with students has me worried that years of "texts being read" and "tests being taken" have created the sense in them that whatever they're devoted to doesn't matter much to the rest of us – so long as they know the answers to our questions, so long as they pass the test.'

Korb's piece is an interesting one and if I keep sharing excerpts, I will end up sharing the entire article. However, for the sake of brevity here I'll emphasise a point that aligns with the main idea of this book. As I mentioned earlier, indoctrination is reflected in the little things – and in Korb's case, it's even more telling in the way the students write essays about themselves. Scott Korb teaches writing to first-year college students, and he witnessed firsthand the effects of indoctrination on his students. These students have, over time, learned to divorce themselves of reality in their essays. They have been taught to focus only on getting the 'right' answers – because they know this is only what the teacher wants.

Korb goes on further to explain that his students write as if waiting for a momentous event in their lives, rather than having the courage and confidence to write as they should. This validates what I said earlier about societal and academic validation being tied to achievements. Korb's students have imbibed the idea that they cannot share their stories unless those stories are 'worthy' of recognition. I believe that they feel no-one would read or enjoy their stories if the stories didn't contain their accomplishments. This is perhaps why so many professionals today feel uncomfortable sharing the adversities and challenges of their personal stories in their blogs, content or speeches.

INTELLECT (MEMORY RECALL) PRIORITISED OVER CREATIVE IMAGINATION

Examinations in conventional schools are tests of memory and analysis, not creativity or imagination. Intelligence is a blend of creative thinking and imagination. It involves using knowledge as a raw material for creation and results. Students today are not really encouraged to use their creativity in schools, because as Korb rightly notes, they are expected to *regurgitate* the teacher's ideas.

But is this sufficient? Couldn't a teacher's job involve more than simply teaching the student the subject matter, perhaps guide them to develop their own thoughts and concepts about the subject? Could they be encouraged to look at the world around them and find applications to what they've learnt? During examinations could teachers look more for the students' ideas – and not the exact repetition of what they have in their notes? Could we shift the emphasis from simply being right or wrong and place more importance and weight on 'original thinking'? Indeed, if this were the case, then I think we would produce more entrepreneurs, creators, inventors, discoverers, innovators and disruptors of the future ready to forge their own path, instead of entire generations of students more comfortable following an existing system.

Schools would most certainly do a better job by empowering students to discover and accept their unique identities, and promoting creative imagination is a veritable approach to achieving this. Do great students live under the shadow of their teachers? Or are they capable of processing their learning through their own perspectives to carve out a unique path or strategy?

FEAR OF FAILURE IN EXAM PERFORMANCE

When a student asks a fellow student for answers during an exam or uses the internet to get answers, this is not just examination malpractice – the student is sending a message, making a statement and a cry for help. The student is saying, 'I am afraid of failing. I am in a society that forces me to learn and grow at a pace uncomfortable for me – and because I have to conform to its expectations, I have no choice but to cheat.'

Isn't it ironic that motivational speakers, celebrities and other public figures keep reminding us that it is okay to fail and get back up, while the counter-narrative could not be further from the truth? I can find countless motivational and inspirational articles and quotes, yet what strikes me most is how these messages only seem to apply to entrepreneurs and any other area excluding academia. When it comes to school students, we completely forget this message that it is okay to fail, and instead expect them to perform well at all times. We teach students to fear failure. We would rather have the students produce good grades, 'the right grades' – even if they cut corners to get them – than to acknowledge their need to learn at their own pace.

This unrealistic expectation *needs* to change. I believe more students would perform well at exams if they were not already under the weight of pressure to do well. When students are equipped with self-awareness and self-management training, they are more likely to excel through pursuing subjects that are in alignment with their inner values, passion and strengths. When students understand that failure is a necessary prerequisite to success, they will seek feedback instead of avoiding temporary failure.

RISK-TAKING IS RARELY DISCUSSED OR ENCOURAGED

Because the school environment is a hotbed for conformity and where conformity is most heavily promoted, students are not encouraged to take risks. They are not taught that sometimes success in life comes from trying something new and unpredictable, or taking a risk to see where it leads. Rather, curiosity is stifled and they are trained to see any deviation from convention as high risk. I personally believe this reflects the biases of many teachers who similarly choose the 'safer' career path in teaching because of niggling doubts and personal insecurities surrounding failure if they had dared to seek unconventional or less conventional career paths.

The school environment is a farm for cultivating fears. Since students are taught to fear failure, they automatically become unwilling to take risks. Students wouldn't want to take a risk that would yield no success, so they stick with what they know and validate their stance with certain overused clichés such as 'the devil you know is better than the devil you don't'.

I think we need to allow ourselves to stop for a minute, take pause and ask ourselves/examine what this really means. When someone says that the devil you know is better than the devil you don't, I will argue this: why know the devil at all? Why should risk be seen as something dangerous, or devilish, and why is it presented in this way? When we come to unpack certain clichés like this, what we actually find is the opposite meaning – but we need to access the content of the expression, not rush to judge it if we are to uncover its true meaning.

Similarly, I am sure you have heard of other negative clichés, such as 'pick your poison' – why do we need to see something in this way, as something being the lesser of two evils? Maybe there was no poison to begin with? Or if there is a suspected poison, why have to pick one at all? This is germane to the concept of indoctrination; we mouth certain beliefs without actually stopping to analyse them. Yet when we are able to look at things outside of our indoctrinated minds, we can see more clearly just *how* indoctrination truly works and *how* it influences our everyday thinking in the subtlest of ways. This is our true poison.

PUNISHMENT IS ALLOCATED FOR QUESTIONING AND STANDING UP TO AUTHORITY (DISRUPTION IS DISCOURAGED)

I think that conventional education is structured somewhat like a master-slave relationship. Students (especially in state run schools or schools in emerging countries) are rarely allowed or encouraged to express their opinions or stand up to authority. Questioning the status quo and speaking out against the school administration is considered an act of rebellion and more often than not leads to a student's suspension or expulsion.

Schools are a breeding ground for silence. Students are taught to cower to authority, where challenging conventional educational methods is frowned upon. Suffice to say, conventional educational methods still exist today *because* of this lack of resistance, this inability to disrupt or question. If we were to survey a cross-section of students, I am confident we would discover that a very high percentage are dissatisfied and dislike the way current educational systems are set up. Yet, without any formal avenues open to debate or propose change, a student's only outlet available is to complain on social media or vent their frustrations to their friends or family about flaws in the system. Many times, even the parents of these won't listen, perhaps because they too were conditioned through the same system and can only see things through indoctrinated eyes. Sometimes a student will be seen boldly protesting against some facets of the system, but not the entire system. And even when they do work up the courage to protest against certain facets of the system, there is a pervading fear of punishment that will come from the system in return. In nations where human rights are not recognised, students who have protested against certain school practices have faced severe punishments as extreme as expulsion. Sometimes, instead of expulsion, the teachers or lecturers will intentionally fail the students, thereby forcing them to continually repeat classes until they become so frustrated they leave the school or the school becomes 'compassionate'.

Teachers rarely allow students to air their opinions, even though students *can* speak against what feels uncomfortable without being disrespectful. Administrators and teachers need to be more open-minded to this fact and accept that there *are* things they can learn from students, and that, as I have stated previously, education is always a two-way exchange of ideas. Perhaps it is finally time for schools to be less conventional and more flexible.

Imagine a world that takes young kids in the prime of their lives and puts them through institutions that promote the practice of indoctrination, where they are not taught anything about themselves; they do not learn high-income skills for another sixteen years, then, after crippling them with debt, the system throws these students back out into a world that offers nothing more than depressed wages, financial illiteracy and exorbitant living expenses. You no longer need to imagine such a world. We now live in it.

EMOTIONAL DEPENDENCE IS PERPETUATED

Schools continue to release emotional dependents into the world as a direct result of systems of indoctrination. It is inevitable, really, because what should we expect from a system that breaks down the emotions of the students only to have them rebuilt as part of an indoctrinated system? The system places rigid rules upon their learning without caring or factoring the long-term effects on the psychological and emotional wellbeing of the students. In Chapter Six, I mentioned how St Olave's Grammar School discriminated against the weaker students. Such actions, if not handled correctly, lead to serious esteem issues. This is why we now have so many emotionally deficient youths who seek support through drugs, alcohol, toxic relationships or any other habit they feel brings them succour. Many students seek ongoing validation and acknowledgement from their teachers (which explains why many more are so hesitant to try new things as they grow into adulthood). Could this be one of the reasons why the majority of graduates opt for traditional occupations like medicine, engineering, law, IT or management instead of becoming consultants, trainers, coaches, authors or speakers? Indoctrinated minds clearly prefer the status quo over change.

SELF-EDUCATION, IDENTIFICATION WITH SELF-PASSION, VALUES AND PURPOSE IS NON-EXISTENT

I have emphasised the current lack of identity and passion that emerges as a result of being in a highly indoctrinated system. Conventional education systems indoctrinate students to hide from themselves. There might as well be a welcome sign at the school gates that reads: 'PLEASE REMEMBER TO DROP YOURSELF AND YOUR UNIQUENESS OUTSIDE'. Sarcasm aside, this makes perfect sense because the school system expects conformity – and conformity cannot exist if variety and uniqueness are allowed to thrive. The result? Schools quell individual thought and encourage groupthink, while students are expected to suppress their passion, values and purpose. As a matter of course, students will then often align their purpose and passion according to their expectations. A student good at maths and physics is expected to be an engineer. No-one bothers to ask if they would prefer to pursue a career in music (even though they sing every day in their bathroom and when they walk to school). As a result, so many students end up taking on careers they were just not cut out for. They have simply responded to the demands of society. Conventional education doesn't teach students how to monetise their passion, even though most, if not all, passions can be monetised through the understanding and application of marketing, branding, promotion, sales, positioning, persuasion, copywriting, negotiation and closing. However, many of these commercial high-income skills are noticeably absent from most school and university curriculums. What could be the reason? Could it be that indoctrination actually results in choosing familiarity?

Furthermore, the school system does not allow for students to embrace self-education. Instead, they expect students to learn and stick with only what they are taught in school. This form of indoctrination is cemented in the fear of failure. When a teacher encounters an idea different from what they have taught in class, they almost always automatically fail the student. So, throughout their school year, students become confined to a limited curriculum and are rewarded only based on what they learn in school.

PANDERING AND APPROVAL-SEEKING BEHAVIOURS ARE ENCOURAGED

Approval-seeking is the consequence of almost every other form of indoctrination. In an environment where conformity is promoted, and collaboration and individual expression are discouraged, a student will most likely model behaviours outside of their true self to seek and gain approval from others. They are unlikely to don their creativity or imaginative cap because they have to learn by rote – like everyone else – and all this, because they are afraid to fail. This same reasoning can be applied to explain why they shy away from taking academic risks.

So many students today are afraid to stand up to authority because they don't want to be viewed as eccentric. In a system where everyone conforms, it falls back to human nature to not want to be seen as the odd one out. These students will instead dwell in their shell till they morph into an emotional mess. They feel different and alone because they are different and alone in a system that singles them out and isolates them for their differences. The more students become divorced from their identity, passion, purpose and values, the more they have to pander to the dictates of others – and seek validation to achieve emotional stability.

*

Indoctrination is, to use a metaphor, like sculpting an object out of concrete. When the object is first formed, it is wet, soft and malleable – and can crumble easily. But when left for a long time, the object becomes dry, hard and difficult to crack.

It is impossible to pinpoint exactly the period when such nefarious indoctrinations began to plague the modern world. However, what we *do* know with some degree of certainty is that when they began, the majority of people in society in that period did nothing to push back. Instead, what we are now left with are indoctrinations that have normalised – and even become crystallised over time – to the point where, like hardened concrete, they are now difficult, if not impossible, to crack.

CHAPTER EIGHT

The Three Arms of Indoctrination

Wars and activism continue to plague the world because human beings are hardwired to resist change. And this resistance is the reason why indoctrinations still exist. (Note: War and activism can be products of indoctrination. People fight for or against a system where indoctrination thrives.) Resistance to change often comes in the form of criticisms and could also take on the form of arguments and nitpicking. But it is my belief that indoctrinated individuals resist change for one of three reasons. I call them 'The 3s' or 'The Three Arms of Indoctrination'. With these three arms in place, indoctrination can quite literally lock itself firmly into the minds of people. They are:

1. Status quo is comfortable (or, The Comfort of Status Quo).

2. Supposed rewards are alluring (or, The Allure of Supposed Rewards).

3. Supposed consequences are scary (or, The Fear of Supposed Consequences and the Unknown).

THE COMFORT OF STATUS QUO

Newton's first law of motion states that a body at rest will always remain at rest until an external force acts upon it. And even when the external force acts, the body will resist the force unless it is a force greater than the force exerted by the body. This law is not limited to inanimate objects but to human beings as well. The human mind has evolved to seek survival and stimulus, but not massive change, and so it is we find ourselves resisting significant change when it presents itself.

Psychologists and behavioural scientists have studied this process in detail; that when we humans receive new information that aims to alter what we know, we process this information in one of three ways. We either *generalise* the information, *delete* the information or *distort* the information.

Generalisation

When entering into a state of generalisation, the indoctrinated person will conveniently lump the information with a general view. The individual does this by relating new information to an experience and giving meaning to the information based on the outcome of this experience. For example, if you tell a teacher that they need to encourage students to eschew rote learning and use their creativity and imagination as tools for learning, the teacher may generalise this information by telling you that they once tried such and such method but it didn't work as the students failed woefully. Such a response contains three possibilities: that they never attempted the teaching method; that they actually did apply the method and the students failed, resulting in the assumption that the problem came from the students, not them; or they applied the method, the students failed, they acknowledged the problem was from their teaching method, but they never bothered to find out what went wrong. In all three possible scenarios we see an unwillingness to go the extra mile, a rigidity and inflexibility with regards to fixing the problem and a resolute resistance to change.

Deletion

The individual can also subscribe to deletion. As the term implies, the person resists new information by deleting specific parts of it to suit a preconceived narrative and/or provide an excuse. Let's assume you approach the teacher and ask them to revamp the teaching method by being more student focused. You comment that this would greatly improve the students' capacity for learning and also make them a star teacher. But you also add that the process would be physically and mentally taxing as it would require individual interaction with each student to identify their specific academic needs. In deletion, a reactionary response would result in the teacher rejecting all suggestions as it would fall on deaf ears. The teacher refuses to listen to positive alternatives and would act to delete vital components of the information being offered, such as possible benefits to both them and the students. They would hold on to the physical and mental demands that come with revamping their teaching method, and instead of being open to accepting this information and finding new motivations for teaching instruction, they would resist the information entirely by deleting the benefits, while stubbornly sticking with the challenges.

Distortion

Distortion is a powerful tool used to interpret and modify the information to suit a particular narrative. For example, if you tell the teacher to improve their teaching method by being student focused, they may tell you that any student-centred teaching is just an attempt by 'woke' generationalists to justify intellectual laziness. Yet intellectual laziness cannot thrive in student-centred teaching and learning, and teachers inherently know this. But in order to dodge the suggestion, the teacher chooses to distort the information by creating unfounded narratives.

An indoctrinated person will unconsciously or subconsciously use any or all of these three mechanisms to resist change and avoid the discomfort it brings.

THE ALLURE OF SUPPOSED REWARDS

People will gravitate towards a particular behaviour because they find it rewarding or think it promises rewards. Most men still resist gender equality not because they don't understand it, but because they inherently understand the benefits of patriarchy. Patriarchy has erroneously taught us that men are sexual beings who are entitled to a woman's body while subsequently sending the message to women that they need to be subservient and align their will according to the dictates of the man. It has also taught women to depend on men for everything. These perceived rewards would make a man or woman resist the idea of patriarchy tenaciously. The man still wants to be reverenced by a woman, yet he also wants to objectify her and use her to satisfy his desires. The woman, on the other hand, understands that patriarchy absolves her of responsibility or the need to provide for herself, allowing her to escape. She has the mindset that she does not need to suffer when someone can provide for her.

Supposed rewards are not only specific to social indoctrinations, it is also seen in religious indoctrination. The promise of supposed rewards is one of the key strategies terrorist groups like Al-Qaeda use to recruit their members. Suicide bombers are promised the reward of eternal life in the afterlife, a heavenly paradise of seventy-two wives. The promise of such high reward is the belief system terrorist groups have eagerly adopted; they are willing to die because they believe death paves the way to their reward.

However, sometimes indoctrination does not offer the promise of reward; rather it instils the opposing fear of failure, which is a different kind of motivating force and one which assures the indoctrinated person never deviates from this path.

THE FEAR OF SUPPOSED CONSEQUENCES AND THE UNKNOWN

Fear is an incredibly powerful and common tool used by indoctrinators. They know that the indoctrinated individual may one day see through their falsehoods and so they prevent this by using fear and intimidation to threaten the individual with consequences that will befall them should they deviate from the path. Shaming people through labels is similarly used in indoctrination practices to dissuade, deter and control people from challenging the narrative. We see this play out in all forms of indoctrination. For example, a person of one religion would tell his followers not to relate with people from other religions because they are immoral/dangerous/ignorant. In the current wave of the COVID-19 pandemic, pro-vaxxers are quick to label anyone who is hesitant about a particular vaccine as an 'anti-vaxxer' – a negative and derogatory term used to ostracise them and make them feel guilty about their choices. Parents with kids who are excelling academically may be discouraged from hanging around kids with low IQ or from a lower socioeconomic demographic. For generations now, IQ has been assumed to be the primary and correct basis for measuring intelligence.

Similarly, in India, parents use coercion to indoctrinate their children by attaching consequences to choices that do not abide by that parent's wishes. In Indian culture it is commonplace to induce guilt into the child by making them feel selfish about exploring any other choice than that which is given to them. If this fails, the family will threaten to ostracise and abandon them, having nothing to do with the child if they exercise a choice different to the parents' wishes. So if, for instance, a young person from a particular culture or race feels attracted to a person from a different culture or race, they face a conflict. They know this person is cool and sweet but they never feel truly convicted about their choice because they know that their family will have the final say. They also anxiously wonder if they will ever be accepted into the other person's family or culture. Superficially they may play down or even dismiss these thoughts, telling themself that no real harm will ever come to them; yet the nagging fears remain, and they will wonder what the repercussions will be, and what impact it will have on their family – what will happen to them if their family, friends and the entire community they belong to finds out about their budding relationship? Unable to provide satisfactory answers to these concerns, they ultimately decide to keep away from the person they have attraction towards, so embedded and indoctrinated are they in their culture.

Fear as an arm of indoctrination does not only appear in the form of threats; in other cases, it manifests as fear of the unknown. People often resist change because they do not know for sure what lies on the other side. The indoctrinated person fears what will become of them if they drift away from the life they've always known. The patriarchal man wonders if he will still be respected if he breaks free of patriarchal constraints to see himself as equal to the woman. The patriarchal woman wonders how she will survive if she moves beyond the patriarchal structure and no longer has a man to take care of her. The terrorist, buried deep in the indoctrinated beliefs of their religion wonders if they will ever be able to fit into society again. The racist wonders if people of colour can be trusted. The professional looks to rationalisations to maintain their fear of entrepreneurship.

The fear of the unknown may be valid, but it is not enough of a reason to remain indoctrinated, because remaining indoctrinated means positioning and preparing yourself – and the world – for stagnation.

CHAPTER NINE

Consequences of Indoctrination: The Centre Cannot Hold

S ix famous lines in William Butler Yeat's 1919 poem, *The Second Coming* would come to summarise the effects of indoctrination:

Things fall apart; the centre cannot hold;
Mere anarchy is loosed upon the world,
The blood-dimmed tide is loosed, and everywhere
The ceremony of innocence is drowned;
The best lack all conviction, while the worst
Are full of passionate intensity.

Yeat's poem is profoundly prophetic. Indoctrination causes things to fall apart. It dampens our emotions and humanity, and once this is done, the centre cannot hold. The most captivating and profound lines in the poem reads: *The best lack all conviction, while the worst / Are full of passionate intensity.* And this is true. The people who understand how the world can heal are silent because they lack conviction. Would the world accept their truth? Would anybody listen? How can an indoctrinated mind be changed? Such are the questions that hover in the minds of those who think with great intensity as seekers of truth, yet at the end of the day lack the conviction or courage to spread their message. Meanwhile, the non-thinkers may be full of passionate intensity and wreak havoc on the world, but their words are loud, mere noise, lacking in true substance.

Earlier I mentioned that indoctrination begins like a malignant tumour, and if not caught in time, it spreads. It unleashes anarchy in the individual before spreading to wider society.

THE INDIVIDUAL'S CENTRE CANNOT HOLD

A person divorced from his emotions will have no regard for humanity. He becomes a savage being, akin to the terrorist who does not hesitate to hijack a plane and destroy a building with people in it. This is why the patriarchal man does not think twice before using his power to obtain sex. This is why a racist can kill a person from another race as 'honour killing'. This is why the corrupt politician will divert funds and palliatives meant to take care of their constituency during the COVID-19 pandemic. This is why the religious person will readily discriminate against others because they are 'infidels'. And this is why people will collect sewage water and use it as a religious artefact.

SOCIETY'S CENTRE CANNOT HOLD

Society is a collection of human beings. But when we have a lot of dysfunctional people as a result of indoctrination making up a large portion of the population, what we are left with is a dysfunctional society. This is why Los Cabos, Mexico, is the most dangerous city in the world.[1] This is why countries like South Sudan and Somalia rank highest as the most fragile and dysfunctional countries, scoring very low for human rights.[2]

A dysfunctional society is a direct product of its dysfunctional individuals. This means that for a society to heal, the individuals must first heal. And in order to heal we must be able to identify what it is that made us sick in the first place. Then, and only then, will we be able to make the conscious first steps towards overcoming indoctrination that will ultimately put society on the path to healing.

Overcoming Indoctrination: Unlearning, Learning, Relearning

```
                    X
                  /‾‾‾\
                 /     \
               A         B          Political,
Information → Knowledge  |  Wisdom → social,
                         |          economic,
                         |          enviormental
```

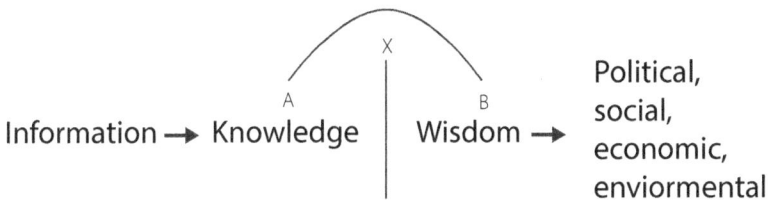

Figure B: The Barrier to Wisdom

The above pictorial representation shows the relationship between information, knowledge, wisdom and indoctrination. Notice that indoctrination is a wall. In normal situations, a person needs to scale a wall to get to the other side; but when it comes to indoctrination, the only way to get to wisdom is to demolish the wall.

The walls of indoctrination are so high that without exceptional self-awareness of one's own biases, it can be extremely challenging to scale it. The walls of indoctrination are made up of blocks and blocks of falsities stacked upon one another over a long period of time. And for as long as the wall remains, humanity continues to be stuck in a place far removed from wisdom.

Overcoming indoctrination is like loosening braided hair – you have to follow the same path to unravel it, reversing the methods.

To overcome indoctrination, we need to follow the same path back through the indoctrinating methods and tendencies, but replace falsities with truths. This can only be achieved through the three-step process of unlearning, learning and relearning.

UNLEARNING

It takes a conscious effort to learn something and even a greater effort to unlearn it. To unlearn, you need to consistently make the decision to rid your mind of the untruths you have imbibed along the way. In their article titled, 'Why the Problem with Learning Is Unlearning',[1] *Harvard Business Review (HBR)* explains that unlearning is the *ability* to *choose* an alternative mental model or paradigm. 'When we learn, we add new skills or knowledge to what we already know. When we unlearn, we step outside the mental model in order to choose a different one.'

One cannot choose an alternative paradigm without first coming to the conclusion that the old paradigm is faulty. This is where ability comes into play. *HBR* directs their article to business managers, teaching them how to move on from long-standing dysfunctional systems to alternative models. It is not easy to unlearn dysfunctional ideologies or models, but it becomes even more difficult when it is an ideology that that person perceives to be functional or beneficial. This is the same with indoctrination.

It is difficult to unlearn indoctrinated ideologies because indoctrinators often get their minions to believe that their ideologies will always be functional and beneficial. For the racist, racism is a functional ideology that gives them an upper hand in the world because of skin colour. The rapist believes that forcefully sleeping with someone is the gateway to satisfying a sexual urge without having to woo them. The robber sees robbery as a functional method for getting rich quickly. To the politician, being corrupt and taking advantage of the masses is the surest route to achieving power and status. The young hacker who indulges in cybercrime thinks that wealth is the only way to earn the respect and admiration of society. The suicide bomber will always aspire to inflict pain on people to earn what they believe are rewards in the eternal life.

Such perceived functionalities and their benefits are ideologies that have affixed themselves firmly in the minds of indoctrinated people. This is why it takes a great deal more effort to *unlearn* what has effectively become embedded in their psyches. Unlearning is difficult; but it is not impossible. Unlearning requires self-evaluation, intentionality and patience, as seen in the story of Daryl Davis.

Daryl is a musician; however, he's not as famous for his wide range of musical expression on the piano as he is for something far more strange and peculiar: converting members of the Ku Klux Klan. One fateful night in 1983, Daryl had gone to the Silver Dollar Lounge in Maryland for a country gig. He was the only black man there, but this didn't bother him. After he was done with his performance, the patron of the lounge approached him. The patron praised Daryl's prowess and told him that he had never seen a black man play like the American singer, songwriter and pianist, Jerry Lee Lewis.

Daryl was more curious than offended by the man's statement, yet he took the time to explain to the man that Jerry Lee Lewis had been influenced by the same black pianists that had influenced him. He went on to say that he was friends with Jerry Lee Lewis. Fascinated by Daryl, the patron asked him to join him for a drink. As they drank, the patron said to Daryl, 'You know, this is the first time I ever sat down and had a drink with a black person.'[2] When Daryl asked him why, the patron hesitated at first, then admitted that he was a member of the Ku Klux Klan. This revelation marked a significant turn in Daryl's life and career.

Daryl had *long conversations* with the patron which untangled, in the words of *The Guardian*, 'a knot of hate that had coiled for decades'.

He extended the conversation to other members of the organisation who later became his friends. He met with Klansmen of different ranks and also attended cross-lighting rallies. His dialogues with these men made them renounce the Ku Klux Klan and its tenets. He even got a highly placed Klansman, Robert Kelly, who later became the Imperial Wizard of Maryland to quit the organisation. Daryl had set up a meeting with Kelly without letting the latter know that he was black. When Kelly eventually met with Daryl, he was shocked. Despite the tense atmosphere, the two men were able to converse, and this meeting birthed more meetings. Kelly even invited Daryl to his home and Klan rallies. Kelly held nothing back and shared with Daryl the racial stereotypes that inspired the Klan's hatred. Daryl listened, took notes and asked questions. Then, *picking off each stereotype one by one*, he riddled holes in them, revealing their flaws. Kelly eventually quit the organisation, shut down his Maryland chapter and gifted his robe to Daryl.[3]

In Daryl's story we can see that the process of unlearning is a gradual, intentional process. One remarkable quality about Daryl was his ability not to be confrontational towards men whom the black community saw as oppressors. Daryl also had this empathetic quality to him, and it was his empathic nature that made him listen to the Klansmen to get their side of the story, learn what fuelled their hate and understand where they were coming from. It was then easy for Daryl to dispel the racial stereotypes because he knew that these stereotypes had been built on sand.

When Daryl was ten years old, he was racially abused. He was in a parade as a Cub Scout when people began to throw rocks and stuff at him. Recounting the incident, Daryl said: 'I didn't understand why people would do that, and I formed a question: "How can you hate me when you don't even know me?" The answer was always, "There's [sic] some people who are just like that." Well, that wasn't good enough for me. What does "just like that" mean? Where does that come from? You're not born "just like that". I've been curious about racism ever since, but even still, nobody can seem to answer the question.'[4]

By now, you should know why no-one could give Daryl a logical answer to his question. Indoctrination implants ideologies into our minds and removes our power to question. We simply align ourselves to the status quo without ever questioning why the status quo exists in the first place. So, for Daryl to get the Klansmen to *unlearn* their racist ideologies, he had to go through a three-step process. First, he had to diagnose the problem by understanding the foundations of their racist tendencies. Second, he had to *slowly* dispel these stereotypes. Lastly, he presented new and irrefutable truths to them.

This pathway of unlearning provides us with a perfect template for overcoming any form of indoctrination. We could understand what motivates that person to rape, or what possesses the young child to steal, or why that corrupt politician felt the need to steal from their constituency, or what impelled that young person to be an online scammer and that suicide bomber to consciously and willingly destroy innocent lives and properties. In Chapters Eight through Ten, I explored the diverse motivations for people who choose to live their lives based on indoctrinated ideologies and principles. Understanding their motivations is how we are able to gradually dispel the forces at work that resulted in their indoctrination in the first place.

It is critical to understand that unlearning takes time. Just as it takes time to build a house, it takes an equal amount of time to knock it down. The indoctrinated person has to do away with untruths that have been cemented in their minds for years. These untruths have governed their lives for so long that embracing change becomes a scary, if not herculean, task. This is why we initially see such high resistance through generalising, deleting or distorting any new information that is presented and challenges the indoctrinating principles so ingrained. Thus, we must endeavour to be models of patience and tolerance as we allow the indoctrinated person time to replace faulty ideologies with the truth. The process of unlearning and relearning is laborious, tedious work, yet it remains the only thing that can reverse the damage of indoctrination.

LEARNING AND RELEARNING

In the process of overcoming indoctrination, learning may seem difficult because most people tend to skip the unlearning phase and go directly to learning. This is like trying to fill a bucket with the lid on top of it. It is a waste of time, water and energy. Learning can only be effective when the individual has emptied themselves of their old ideologies first.

Teaching individuals to embrace and employ their cognitive abilities is a mammoth task. Though you are presenting the truth to them, you must ensure that the person sees and understands this truth for themselves and not just because you said it. Do not rely on logic to get people to accept the truth. Establishing an emotional connection with the message is important for the receiver to shift their paradigm, because this is exactly how they became indoctrinated in the first place.

Just like unlearning, the learning phase also requires consistency. Exposure to a message is not enough. The new message must be repeated often.

In overcoming indoctrination, we must bear in mind that we are not overcoming indoctrination for ourselves alone, but for the world at large. As we teach people to imbibe new tenets, our primary objective should be to birth a better world. If we teach people to place themselves before the world, they will only seek solutions that will benefit them alone. But if the world can benefit from this solution, then good for it; if not, they don't care. If the latter is true, this resets our effort to zero since one of the key drivers of indoctrination is selfishness – blinding oneself to the humanity of others and focusing only on (supposed) personal gains. Getting the learning phase wrong the second time around will only revert us once again to the status quo.

So, it's important to never rush the learning process. Sometimes, people do need a reality check before they can recognise and accept the truth, and we saw this happen during the COVID-19 pandemic in 2020. Companies that were sceptical about allowing their staff to work remotely prior to the pandemic had no choice but to allow them to work from home. They saw it was beneficial not just to their employees but to their companies. FlexJobs, the company where people can find the best remote and flexible jobs, reported that during the pandemic, employers in the United States saved up to $30 billion every day by allowing their staff to work from home. FlexJobs itself saved more than $5 million.[5]

Before the pandemic, only a few companies allowed their staff to work remotely. In a survey carried out by *Pew Research Center*, it was reported that prior to the pandemic, only 20% of workers worked from home. A greater percentage of workers never worked from home even though their job responsibilities could be comfortably carried out at home. But with the pandemic, the number of workers that worked from home increased to 71%.[6] In a similar survey, *Forbes,* in their article titled 'Remote Work: The Biggest Legacy Of Covid-19', report that a survey conducted among US HR executives showed that only 5% of these executives had 40% of their workers working primarily from home before the pandemic. However, by September 2020, this figure increased to over 33%.[7]

Sometimes learning can be painfully and arduously slow and it requires a significant or major event to effect change. Businesses in the pandemic were slow to embrace remote work, but as new work-at-home models were presented, most companies now want for a large percentage of their employees to work remotely. As the tide of the pandemic ebbed, some big tech companies extended the remote leave to their workers. (The same companies that did not see any feasibility in remote work prior to COVID-19.) Facebook and Google extended worker leave to the end of 2020, while Twitter and Square told their workers that they could work from home 'forever'.[8]

The global acceptance and movement towards working remotely proves that learning new ways might take time but it does eventually materialise with consistency, better ideologies and newer systems and methods in place. There is no shortcut to learning: just put the truth out there always. Truth may be rejected at first; but truth eventually does win.

Teach people to think for themselves. Teach them never to depend on the ideas of another even if the person is superior in rank, position or authority. Teach them to filter every piece of information using the sieve of truth. People need to become more adept at asking themselves key questions such as: *is the information* true? *Is the information beneficial or harmful to me and humankind? Do I believe this information because I am convinced about it – or because the information comes from someone I respect and revere? Would acting on this information make me undervalue myself or human life? Do I believe and agree with this information because it is conventionally accepted or because it is wise and true?*

Based on this approach, we can deduce how unlearning and relearning can illuminate some of the blind spots we discovered earlier.

- **Racism:** Learn to see the world through the lens of humanity and not skin colour.
- **Crime:** People tend to commit crimes because they feel they can justify it, so the criminal needs to understand that there is no justifiable basis for crime – not lust, not hate, not poverty.

- **Political malpractices:** Politicians should learn that power is not a means to building wealth. They should seek power not because they want to rule and oppress, but because they want to lead and serve. They should learn to see political positions like a business where the onus of responsibility rests on them to *satisfy* the public.
- **Sexism:** Gender does not make anyone superior or inferior to another. Men and women were created different, but they are equal. They do not need to be the same to be equal. The indoctrinated mind doesn't comprehend this distinction.
- **Religion:** Desiring a divine relationship with the metaphysical world and a supernatural being does not mean severing human relationships. Being religious does not translate to being fanatical. Religious ideologies and doctrines that undervalue life may need to be questioned.
- **Finances:** People should learn that getting a degree and a job is not the path to financial success, because the skill to making money is far different to the skill required to keep and grow money.
- **Education:** Students should be taught that real education goes beyond academics. If personal development, spiritual awareness and financial/business education is not taught, the academics is rendered ineffective.

Teaching people to think and question are the greatest tools they can equip themselves with for learning. Your duty is to hand them the tools and remain patient with them until they can use them effectively. You should also be on standby to reinforce your message in the phase of relearning. Learning and relearning go hand in hand. If you tell a child not to play with your computer, you will most definitely need to repeat the same information tomorrow, next week and probably next month. This is typical of human nature; our minds do not store new information for long. Old information needs to be nudged out and replaced gradually by new information, especially if the mind still sees the old information as beneficial. Thus, we have to learn – and relearn – through a process of sorting old ideas from new, fighting and challenging the old status quo, and reinforcing new ideologies through the continuous pushing back and edging out of falsehoods long stuck in the indoctrinated mind – and we do this by utilising and actively engaging in one's true autonomy of thought.

CHAPTER ELEVEN
The Autonomy of Thought

*'The masses have never thirsted after the truth. Who-
ever can supply them with illusions is easily their
master; whoever attempts to destroy their illusions is
always their enemy.' – Gustave Le Bon*

I stumbled upon this story online, titled *Guarding the Concrete Slab*. It has no author, and one cannot tell if it is fictitious or not. However, it carries with it valuable lessons relevant to this chapter, so I am here to share it.

An army barracks had four soldiers guarding a concrete slab in front of the barracks at all times. Different commanders came and went but the tradition remained; the soldiers changed shifts guarding the slab.

After eighty years, a new commander was assigned to the barracks. One of the things he did was to ask why things were done the way they were. When he asked why soldiers were guarding the slab, he was told, 'We've always done it this way. It's our tradition. Our former commanders instructed us to do that.'

The commander was bent on finding out the reason for this practice. He went to the archives to look for answers and came across a document that had the explanation.

The document was very old. It had instructions written by one of the retired commanders who had passed away. The new commander learned that over eighty years ago, the barracks had wanted to build a platform where events could be performed. When the concrete slab was laid, however, wild animals would walk over it at night before the slab could dry. The soldiers would fix it the next morning, but when evening came the same thing would happen. So, the commander ordered that four soldiers should guard the concrete slab for three weeks to allow it to dry.

The following week the commander was transferred to handle another assignment elsewhere, and a new commander was brought in. The new commander found the routine and continued to enforce it without asking questions. And since then, every other commander that came along did the same.

Thus, eighty years later, soldiers continued guarding the concrete slab – an assignment that was ordinarily designed to last just three weeks. Eighty years of ignorance along with hard labour has passed.

Questioning is the first step towards overcoming indoctrination. However, only those with full control of their thoughts have the ability to ask questions. It is often said that nature abhors a vacuum; so, if a person has no control of their thoughts, then they become a slave to the dictates and ideologies of another. Simon McCarthy-Jones writes: 'To lose freedom of thought (FoT) is to lose our dignity, our democracy and our very selves.'[1] No truer words have been said. Many underestimate the power of their thoughts, and so, easily relinquish control of their thoughts to others.

We are undeniably a product of (our) thoughts. Corny, I know – but true. And yet the corniness of this statement does not take away the profundity of it. Every human creation, tangible and intangible, is a product of human thought. The phone you use, the television you watch, the aircraft you fly, the state laws you obey, the books you read, the activisms and demonstrations you partake in – are all thoughts that have come to life. So, what *is* (a) thought?

Encyclopedia Britannica refers to thought as '*covert symbolic responses* to *stimuli* that are either *intrinsic* (arising from within) or *extrinsic* (arising from the environment). [It] is considered to mediate between inner activity and external stimuli'.[2]

I have emphasised certain words and phrases key to this definition. These words serve to explain why thoughts are so powerful, and why we need the autonomy of thought if we are to overcome indoctrination.

THOUGHT EXPLAINED ...

Covert symbolic responses

This is where the strength of your thoughts lie. Your thoughts are covert, hidden. Except when you voice or act them out, you alone have access to your thoughts. Your thoughts are safely tucked away in your mind.

Through our thoughts we are able to process the information we receive from our internal or external environment. This is why our thoughts are also our responses. We receive information, then internalise and respond to them through our thoughts – and since we all process information differently, our thoughts are symbolic and unique to us.

Our personality, upbringing, experiences and environment are factors that shape our thoughts. As Erica Goode explains in a *New York Times* article, 'cultural differences might dictate what people think about. Teenage boys in Botswana, for example, might discuss cows with the same passion that New York teenagers reserve for sports cars.'[3]

Indoctrinators often rely on these factors to override a person's autonomy of thought. This brings to mind a scene in the 2015 war drama film, *Beasts of No Nation*. The movie follows the life of a young boy, Agu, who became a child soldier for a guerilla force following the outbreak of war in his country. In one of the scenes, the guerilla soldiers ambush a convoy of trucks and armoured vehicles. They execute the soldiers; however, when they discover a corporal who has survived, the guerilla commandant asks Agu to kill him with a machete. Agu hesitates at first; but the commandant fuels Agu's rage by telling him that the corporal and his colleagues were the people who killed Agu's parents. Driven by rage, Agu uses the machete to hack off the corporal's head.

Although brief, this scene showcases how indoctrinators are capable of holding such influence over people's minds. In the case of Agu, the commandant used Agu's experience and environment to override his will and implant in him a thought that was not there before. His experience and environment provided the perfect template to process the thought implanted into him, which spurred him on with reasons (justifications) for killing the man.

We see this play out with alarming regularity in real life. Ask patriarchal people why they are sexist and they will tell you that sexism aligns with their *culture*. Their culture is the platform upon which they process their perception and relationship with any gender.

Ask criminals how they got into crime and they would most likely tell you that their financial background or local community lured them into the world of crime.

Ask corrupt politicians why they are high-handed, corrupt and financially dishonest, and they will tell you that that is 'just the game of politics'. They will justify their actions by telling you that, in order to be ahead, you have to cut corners. It is what politicians before them had done as well, so why deviate from the norm? Why think for yourself when you can just follow conventions?

Ask the religious fanatic why they are judgemental and sanctimonious and they'll tell you that that was 'just how they were brought up'.

So, while thoughts are covert, they are responses symbolic to an individual's background, experiences and information they are exposed to. In the context of the relationship between information, knowledge and wisdom, we can say that thoughts provide the platform on which knowledge – which is stored information – is converted to wisdom. Thus, we are able to define wisdom as the overt expression of covert responses to information.

Stimuli

This is the second keyword in the definition. In this case, a stimulus refers to information. This information could be from an external or internal source. Or as *Encyclopedia Britannica* puts it, stimuli could be intrinsic or extrinsic. External or extrinsic sources include information obtained from any of the five senses – sight, smell, taste, sound and touch. Indoctrination most often occurs through the senses of sound and sight.

In the earlier example we saw how the movie character, Agu, was motivated to kill a man because of information he received through his ears. Religious and political fanatics similarly become indoctrinated through the various manifestos and threats they hear. In addition to this, some receive indoctrination through their use of sight – by reading books and so-called holy writs.

Internal or intrinsic sources of information include memories and information imbibed through learning. This means that stimulus is always a merger of external and internal sources. The memories or information we recall all come from an external source. They are products of something we've seen, heard, perceived, felt or tasted. Information obtained through the senses gets stored in our minds and becomes (re)played as thoughts.

HOW INDOCTRINATION OVERRIDES OR SEIZES A PERSON'S AUTONOMY OF THOUGHT

Stimulus or information is an important factor in this discourse of thoughts and how they contribute to indoctrination. This is because it is at this point of stimulus when indoctrinators act. They know that they cannot get a hold of a person's thoughts without first implanting (false) information into them. Without false information, indoctrination cannot happen. And without true information, liberation cannot occur. Just as in the case of Nat Turner we saw outlined in Chapter Three, information gave him the motivation he needed to escape the shackles of slavery. The slave masters understood the inherent power of information, which was why they tried to stop black people from becoming literate.

Indoctrination is like a viral disease. A virus acts by attaching itself and injecting its genetic material into the host's DNA. By injecting its genetic material, it can then use the host's genetic program to replicate itself. This is why viral diseases are difficult to treat – it is hard for the drug to suppress or destroy the virus without causing damage to the host's genetic information. This is unlike bacteria that have weak attachments and do not inject their genetic material into the host.

Similar to a virus, indoctrinators 'attach' and inject information into the mind or thought process of the indoctrinated person. In other words, indoctrinators provide the necessary stimulus. The aim of this is to get the person to use their thoughts to water false information. Once this happens, the indoctrinated person loses their will and autonomy over their thoughts, and ultimately relinquishes control to the indoctrinator. The person becomes a puppet, almost like a robot or zombie. They begin to think and act like the indoctrinator. They lose their autonomy, their ability to question, even, as they carry out the indoctrinator's bidding.

At this point, the indoctrinator does not have to do much since the person is literally zombified and on autopilot. All the indoctrinator has to do is to maintain *and* build upon a newly established foundation. One way to do this is by cutting off every other source of stimulus. The indoctrinator knows that if the person gets access to other sources of information, there is the likelihood of losing the control that has been established. This is why selected censorship is the preferred weapon for indoctrination. The indoctrinator sets up mechanisms for maintaining control even in the presence of a new stimulus, and they do this in two ways, as we saw in Chapter Ten; either they entice the individual with the allure of supposed rewards or they seek to instil fear through supposed consequences. They can even employ both methods to ensure that the indoctrination process is successful. And if the indoctrinated one turns out to be a person who prefers to maintain the status quo, then the path to indoctrination is already well and truly sealed.

A truly intelligent mind understands that the quest for wisdom is a process of continual learning and discovery. Indoctrinated individuals and groups are less likely to question and more likely to subscribe to a belief handed down by institutions and people of authority, especially if the belief has been packaged with data or so-called scientific facts. Human nature and our natural world are certainly not simple, and the truly wise understand this. Data is not always a perfect representation of reality either, but only a mind free of indoctrination can acknowledge this. As it's been said, the most dangerous words in the world of commerce are 'we have always done it this way'. And an autonomous mind will always have a problem accepting this statement as an explanation. An indoctrinated mind will accept the statement as fact and cease to question it. The more indoctrinated a person becomes, the more likely they are to ask 'what' and 'how' questions and less likely to ask the 'why' questions. Why? Because an indoctrinated mind is less likely to question the status quo.

One unique feature of a person lacking autonomy over their thoughts is how quick they are to hand down the indoctrinator's ideas to others. Just as with the soldiers guarding the slab, the indoctrinated person becomes the protagonist in a script they didn't write. Ask them why they support an idea or uphold an ideology – and their response will almost always be, 'That is how it has always been done,' or, 'It is our culture.' 'We have *always* done it this way.'

Unfortunately, indoctrinated people cannot see the level of brainwashing that has been inflicted upon them because they have lost the power to *reason* out the truth for themselves.

RECLAIMING THE AUTONOMY OF THOUGHT: THE WHY

In an exposition titled *American Plantation Slave Culture*,[4] Lindsey Smith reveals some interesting facts about the African slaves in North America. Of these slaves, Lindsey writes: 'Even though slaves were continuously treated as subhuman property, *they kept the idea that they were still human beings.*' In other words, even though they were slaves, they never saw themselves as slaves. They retained their autonomy of thought and refused to take up the identity the slave owners forced on them. Instead, they held tenaciously to their culture and heritage. Over time, their culture mixed with European culture to birth a hybrid. This creation of a new culture was an act of rebellion, the revelation of a defiant spirit. As slaves, they had personal gardens, cooked their cultural foods, practiced their religion and expressed themselves with their own music.

An interesting quality about these slaves was that they were able to see the good in every situation. For example, slaveholders allowed slaves to cultivate small pieces of land next to the slaves' quarters. They allowed this because they *assumed* that allowing slaves to own a property would make them comfortable in their slave and subhuman status; a comfort that would prevent them from seeking freedom and also promote the plantation of the slave owners. This assumption was accurate: the slaves were comfortable. But they were not comfortable as slaves or subhumans, instead, they took pride in the fact that they owned gardens. They planted and harvested corn, tomatoes and greens. These foods were not only sources of extra nourishment but also sources of income. Some slaveholders allowed their slaves to sell or barter their fresh produce at the market. From their sales, these slaves began making plans to save up for their freedom and that of their loved ones.

Yet, even amid their slavery, the Africans managed to protect their mental space and create joy from their chains. As Lindsey Smith aptly notes, [their] 'ability to create a lasting culture under such harsh rule was astounding and no easy feat'.

The slaves were able to create and successfully protect their culture because they still retained the ability to think for themselves. Never did they forfeit their mental independence. Never did they submit mentally and spiritually to the slave owners or their position of circumstance.

You see, we are not born zombies or robots. Our free will and rationality are the very same qualities that distinguish us and elevate us from other animals. When we lose these qualities, we dilute our human essence. Imagine if these slaves had lost the ability to think for themselves – they would have succumbed to their subhuman existence, believing they were subhuman and living out their lives at subhuman levels.

We need to reclaim our autonomy of thought – for without it, we will only live out our lives as edited versions to fit the narratives of others. While the reasons for reclaiming our autonomy of thought are diverse, they can be summarised into four main areas: mental and physical liberation, a better life, progressive systems and a better world.

Mental and physical liberation

When we talk about holocaust survivors, the Austrian neurologist, philosopher and author, Viktor Frankl comes to mind. Nine months after he married his wife in 1942, Viktor Frankl and his family were sent to the Theresienstadt concentration camp. Viktor's father died of starvation and pneumonia in the camp, and by 1944, he and other surviving family members were transferred to the concentration camp at Auschwitz. There, the Nazis gassed his mother and brother. Frankl's wife would later die of typhus and Frankl, all alone, would spend three more years in four concentration camps.

The question: how did Frankl survive these years despite the torture inflicted on his mind and body? Answer: he possessed incredible autonomy of thought.

In his bestselling book, *Man's Search for Meaning*, detailing his life and times in Nazi concentration camps, Frankl explained how we get to choose how to react to situations. Of himself and other prisoners in the camp, he would write: 'Even though conditions such as lack of sleep, insufficient food and various mental stresses may suggest that the inmates were bound to react in certain ways, in the final analysis, it becomes clear that the sort of person the prisoner became was the result of an inner-decision and not the result of camp influences alone. Fundamentally then, any man can, under such circumstances, decide what shall become of him – mentally and spiritually.'[5]

Just like Frankl, having the will to maintain and exercise one's autonomy of thought, despite circumstances or subject to indoctrination, opens unexpected doors to both mental and physical liberation. Since our actions are a product of our thoughts, submitting to the control of another makes us prisoners in mind as well as in body. Imprison a man mentally and it won't be long before you imprison him physically. This was how colonial powers ruled over indigenous lands long ago – first got the indigenous tribes to believe that their culture was inferior and that the ways of the colonial masters were best. This indoctrination was subtle and relentless through oral education and societal pressure, and before long the colonial masters set themselves up as perpetual rulers over the indigenous peoples.

Just as mental slavery can lead to physical imprisonment, mental liberation precedes physical freedom. If you see a prisoner who is mentally liberated, it will not be long before he also sets his body free. This was depicted in the 1994 film, *The Shawshank Redemption*, an adaptation of Stephen King's novella, *Rita Hayworth and Shawshank Redemption*. The movie tells a story of a banker, Andy Dufresne, who was wrongly convicted for murdering his wife and her lover and received two life sentences for his crimes at the Shawshank State Prison. In prison, Andy mostly kept to himself until he befriended another inmate, a notorious smuggler known as Red. Although Andy was incarcerated, he never allowed his mind to be caged. When he overheard one of the captains complain about being taxed on his inheritance, Andy offered to help the captain shield his money legally. When he was transferred to the prison library to assist the elderly inmate in charge of the library, Andy wrote letters every week to the state legislature requesting funds to rehabilitate the library. When the legislature, after months of silence, finally sent a library donation that included a recording of Mozart's *The Marriage of Figaro*, Andy was not scared to lock a guard out and play the record over the public address system. For this, he was punished with solitary confinement; when he got out, he told Red that hope was his coping mechanism and the thing that kept him alive – and so he played the record for other inmates, to raise them up, make them feel hopeful again, keep their hopes alive. It was this hope that continued to keep him sane when the prison warden foiled Andy's plans to escape prison, and again later when the truth of his wife's murder came to light. It was also hope in the end that gave him the strength to dig a tunnel for nineteen years using a rock hammer and make his final escape through the prison's sewage pipe.

Andy's story may be fictional but it is not far-fetched. No-one ever fails by holding on to their autonomy of thought. No-one loses their strength by being able to think for themselves. This autonomy is the critical and necessary gateway to our mental (and physical) liberation.

Better life

As stated previously, our lives are a product of our thoughts. The action you take today is a reflection of what you've thought about. I don't want to sound corny but I still need to state this: you cannot live beyond your thoughts. If you think like a helpless victim, you will act subservient and be a victim. If you think like a king or queen, you will act like a leader. This is the defining principle of life.

Indoctrinators understand this well, that is why their first target is the human mind. They know that one cannot get a person to act a certain way if said person doesn't believe in that action. People do not just act if they don't believe in their actions.

Convince a person that suicide bombing will send them to paradise. Is this destructive act towards humanity good for them? No. So why do they do it? Because they have been led to believe that it is their obligation to appease God. Unfortunately, their belief will result in immense suffering. But indoctrinated minds will never acknowledge this because they are more likely to rationalise their actions.

Letting go of autonomy of one's thought processes greatly reduces the quality of a person's life. The racist carries the burden of hate. They hate because they were taught to hate while never being made aware of their prejudices.

It is the same with a criminal. They may continue to live a life of crime thinking that they are living the good life, but in reality, they are not. The robber and the internet fraudster are forever looking over their shoulders as they live in constant fear of being caught and going to jail. The rapist exposes themself to sexually transmitted diseases and risks being injured or killed by the victim as a means of self-defence.

The politician, by being corrupt, denies themselves the chance to create a legacy. They miss out on the love and admiration of the people and of experiencing the true power of leadership that comes through serving their people. Bad leaders often live unfulfilling lives. Take

Hitler for example. He couldn't accept defeat in the end, so he poisoned himself, his wife and their dogs, then shot himself in the head. It is safe to posit that Hitler was afraid to experience the suffering he himself had inflicted on millions. However, one truth emerges here: that is, for Hitler to feel fear, shame and disappointment shows that there had to have been traces of humanity left in him. It is recorded that he married his wife, Eva Braun, on the eve of their double suicide, evidence that Hitler also felt love – romantic love. In secret, he was an avid painter and poet, and was known for throwing lavish dinner parties and soirées whilst serving time in prison (as they did revere him, despite being incarcerated for his crimes). For Hitler to be the cold-hearted dictator he was purported to be, meant that he would have had to *consistently* suppress his humanity and conscience, which in reality takes a great deal of effort and is no way to live. However, in the presence of indoctrination, people are numb to their humanity and do not care about the consequences of their (in)actions. Yet his loyal German followers would once again welcome Hitler as their leader immediately upon his release from prison, hard evidence of the power of his undisputed techniques in indoctrination.

Still, Hitler, ever the patriarch, would eventually crush under the weight of his pride and ego just to prove that he was a man and did not need help from a woman. (It is also, I suspect, the reason why his patriarchal wife, Eva Braun, would dim her light to accommodate the egoistic desires of her husband and sell herself short because she had been *taught* to think that she could not be more.)

It is the same reason religious fanatics put themselves in harm's way as suicide bombers (because they believe that killing infidels delivers reward in eternity) or collect sewage water (because they believe it has healing powers).

All the above are just a few examples of how Hitler became infamous as the grand master of indoctrination, and how easily the loss of one's autonomy of thought ultimately results in the erosion of conscience and blunts one's thinking whilst maintaining a culture of fear.

For every form of indoctrination we submit to, we ultimately reduce our quality of life. The only way to a better life is by regaining and maintaining our light within – our autonomy of thought.

If Derek Chauvin had held on to the truth that life is sacred he would have been a free man today, enjoying the love of family and the respect of society.

If the robber and the fraudster had endeavoured to make an honest living for themselves, they would have been able to walk the streets as free people with their heads held high. In the same vein, the rapist, if he hadn't felt entitled to a woman's body, could have gone on to live a life full of value and meaning.

If Hitler had been a man of peace like Martin Luther King Jr or Nelson Mandela, just imagine how the mention of his name would have resonated with perpetual praise and admiration. Imagine how he could have been a model leader for many, instead of a master dictator and indoctrinator who himself operated from a place of fear.

If the patriarchal man had understood that a person's worth is not determined by gender or gender roles prescribed by society, he would have been able to live a life of ease knowing that woman was his equal and her independence did nothing to puncture his ego. He would have learned to show his emotions instead of bottling them up, and he would not have associated emotions with being labelled weak. On the contrary, a man able to express his emotions understands that it does not define him and is stronger internally than Hercules, and consequently has no need to seek power through indoctrination because he already knows his own worth.

If the patriarchal woman had understood that a person's worth is not determined by gender or gender roles prescribed by society, she would have lived her best life without dimming her light to accommodate the ego of men. She would have climbed to the highest pinnacle of her career and found self-fulfilment rather than live in the shadows of patriarchy and oppression.

And if the religious fanatic hadn't let religious untruths override their ability to reason, they would have been alive instead of exploding into fragments for their cause.

Progressive laws and systems

The accounts of Hitler's early life reveal that as a child he had lived a lonely and secretive life[8] giving himself over to voracious reading (through which he developed his unconventional political ideologies).[9] In addition, Hitler and the entire Nazi regime were (subtly) indoctrinated by American racial laws. Racism in America gave Hitler a template to follow. About America's influence on the Nazis, Ira Katznelson would write: 'In the 1930s, the Germans were fascinated by the global leader in codified racism – the United States.'[10] Thus, it was only logical for Hitler to institute laws and systems according to what he knew.

Every leader acts based on what they know. Excess governance drives the need to indoctrinate others, and this produces authoritarian governments by which nations become ruled; these rulers know nothing other than high-handedness and total disregard for human rights because they too have been indoctrinated to rule with an iron fist. However, leaders like Jose Mujica, who are able to reclaim their autonomy of thought, can think clearly and logically and implement progressive laws and systems to the benefit of all. This is the reason why we see nations like Norway, Finland, Denmark and Belgium rank highest in the list of best countries to live in the world.

Better world

The totality of our lives as humans leads us to either a better world, or a dysfunctional world. Progressive laws and systems reject corrupt and inhumane systems that negatively affect the quality of our lives and is the fundamental first step to a better world.

Our world is an index of our quality of life. We can use Norway as an example to put this into perspective. In 2016, the Economist Intelligence Unit ranked Norway the best democracy for the sixth time in a row, making Norway the best place to live in the world. The country also ranked first on the Legatum Prosperity Index in 2017 and claimed the top spot in the United Nations' World Happiness Report because it ranked so highly in humanitarian indicators, such as caring, freedom, generosity, honesty, health, income and good governance.[11]

Norway could not possibly rank so high in these indices unless its citizens lived well. These indices reflect the lives and values of average Norwegians who value family and put family first. Parents enjoy paid leave to take care of their newborns, and as a result of the socioeconomic prosperity of the nation, citizens are freer to express genuine love and patriotism to their nation in what is undeniably a most healthy symbiotic relationship between the individual and the state.

One may argue that it is a nation that makes people; people do not make a nation. In other words, Norwegians are happy, healthy, free and honest because they live in a country with effective systems. This statement would have been true if Norway, as a country, could function without its people. However, any country still needs people to create and maintain working systems; systems which mirror the values of Norwegians, from its leader right down to its newborn. These working systems are also a model of proof that shows the average Norwegian has control over his or her thoughts.

The indoctrinated mind says, 'If everyone is doing it, it must be right,' but the independent and rational mind says, 'Just because the majority are doing it, doesn't make it right.'

This is without doubt the template for a better world. From the stories we've read so far, we can see that indoctrination sits at the core of every pathology plaguing the world today. If we must reclaim our world, we must first reclaim our minds – our autonomy of thought. But how does one do this?

RECLAIMING THE AUTONOMY OF THOUGHT: THE HOW

Given that no rational human being can be comfortable with the current state of the world, I do believe a lot of people understand our current need to reclaim our autonomy of thought. We complain about unjust political systems, heightened crime rates, extreme religious ideologies, gender inequality, medical apartheid and other socioeconomic pathologies of the world, and seek out national and international bodies to organise summits, conferences and symposiums to address these issues. Yet somehow, these programs never actually get to the root of the problem. The pathologies of the world can really only be solved when a greater percentage of the world's population are ready to reorient their minds – and ways of thinking. If we cannot do this, we will continue going round in circles like a cat chasing its tail until the end of time.

Reclaiming our autonomy of thought is a necessary venture and a three-step process. These steps are: decision, questioning and action.

Decision

This is the hardest step in the reclamation ladder, because so many are still too reluctant or afraid to take the first step, which is why indoctrination still reigns supreme. People are scared of venturing into the unknown. The racist feels insecure about losing their supposed superiority. The criminal feels insecure being without money and not being able to fend for themselves. The corrupt politician feels insecure about not being able to amass power. The patriarchal woman would rather remain subservient instead of being independent because she feels a man must cater for her at all times. The religious fanatic feels insecure about offending their religious leaders, so they continue to sacrifice humanity on the altar of religion. The academic student feels insecure about disappointing teachers and parents, so they never speak up. The professional feels insecure about failing, so they settle for a dead-end job or mediocre salary. **Insecurity breeds indoctrination**.

The status quo is comfortable, and the indoctrinated mind enjoys comfort and would likely never leave the comfort zone unless pushed. This, coupled with the fact that it is naturally difficult for human beings to make rational decisions, allows for indoctrination to flourish. In the article *The Mechanics of Choice,* Eric Wargo's assertion is based on the idea that, no matter the context for making decisions – whether it's buying a shirt or placing a trade on a fluctuating stock market – humans aren't rational creatures. If we were, we would be able to make optimal decisions and the global world construct would ultimately be a better place.[12]

Making rational decisions is difficult for humans though, because we are hard-wired to enjoy the status quo. Most humans are largely irrational and emotional creatures, and indoctrinated individuals and groups even more so.

In situations where we must make a decision, we will more often than not take mental shortcuts called heuristics, where each heuristic reflects our predisposition towards what is easy and comfortable. Eric Wargo lists four types of heuristics, namely:

Representativeness, anchoring, availability and affect.

Representativeness is a convenient heuristic. The individual relies on stereotypes and ignores facts and statistics. For instance, people assume those who are shy and introverted are more artistically inclined. We've seen parents and teachers suggest students study a particular course because it fits their personality, even when the student has no interest in that course. These parents and teachers are using stereotypes as a shortcut to make an assumed decision for the student.

For the indoctrinated person, representativeness is the most convenient heuristic, since indoctrination already uses stereotypes to (re) program the mind. Representativeness is closely associated with the next heuristic – anchoring. Anchoring as a heuristic is defined as the tendency of a person to *anchor* their decision to the first piece of information they receive. Anchoring and representativeness work hand in hand. Most times, when an individual is in the throes of indoctrination, they will anchor their decision to the first information they receive, which is almost always a stereotype. See the following examples:

• Most criminals and drug offenders in America are black **(stereotype/representativeness).** A white officer hears of a robbery in a neighbourhood. They arrest or even shoot the first black person they see **(decision)** because most criminals and drug offenders in America are black **(anchoring).**

• Women are sex objects **(stereotype/representativeness).** A man sees a woman and asks her out, and she refuses. So, he corners her to rape her **(decision)** because women are sex objects **(anchoring).**

• Politicians get into power for private gains **(stereotype/representativeness).** A person gets into power and launders money in the national treasury **(decision)** because politics is a place for enriching oneself **(anchoring).**

• A man must provide for a woman **(stereotype/representativeness).** A woman chooses to be a housewife **(decision)** because she believes her man must provide for her **(anchoring).**

• Infidels are enemies of God **(stereotype/representativeness).** A religious fanatic bombs a market **(decision)** because they need to kill the enemies of God if they are to receive an eternal reward **(anchoring).**

- Professionals settle for uninspiring jobs because they view entrepreneurship as a risky venture and sales as slimy **(anchoring)**.

Indoctrinated people often anchor their decisions to stereotypical information because: (1) this is the only information available, and (2) it is the only information they do not perceive as risky. By virtue of how indoctrination works, stereotypes are readily available to the mind because indoctrinators close every 'loophole' that can expose the indoctrinated person to something new. This lack of alternatives provides *subtle* reinforcement upon the indoctrinated person to rely on the *availability* and *perceived safety* of the information as the heuristics for decision-making. This means that representativeness, anchoring, availability and affect heuristics are interconnected. The indoctrinated person anchors their decision to the only available information (which is, of course, stereotypical) because over time, their minds have learned to perceive and accept this information as safe and correct. Linking these four heuristics together, we are able to modify our previous examples.

- Most criminals and drug offenders in America are black **(stereotype/representativeness)**. A white officer hears of a robbery in a neighbourhood. They arrest or even shoot the first black person they see **(decision)** because most criminals and drug offenders in America are black **(anchoring)** – and because this is the only information that comes to their mind with ease **(availability),** they feel that the information and the resultant decision they derive from is safe for them and the white community **(affect)**.
- Women are sex objects **(stereotype/representativeness)**. A man sees a woman, asks her out, and she refuses. So, he corners her to rape her **(decision)** because women are sex objects **(anchoring)** – this is the only idea he knows **(availability),** and therefore because of this it is also the only idea that can satisfy his sexual desires **(affect)**.

- Politicians get into power for private gains **(stereotype/representativeness)**. A person gets into power and launders money in the national treasury **(decision),** because politics is a place for enriching oneself **(anchoring)** – this is the common narrative about politics **(availability)** and it is therefore this narrative that fuels their greed **(affect).**
- A man must provide for a woman **(stereotype/representativeness)**. A woman chooses to be a housewife **(decision)** because she believes her man must provide for her **(anchoring).** Feeling inferior and being submissive are the gender ideas she has been exposed to by her society **(availability)** – and these ideas fuel her tendency to be dependent **(affect).**
- Infidels are enemies of God **(stereotype/representativeness).** A religious fanatic bombs a market **(decision)** because they need to kill the enemies of God if they are to receive the eternal reward **(anchoring).** These are the teachings they know **(availability)** and therefore they believe these teachings will give them eternal security and reward **(affect).**
- Being a professionally qualified employee in a large corporation is the way to career and financial success **(stereotype/representativeness).** Entrepreneurship and investments are only for those with capital and who are willing to take high risk **(anchoring).** By working their way up the corporate ladder and focusing on income and titles, one can become successful in society **(affect).**

Since decision-making is the most difficult step in overcoming indoctrination (and humans depend on heuristics to make wrong, deep-rooted decisions), we can modify these heuristics to overcome indoctrination. However, this time, the information available is new and holistic. Unlike indoctrination (that creates falsities from partial information and peddles them as truths), we present truths as truths – allowing for the facts and everything in-between to hold weight towards correct decision-making. We evenly weigh all the pros of making the right decision *and* the cons of making the wrong decision. In this way, the truth becomes the only information the mind can rely on. It becomes the only available option. The option with no risk.

Let's see how the truth transforms the previous hypothetical examples:

• Criminals and drug offenders in America can be people of any skin colour **(fact).** A white officer hears of a robbery in a neighbourhood. They investigate, question and arrest suspects irrespective of their race **(new decision).** This is because criminals and drug offenders in America can be people of any skin colour **(new anchoring).** This is the only information that comes to their mind with ease after all falsehoods have been erased **(new availability)** and they feel that this information and the decision that has birthed from it is safe for them and all Americans **(new affect).**

• Women are not sex objects **(fact).** A man sees a woman, asks her out, and she refuses. So, he lets her be **(new decision)** because women are not sex objects **(new anchoring).** This is the only idea he knows **(new availability).** It is also the only idea that can keep him and the woman safe **(new affect).**

• Politicians enter into power to serve **(fact).** A person gets into power and uses money in the national treasury to serve **(new decision)** because politics is not a place for enriching oneself **(new anchoring).** This is the new real fact about politics **(new availability),** and it is this fact that fuels their service to the people **(new affect).**

• Adult humans must provide for themselves **(fact).** A woman chooses to work **(new decision)** because she believes it is her responsibility **(new anchoring).** Gender equality is the only gender idea she knows **(new availability),** and in this idea births her new tendency to be independent **(new affect).**

• Unbelievers are human beings who have the right to choose their faith **(fact).** A religious faithful worships their deity without minding if others believe in their deity **(new decision)** because they understand that unbelievers are human beings who have the right to choose their faith **(new anchoring).** This is the truth they know **(new availability)** and they feel this truth will bring them and others peace **(new affect).**

• Career and financial success is more likely to come from developing in-demand skills and applying those skills to solve problems for others **(fact).** Anyone can learn how to develop high-income skills, market their skills, build a low-risk business around one's passion and invest wisely to achieve career and financial success **(new affect).**

Once the individual can walk themself successfully through the decision phase, they can then progress to the next step: questioning.

Questioning

This step follows immediately after the decision-making phase. A person's ability to question is a cardinal sign that the person has successfully freed themselves from indoctrination. Questioning is evidence of the fact that the person has regained control over their cognitive faculties and is able to scrutinise the rationality of their perspectives, beliefs and ideologies.

Questioning is a continuous process and an important step in overcoming indoctrination because indoctrinators work round the clock to generate new ideologies that will get a hold of minds to promote different agendas. The only way to uncover the dangers behind these ideologies is through continuous and repeated questioning.

To explain the concept of questioning, I have created the following hypothetical dialogues from the previous examples:

The racist indoctrinator vs. the autonomous mind

Racist indoctrinator: White people are superior to black people because white people are smarter and more creative.

Autonomous mind: But weren't scientists like Daniel Hale Williams, Charles Drew, Benjamin Banneker and Mae Jemison black?[13] Aren't there books written by renowned black writers, like James Baldwin, Toni Morrison, Maya Angelou and Gwendolyn Brooks?

Racist indoctrinator: Okay. But you will agree with me that the average African-American woman is aggressive, loud, demanding and physically abusive?

Autonomous mind: No, I don't agree with you. Aren't there white women who are also aggressive, loud, demanding and physically abusive? Is bad behaviour race specific?

Racist indoctrinator: You may be right, but it does not erase the fact that black people are dangerous and criminally minded.

Autonomous mind: Are crime and wickedness racial flaws? Are men like Al Capone, Adam Lanza and Jim Jones – some of the worst criminals in American history – black?

The rapist vs. the autonomous mind

Rapist: You cannot allow her to go just like that. Women are supposed to cater to the sexual needs of men, and if they cannot do so willingly, then they must be forced to do it.

Autonomous mind: What law says women must cater to a man's sexual needs? Who turned women into objects and sexual dolls? Since women have sexual needs too, would a man be comfortable if a woman were to override his will and force him to have sex with her?

The political indoctrinator vs. the autonomous mind

Political indoctrinator: As a politician, you have only two objectives: first, you have to ensure that power never leaves our political party. Second, you have to enrich yourself.

Autonomous mind: If I fulfill these objectives, what becomes of the nation? What will happen to the numerous men, women and children who look up to me to enhance their life as their leader? How will my own future generations be affected by my actions? Will I feel fulfilled if I generate wealth and power, yet know I betrayed my own conscience? Will I be happy if I remain a citizen if the leader I elected doesn't fulfil his campaign promises but instead enriches himself with national wealth?

The sexist indoctrinator vs. the autonomous mind

Sexist indoctrinator: A man and a woman can never be equal. A woman is inferior to a man. Her place is in the kitchen to feed her family and also in the bedroom to procreate and preserve the human race. She cannot lead. She cannot be outspoken. She can only attain heights in society through a man as he allows.

Autonomous mind: What is the basis for determining superiority? The sex organs? Does any human being have a say on their gender when they are born? How do you label some people superior and others inferior on the basis of characteristics they had no control over or say in at birth? If you come into the world as a woman, is it fair to be discriminated against just because you possess a vagina instead of a penis?

The religious indoctrinator vs. the autonomous mind

Religious indoctrinator: We are the only holy people on earth. We are God's people. We should rule the world. Anyone who doesn't conform to our doctrines is an infidel, and all infidels should be exterminated.

Autonomous mind: Doesn't everyone have the right to believe or not believe? If you believe that God created humans, would He want you to destroy His creation, whom He gave free will to choose their lifestyle – which also includes choosing their religious belief? If you weren't part of this religion, would you want someone else to kill you just because you don't share their belief?

The educational indoctrinator vs. the autonomous mind
Educational indoctrinator: Get good academic grades at school, obtain a degree from a prestigious university and get a good job.
Autonomous mind: How many people who achieve academic excellence are working in inspiring careers and have financial abundance? If academic achievement is the only thing that equips one for career success, why is it that so many students who work in professional jobs still lack the confidence, direction and the time/money freedom that they actually desire?

Through these dialogues, you'll notice the questions that immediately follow flaw the logic of the indoctrinator. Indoctrinators have a unidirectional line of thought; they never ask themselves the question: 'What if I'm on the receiving end?' and intentionally obscure facts which would erode the basis of their ideologies and cause the collapse of their arguments. Questioning is a most powerful tool as it uses logic to uncover the facts and motives behind a flawed argument and pressures the individual to face the holes in their argument and then *do* what is right – which is the final step towards overcoming indoctrination.

Action
Any thought that is not expressed remains dormant. And as long as a thought remains dormant, we cannot know its capacity for evil or good. Every expressed thought usually follows the path of decision,

speaking/questioning, action. Decision-making takes place in the mind, speaking takes place in the mouth and action takes place in the body. These levels are hierarchical, with decision-making occurring at the lowest tier and action resulting at the highest tier. In other words, thinking is tier one, telling is tier two and doing is tier three.

Action is the highest of all three levels. All the examples we've looked at, whether real or hypothetical, were about people who *acted* on their thoughts. Criminals are arrested and sentenced because they carry out a criminal thought; that is, their thought manifested to action at the highest tier. No-one has ever been arrested for thinking about murder or theft or rape. Some have, however, been arrested for thoughts that manifested at the middle level; for example, if a person made inciteful statements such as a threat to kill someone or cause bodily harm, because such threats progressed beyond the stage of thought (tier one) to telling (tier two). Punishment for incitement is a grey area, because there is no way to ever ascertain whether they would have acted (tier three) on such thoughts.

There is no way a person can conclusively prove they have overcome indoctrination if they do not demonstrate it in their decisions and actions. A person must be able to show that they have overcome indoctrination through actions, not just words. Indoctrinators need to ensure their puppets act on their ideologies – because they know that without action, they cannot effect change. Likewise, if you know the truth and refuse to act on what you know, then the world will remain the same. *Action* is the ultimate proof of your reclaimed autonomy, and the key to physical and mental liberation, progressive systems, a better world and a better life.

CHAPTER TWELVE

Sixteen Desirable Skill Elements

*'Nature abhors a vacuum: whenever people do not
know the truth, they fill the gaps with conjecture.'*
— George Bernard Shaw

You must have heard of the idiom: nature abhors a vacuum. It's true. The Latin term, *'Horror vacui'* is one frequently used by scholars and is attributed to Aristotle, the Greek philosopher, from 300 BC who coined the postulate. He articulated a belief (that would later be criticised by the atomism of Epicurus and Lucretius), that nature contains no vacuums because the denser surrounding material continuum would immediately fill the rarity of an incipient void. Think of this concept in terms of natural law, or nature. Any gardener knows that if you leave a plot of ground open and unfilled, weeds or other plants will creep in to fill the void.

But it also applies in social systems to humans. Watch what happens when a leader steps down in government or business, either to retire, finish a term in office or even when a supervisor goes on vacation — once there is a space, colonisation and growth happen. This is why a deserted house is filled with cobwebs and a fallow land is overtaken by weeds. In the same vein, once the mind has been released from indoctrination, the mind must be consistently filled with fresh knowledge and skills, or else the individual may return to indoctrinated ways.

In order to overcome and break the cycle of indoctrination (and teach others to do the same), our next step is to replace indoctrinated thoughts with rational values and skills. While I have implicitly discussed some of these skills in previous chapters, it is important to elaborate on them here. Following are sixteen desirable skills everyone should possess:

1. OUT-OF-THE-BOX THINKING

'Men are born ignorant, not stupid; they are made stupid by education.' - Bertrand Russell

'Some ideas are so stupid that only intellectuals believe them.' – George Orwell

'Two percent of people think, 3% of the people think they think and 95% of the people would rather die than think.' – George Bernard Shaw

The metaphor 'out of the box' originated with John Adair's famous nine-dot puzzle, a study on creativity that challenged research subjects to connect nine dots arranged in an imaginary square using four straight lines and without lifting the pencil from the page.

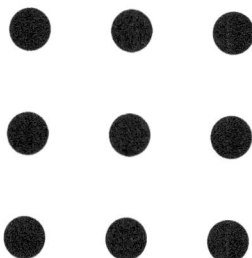

The first attempts the subjects made involved drawing lines inside the imaginary square. But this was never the solution. The solution required that the person extend the lines beyond the imaginary perimeter defined by the dots. Because subjects limited themselves to solutions within these so-called imaginary lines, they were advised to 'think outside the box' to find the solution to the problem. Ever since, thinking 'outside the box' has become a popular metaphor used in all spheres of life to motivate and encourage people to unlock their creativity and think beyond their own boundaries.

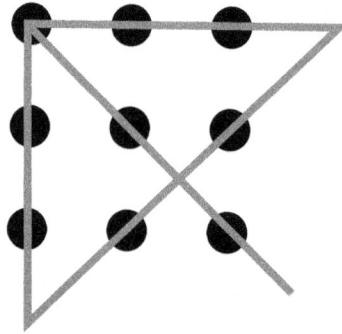

It is not out of place to say that this metaphor is suggestive of directly opposite thinking to that of indoctrination. Indoctrination forces a person to think in a particular direction. It limits thinking to stay within the confines of indoctrinated ideologies. However, many have rightly opined that going by this nine-dot puzzle, the metaphor is inaccurate. Why advise people to think outside the box when there may actually be no box? The nine dots weren't actually placed in a box. In a bid to solve the puzzle, most people create an imaginary box in their minds and confine themselves to this box.

Like their subjects, indoctrinators create boxes and cage themselves and others in such boxes. But we humans are not wired to think in boxes. Our minds are designed to think boundlessly. This is evident in the many technological and social innovations we have come up with and continue to create. Indoctrinators, however, create imaginary boxes in the form of stereotypes and ideologies and pass down these imaginations from one disciple to another.

For instance, there's no law that states that people with a particular skin colour are superior to others, nor is there any law that defines a man as a superior member of the human species. There is no evidence that a person with a degree makes a better executive, leader or entrepreneur. Such parameters for distinction and segregation were not there initially, and are all boxes instituted by humankind. Yet traditionalists hinge on them to protect instituted stereotypes and sustain models of indoctrination.

In the absence of indoctrination, an individual's perspective becomes broadened. Their thoughts become boundless – boxless. They can pick up ideas from diverse sources, analyse and integrate these ideas, filter the chaff, and arrive at rational conclusions. As Chuck Swoboda rightly said, 'You'll never find the best ideas until you recognise there is no box.'[1]

Unfortunately, educational programming through institutions creates an attachment to protocols and rules to the point that a person will relinquish their autonomy of thought. Institutions are less interested in discovering the truth and more interested in instilling compliance and obedience until the indoctrinated person cannot even conceptualise what true freedom is. Indoctrinated people believe in silos. They have a view that everything exists in a state of separation because they can't properly see the interconnectedness between different parts. This can contribute to self-centredness, along with a propensity to make their choices from a place of fear instead of arriving at new places from their vision. This cycle keeps them perpetually trapped in an indoctrinated state.

2. ORIGINAL THINKING

Out-of-the-box thinking became a popular motivational tool for creative thinkers because it encouraged humans to deviate from original thinking. Herd mentality made us do away with original thinking so that our ideas could conform to indoctrinated ideas and conventional wisdom. Normally, we would have been expected to *independently* think, inquire and arrive at our own conclusions about the world and its elements. This was how Isaac Newton figured out gravitational force. Apples have been falling from trees since before Newton was born, though people in Newton's time didn't pay attention to the fallen apples and probably dismissed it as a natural, unexplainable phenomenon, or even an act of God. But Newton was different. Sitting in his garden under the shade of an apple tree, his first question of the fallen apple was: why did the apple fall? It was a question that reflected original thinking; a thought not governed or influenced by any preconceived notions or conventions.

We are all capable of such thoughts, but we suppress them because: (1) we want to conform to general beliefs and ideologies, and (2) we have been indoctrinated to suppress our essence and originality.

Data is all about facts and figures. Information asks *who, what, when and where?* while knowledge asks *how?* and wisdom asks *why?*

In the article, *Original Thinking: How to think like an entrepreneur!* Helmut Schuster concisely captures the concept of original thinking. He understands that original thinking is important because the problems of tomorrow cannot be solved with the mindsets of today. He further outlines and explains four ways individuals can cultivate original thinking. They are: curiosity and mix, vuja de, thinking in a higher dimension and flying out of one's comfort zone.[2]

According to Schuster, Leonardo da Vinci was a prolific inventor, architect and scientist, not to mention one of the greatest artists of the Renaissance due to his 'unquenchable curiosity'. Of Leonardo, Schuster writes: 'He had an unquenchable curiosity and questioned everything. His creativity gave us inventions like the helicopter and parachute, all while he was creating exquisite works of art like the

Mona Lisa and *Vitruvian Man.'* To develop a mindset of curiosity, Schuster states that an individual must mix two ingredients: one, the individual should ask why things are the way they are, and then allow their imagination to flow; two, the individual needs to step out of their comfort zone and explore new environments in search for better alternatives. People need to mix up their social and work circles with people from other backgrounds because it sparks curiosity and challenges them to see the world differently.[3]

Indoctrinators understand the power of mixing up social or work circles; this is why they prevent their adherents from being in touch with others. We see this happen frequently in religious indoctrination. It is also seen in universities where commerce students are not encouraged to spend time with arts students. In corporations, where business units work in silos and do not care to understand how other business units work, all under the pretext of 'it's not a part of my job'.

As a digression, it is worthy to point out that the word 'environment' isn't limited to our physical environment; it includes our mental environment. Some ways to explore new mental environments include reading and watching movies and documentaries. This is the reason why indoctrinators discourage activities or learning that doesn't correspond to their agendas and why they limit their adherents from having access to new sources of information or communication. They understand that exploring new environments in any form would make one see the world differently and find out the truth for themselves. Indoctrinators are indeed smart. They create a problem, predict the solution to the problem, block every channel that leads to the solution, and then convince their adherents that there is no solution.

Vuja de is the opposite of deja vu. It means experiencing something familiar as if it were strange. Schuster advises individuals to approach familiar concepts with a fresh perspective because it can help them unlock new possibilities. Shuster advises [that the] 'answers to many of your questions may already be around you – it just takes a fresh perspective to connect the dots and find the answer'.[4]

The inability of many to revisit familiar ideologies is the reason why conventional yet redundant wisdom still thrives in the world. Many assume these conventions to be true because they have existed for a long time. But if they revisited these ideologies and examined them from a fresh perspective, they would ask pertinent questions that would lead them to the truth. Consider this:

Many times, when I post on social media espousing the virtues of entrepreneurship, inevitably, I have a few professionals who make the argument that 'if everyone became an entrepreneur, how would entrepreneurs find employees to work for them?' It doesn't even dawn on the individuals who ask this question that, while joining the ranks of hundreds of millions of students and professionals by choosing the same career path as them, the concern of 'oversupply' never occurred to them. I usually respond by asking, 'Why did this same concern of oversupply not come up when you chose your degree or an occupation that hundreds of millions of other graduates and professionals picked as well?' Why is that only when certain topics like 'entrepreneurship' or 'investing' are brought up, the individual is inclined to affirm 'but not everyone can be an entrepreneur/investor?' Is it the individual's way of rationalising their unexamined choice? Defence and denial are the tools indoctrinated minds use instinctively and regularly fall back on.

The ability to put our own choices, beliefs and biases under the microscope is how we evolve past groupthink.

If only we looked at the tenets of our laws, traditions and religions with fresh eyes; if only we diversified our perspectives; if only we questioned conventions no matter how long they've been in place.

Schuster describes thinking in a higher dimension in three words: pause and think. 'Take time just to sit down, slow down, take a breath and think. Don't meditate, don't let your mind wander, don't brainstorm with others – just sit alone quietly, and think.'[5]

Thinking in a higher dimension involves finding time and space to think without being interrupted. It involves thinking about concepts, ideologies and projects to check that you are moving in the right direction. Think about life now and think about the future. Consider how the choices you make now will impact the future. Reflect on the alternatives and do not limit your thoughts. Thinking in a higher dimension helps you look at the world differently and gives you new insights into old problems.

Oftentimes, to think in a higher dimension requires that we leave our comfort zone and allow ourselves to feel uncomfortable about our past choices. To explain this, Schuster highlights an amusing study by Adam Grant, a professor of organisational behaviour at Wharton Business School. Through his studies, Grant discovered that Firefox and Chrome users were better thinkers than Internet Explorer and Safari users. While Internet Explorer and Safari users would accept the default option in any area of their life, Firefox and Chrome users asked for better options.[6]

If you are not conversant with internet browsers, then the significance of this study and the underlying humour in it may be lost on you. Allow me to provide a context. Internet Explorer and Safari are default browsers developed by Microsoft and Apple respectively – and they both are slow. This led to the development of Firefox and Chrome browsers by Mozilla and Google respectively. Clearly, the users who moved onto the faster browsers are also quick by nature to leave dysfunctional systems, no matter how comfortable these systems may be, and move to working solutions.

Our thoughts should come from within. At one time, our minds were blank slates – tabulae rasae – when we came into the world. We didn't come into the world with pre-installed thoughts or ideologies.

Nature's aim was to give us a pristine platform for applying our rationality and autonomy of thought. We were to look at the world and understand it by and for ourselves. Institutions like family and schools were there to guide us forward in the right way. Unfortunately, we were then taught – or more aptly put, indoctrinated – to discard original thinking and adopt the inauthentic ideologies of others.

We need to go back to the drawing board. We need to embrace our true selves as well as the intrinsic nature of original thinking. So how do we do this in a world where there are already instituted ideas and laws we live by? How do we rediscover the truth for ourselves? The answer lies in what is called the first-principles approach to problem-solving.

3. FIRST-PRINCIPLES APPROACH TO PROBLEM-SOLVING

In the 2006 movie, *Akeelah and the Bee*, there is a scene where Akeelah tries to convince her spelling coach, Dr Larabee, to teach her to spell a number of big words because her major opponent, Dylan, knows how to spell a lot of big words.

I feel it important to mention this scene because it encapsulates the entire message of this book. Also, a part of the conversation is a springboard towards explaining the first-principles approach to problem-solving. But before we go into the first-principles approach, let's discuss what takes place in this scene.

If you watch the movie, first we see Akeelah arguing with Dr Larabee about rote memorisation being the perfect method for learning words. She does not suggest this because she wants to learn, but because: (1) she wants to win, and (2) she wants to be like Dylan, her opponent who is a champion and also defeated her. As Dr Larabee says, Dylan can spell a lot of words but those words mean nothing to him. They are only tools used to claim the prize.

Dylan subscribes to rote memorisation to learn words because that's the type of society he finds himself in; he lives in a society that does not care about methods, only results. Thus, it makes sense why Akeelah doesn't want to go through Dr Larabee's method which asks her to deviate from the current societal indoctrination and learn words she can use to change the world. Indoctrination normalises the wrong things so that it becomes difficult not to accept them. Fortunately, for Dr Larabee and Akeelah, he convinces her to learn the right way. And one way he does this is to introduce her to the first-principles approach of problem-solving.

Solving problems with the first-principles approach requires that one breaks down a complex problem or concept into its foundational components. It requires reducing the problem to the most basic elements and working your way up. This makes room for original thinking because when you reduce problems to their foundation, you do away with assumptions and conventions associated with the problem. Sahil Bloom's interesting exposition about first-principles thinking highlights key points about the approach. First, Bloom defines a first principle as 'a foundational assumption or proposition ... [that] cannot be deduced from other assumptions or propositions'.[7] He further notes that first principles thinking require you 'to ground yourself in the foundational truths and build up from there'.[8] In other words: discard all indoctrinations, understand the truth for yourself and build your ideology from there. This is the significance of the first-principles approach.

According to Bloom, when we encounter complex problems, we tend to rely on assumptions that we have been told are true or that we believe to be true. But relying on these assumptions only leads to 'unimaginative and linear solutions that closely resemble all that has been done before'.[9] He describes this as 'reasoning by analogy', which 'leads to solutions that are like something else. It can be a useful heuristic when speed is required and novel solutions are not the goal. But it falls short when dealing with complex problems in need of imaginative solutions'.[10]

The first-principles approach is a fundamental step to reclaiming our autonomy of thought. This is why a key feature of the approach is questioning. Just as we saw in the previous chapter, questioning is one of the three steps to reclaiming our autonomy of thought. When you reduce the problem to its basic components, the next step is to ask vital, unbiased questions. Some of these questions, according to Bloom, include:

- Why do I believe this to be true?
- How do I know this is true?
- How can I support this belief?
- What alternative viewpoints might exist?
- Am I biased towards a certain viewpoint?

These are just some examples of questions to ask – but do not stop there! As Bloom says, 'Become an endlessly curious child again! Question anything and everything. Ask why!' The truth is, one can never ask a bad question; on the contrary, there is much truth to the sentiments expressed in *21 Lessons For The 21st Century* by public intellectual, historian and professor, Yuval Noah Harari. Harari states: 'Questions you cannot answer are far better for you than answers you cannot question.' This is a great articulation of the importance of cultures and belief systems that lend themselves to being open to curious inquiry. Even if we think we know something, we should never be afraid of doubting our opinions or asking questions and checking, for the humble man seeks truth always with a curious, humble and open mind. Even if temporarily you run into a dead end, this is still preferable to having never asked the question at all – or worse, never being *allowed* to question. Such is the silencing nature of indoctrination.

NB: If you observe carefully, you'll see that a relationship exists between out-of-the-box thinking, original thinking and the first-principles approach to problem-solving. If there is a problem that requires innovative solutions, the first step to take may be out-of-the-box thinking. This is you thinking outside the assumptions, preformed opinions and stereotypes about the subject. However, this may not yield the result you seek because you are using these assumptions, opinions and stereotypes as background for your thought and decision-making. The next step is to use original thinking. But this cannot happen without first isolating the assumptions and opinions, then reducing the problem to the basics. Let's see an example or two with our hypothetical scenarios.

Problem: How do you convince an Indian (who is indoctrinated to believe in caste segregation) to see the evil in the caste system?
Solution 1: Try out-of-the-box thinking.

What is the (imaginary) box? Skin colour and caste determine social status, hence, certain castes are superior to others.

Using out-of-the-box thinking, the individual challenges themself to think outside the boundaries of these theories. They then begin to understand that humans are equal, and that caste is not a yardstick for measuring capability and intelligence. But there is still a problem. While they may have learned not to segregate on the basis of skin colour or caste, at least publicly, they may still internally feel that as a middle-class educated Indian, they are superior to the lower class. This creates a new problem that requires more out-of-the-box think-ing. So, does this mean, for every new problem, there must be an out-of-the-box solution? Is there no one-size-fits-all approach to every problem? Well, actually there is.

Solution 2a: Original thinking.

In this challenge, the person has to think for themself. They have to let go of every assumption and idea they have about caste and its workings. To do this, they need to adopt another solution to augment original thinking.

Solution 2b: First-principles approach to problem-solving.

They reduce the complex problem of caste, skin colour or socio-economic status to one question: at the start of the human race, did nature provide any rational basis for segregating people? The obvious answer is no. However, if the person thinks that there is a natural basis for inequality, then they should ask themself the following questions:
- Why do I believe that there is a natural basis for inequality?
- Can I support this belief?
- Why am I hanging on to this belief?
- Are there alternative viewpoints I should consider?

Sometimes, breaking the problem down to its simplest compo-nents by asking pertinent questions may not yield fruit, especially when it comes to social problems like caste, race, socioeconomics and religion. This is because the person may know the solution to the problem yet decide to hold on to doing the wrong thing. You see, it requires a high level of intelligence to deduce the truth and stick to the truth. And one form of intelligence many lack, especially in social issues, is emotional intelligence.

4. EMOTIONAL INTELLIGENCE

Conventional education ignores the fact that intelligence has different facets. It concentrates only on cerebral power and teaches people to do the same. Thus, there are more talks about IQs than any other type of quotient. Technically speaking, there are four types of intelligence:

intelligence quotient (IQ), emotional quotient (EQ), social quotient (SQ) and adversity quotient (AQ). I will explain these later in more detail.

While IQ measures a person's ability to comprehend, memorise and recall subject matters, EQ measures one's ability to understand and manage their emotions positively to communicate effectively, show empathy and resolve conflicts. Many focus on improving their IQ while they put no effort into developing their emotional intelligence. For some, they do not even know that there is such a parameter for intelligence.

Original thinking and the first-principles approach yields little or no result in resolving a social issue if the individual is not emotionally intelligent. A person's IQ can help them deduce the truth through original thinking, but only their emotional intelligence can *motivate* them to adopt and stick with the truth. For instance, recalling anthropological knowledge gained from different informational sources can help a person to deduce that all human beings are equal and that skin colour is only a product of biological diversity; however, the person can only *accept* this truth if they are emotionally intelligent.

Through emotional intelligence, the person is able to take off the blinders that make them see another human as unequal because of their skin colour. Their emotional intelligence will enable them to navigate and break down the walls of selfishness and instituted privileges built up and associated with racism. They simply cannot rely solely on their IQ for this.

The human species is regarded as the most rational of all species. This is not because we are highly cerebral (although this is part of it) – it is because we are highly emotional beings, and our emotions work to keep us in touch with reality, keep us in check.

So, if one can develop their IQ by reading, studying and digesting information through different media, how can one improve their EQ?

To answer this, it is important to point out that emotional intelligence is defined by four components: self-awareness, self-management, social awareness and relationship management. This means that to improve your overall emotional quotient, you need to concentrate on these four components. The good thing is that all these components are interrelated, so improvement in one component naturally leads to improvement in other components.

Self-awareness and self-management are like identical twins. They are different yet so similar. The understanding of one leads to the application of the other. Self-awareness is about understanding oneself, preferences and behaviours. Self-management, on the other hand, is one's ability to use this understanding to manage one's behaviour and emotions. A person who knows they get angry easily is self-aware. If they are also able to control their anger and prevent themselves from being aggressive, then they also know how to manage themselves.

Social awareness is one's ability to see the perspective of others and empathise with them; to understand the emotional needs of others and pick up on emotional cues; to be conscious about one's social environment and social standing. Sometimes, if not all the time, self-awareness and management are the precursors to social awareness. When you understand yourself and your behaviours, you'll become careful not to negatively impact other people with your behaviours – that is, if they are bad behaviours. If the behaviours or preferences are good, you will be eager to positively impact others. This tendency to be mindful of others already makes you more socially aware; and because you are socially aware, you are more likely to build and manage healthy relationships.

Relationship management deals with one's ability to build and maintain healthy relationships, influence others and manage conflict. This ability is powered by the individual's social awareness. A socially unaware person will have strained relationships with others.

Emotions are complex, but are powerful, defining features of a person; thus, people prefer to be around a person that understands their emotions and allows them the freedom to express their emotions. Someone who is often happy doesn't want to be around a person that dampens their mood. An unhappy person looks to someone who can uplift their spirits.

Improving self-awareness, self-management, social awareness and relationship management all work to increase your level of emotional intelligence. If you can get the racist to increase their emotional quotient, they will understand that their negative bias against another human being negatively impacts the energetic interaction with another person. If you can get the patriarchal man to increase his emotional quotient, then he will come to realise that subjugating a woman will make her feel unhappy and worthless and that he has no right to squash someone else's spirit. If you can get the patriarchal woman to develop her emotional quotient, then she will know that she can derive immense joy and satisfaction by thinking of herself as more and being more. She will also know that her unnecessary dependence on a man can overwhelm him and leave him feeling pressured. If you can get the religious fanatic to up their emotional intelligence, then they'll understand that fanaticism can drive dangerous behaviours.

Emotional intelligence may or may not come through books, but one sure way of developing emotional intelligence is by asking the question: if this were to happen to me, how would I feel? The answer to this question does not lie in a book or a video on YouTube; it lies within you. It is time to pay attention to your intuition.

5. INTUITIVE SKILLS

Encyclopedia Britannica defines intuition as the power of obtaining knowledge that cannot be acquired by inference or observation, reason or experience.[11] It is your gut feeling, that visceral mechanism that lets you know something is true even if you have not yet learned or experienced it. Suffice to say, intuition is the first level of education and the highest form of intelligence.

In her article about intuitive children, author, spiritual counsellor and founder of the Academy of Intuition Medicine, Dr Francesca McCartney shares some fascinating stories about intuitive children and sheds light on how intuition manifests in the early years. Innate intuition was seen in McCartney's daughter. When McCartney took her daughter, who was five at the time, for a horseriding lesson and the teacher introduced the little girl to a cream-coloured pony, the girl stared at the pony and reportedly said, 'Where is the black horse?' The teacher, surprised, turned to McCartney and told her that the pony's offspring was a pure black son who was back at the stable. The teacher said that she had planned to saddle the black pony for the lesson, but changed her mind at the last minute.[12]

How did the little girl know about the black horse when it was her first lesson? Intuition. Innate instinct. Sounds weird, right? This is why the knowledge gained from intuition can rarely, if ever, be explained. In another case, a six-year-old child in the Montessori school where McCartney taught asked her teacher, 'What is your baby's name?' even when no-one in the school knew that the teacher was pregnant. McCartney states such intuitive skill is 'clairvoyance, clear-seeing, perceiving energy patterns and information'.[13]

Intuition isn't only limited to knowing the present; it extends to accurately knowing or predicting the future. To explain this, McCartney relays a story told to her by the mother of one of her students, a four-year-old girl. The mother and daughter were driving down a winding road one day, and as she drove the young girl to school, the girl suddenly asked, 'Mommy, how did the deer die?' The mother was confused for a while but when she turned the corner, there lay a dead deer on the road. This event left the mom shaken and a bit frightened about the girl's perception. McCartney calls this intuition skill precognition – 'seeing what lies ahead of you on the road, in your life, the next day or the far future'.[14] McCartney rightly notes that children have great intuitive skills but 'soon learn from adults and society that the only valid ways to receive information about their world are through an analytical process and the other five senses'.[15]

And if we look for answers as to why our intuition is today in a state of serious disconnection and neglect, it is indeed what we have been looking at through this entire book: indoctrination. In a world of lies and stereotypes, intuition has the power to uncover truths and reveal our originality. By trusting his intuition, Henry Ford doubled the wages of his employees at a time when the demand for cars was declining alongside high worker turnover. With Ford's intuition, he was able to reduce turnover by a factor of over twenty, while productivity almost doubled and produced a massive demand for Ford cars because the company's workers could now afford what they made.[16] Bill Allen, the CEO of Boeing in the 1950s, was also a man of great intuition. While the airline company was making plans for the defence industry, Allen had an unconventional idea: he wanted to build a commercial jet that would serve civilian air travel. Confident in following his intuition, Allen got the board to believe in his idea and risk $16 million for the new airliner – the Boeing 707 – that would turn heads and revolutionise not just the company but the future of air travel.[17]

The voice of intuition leads to the path of truth and offers solutions to not just our personal problems but to our collective challenges as a society. Most times, intuition is the starting point of our creativity.

For an innate quality with great value, it is sad that many neglect their intuition. Sadly, the conventional education system places so much emphasis on the development of the intellect that it totally dismisses the power of our intuitive faculties. Talk to professionals about intuition, and many will mock it as pseudoscience and completely dismiss it. Most people are never taught to recognise the voice of intuition. Spiritual intelligence is real, but indoctrination can result in a high level of scepticism around anything of a metaphysical nature that cannot be verified by physical evidence or through one's sensory capability. The indoctrinated mind faces a huge blind spot in this area; it fails to recognise that many real and powerful frequencies also fall beyond human sensory identification capabilities. A mind indoctrinated through the academic education system will take pride in citing 'scientific basis', again failing to connect that science itself is based on hypothesis and even much of the science proven in one era, was proven false in another era. Scientific experiments have shown that even physical matter which can be identified through one's sensor factors is made up of energy waves at the subatomic level – the mere act of observing an electron can change its characteristics. If an individual who prides themselves on relying on science investigates the work of the HeartMath Institute, they can familiarise themselves with the concept of heart frequency. Indoctrination results in closing the mind to new developments and anchoring to information one was conditioned in, in their formative years. Indoctrination at its worst can breed intellectual arrogance. Professionals need to realise that academic or professional qualifications may not be sufficient grounds for considering someone intelligent. True intelligence goes beyond reasoning, analysis and memory recall. It also involves lateral thinking, creativity and imagination.

Humans are emotional and intuitive entities. To assume that the highest form of education has to carry physical evidence or scientific rationality for it to be regarded as true, is the basis of all academic education and IQ development. Many professionals are quick to overemphasise data or scientific evidence, not realising that data and science can also be wrong. To insist that data or scientific evidence in isolation provides absolute closure, does not factor in the complexity of the world and human nature.

There are many instances in history where intellectuals and scientists have assumed conclusive resolution to an issue only to discover years later that those issues needed to be reconsidered. Some common examples are: the absolute nature of time and space, earth being the centre of the universe, smoking tobacco not being harmful, the efficacy of vaccines, the infallibility of the financial system and the causes of disease.

6. CREATIVITY AND IMAGINATION

Creativity would be synonymous with intuition if not for the fact that creativity applies to producing novel results. It is one's ability to produce something entirely new or use new methods to reform old ideas. Creativity and intuition are both visceral; however, while intuition may or may not surface in the presence of problems or challenges, creativity always comes into play when there is a problem. For instance, the intuitive little girl who knew her teacher was pregnant didn't solve any problem. There was no display of creativity. However, William Kamkwamba, the boy who harnessed the wind (who we will learn more about in Bonus Chapter Two), was a model of creativity, solving a problem by creating a windmill from scraps, bicycle parts and blue gum trees.

There are two ways to fuel creativity; intuition is the first. The second is imagination. Through intuition, we derive knowledge unassociated with reasoning, experience or analytical processes. Imagination, on the other hand, asks us to employ our use of reasoning, experience, inference and observation to create *images* in our minds that can or cannot be actualised. So, while intuition inspires creativity from the inside out, imagination inspires creativity from the outside in.

In William's case, intuition and imagination fuelled his creativity.

Through intuition, he realised he could build a windmill from scraps. However, he did not know the processes he had to go through to achieve this at the time. As we saw in Chapter Two, William *modified* ideas he got from a book in the library. We are certain that this book did not teach William how to build a windmill from scraps and gums, and that such a book exists that would outline processes and the actual materials to be used. So how did William know what to do with his scraps, bicycle parts and gum trees? Imagination.

Since he couldn't get the actual material to build the windmill, William *imagined* how the materials could be improvised to the ones outlined in the book. Allowing for free expression of his intuition and imagination led to William being able to tap into his creativity. Furthermore, William had no formal education. If he had relied on formal education, he would probably have thought that creating a windmill out of scraps was an impossible feat, since he did not have the required materials as outlined in the book.

From William's story, we can see how our imagination and creativity is able to flow in the absence of indoctrination and/or the rigidity of formal education. Allowing for free flow of our creativity is vital because with nothing new under the sun, the current challenges we face in the world needs new thinkers and innovative solutions – solutions inspired and propelled by creativity and lateral thought.

7. LATERAL THINKING

Riddle 1: A woman had two sons who were born on the same hour of the same day of the same year. But they were not twins. How could this be so?

Lateral thinking means solving problems using indirect and creative methods that are not immediately obvious. Phil Lewis in a *Forbes* article describes lateral thinking as a 'person's capacity to address problems by imagining solutions that cannot be arrived at via deductive or logical means. Or, to put it in simpler terms: the ability to develop original answers to difficult questions'.[18] Coined in 1967 by psychologist Edward de Bono in his book, *The Use of Lateral Thinking*, this concept differs from critical thinking in that while the latter seeks to find the validity of statements or problems, lateral thinking uses known ideas to find subtle solutions. In his book, de Bono cites the popular Judgement of Solomon[19] as one example of lateral thinking.

Riddle 2: A man falls out of a thirty-storey building but survives. He does not use a landing pad, neither is he lucky, so how does he survive the fall?

Edward de Bono outlines four techniques for lateral thinking:

1. Awareness: Understanding how our minds process information and resisting or doing away with established patterns.

2. Random stimulation: Letting in a variety of information from different sources – from having a conversation with a stranger to listening to podcasts.

3. Alternatives: Approaching problems from all angles and deliberately considering alternative options even in the presence of the usual solution.

4. Alteration: Reversing the relationship that exists between components of a problem; thinking in the opposite direction of what's implied; reducing patterns to smaller components; translating problems into analogies, then translating them back to solve the problem.[20]

Lateral thinking, in conjunction with other problem-solving skills, allows for a person to be able to solve any problem – including the aforementioned riddles. Here are the answers to those riddles:

Riddle 1: A woman had two sons who were born on the same hour of the same day of the same year. But they were not twins. How could this be so?

Answer: The boys were part of a set of triplets or quadruplets.

Riddle 2: A man falls out of a thirty-storey building but survives. He does not use a landing pad neither is he lucky, so how does he survive the fall?

Answer: The man fell from the first floor.

8. NEGOTIATION

Negotiation is a strategic conversation between parties to reach an acceptable agreement. Throughout the process of a negotiation, the parties involved try to persuade the other to agree to their point of view. The aim of negotiation is to reach a compromise that both parties are satisfied with.

However, the parties involved in a negotiation cannot reach a satisfactory compromise if they lack empathy. Empathy – the ability to understand the thoughts, feelings and emotional states of the other – is a sign of a high social quotient. When you can place yourself in the shoes of others, you are able to sympathise and realise that they are probably more disadvantaged than you. You become motivated towards reaching agreeable compromise – not just for your sake, but for theirs. Remember that the non-indoctrinated mind thinks about the collective good and not only personal gains. This is the distinguishing feature of a good leader.

9. LEADERSHIP AND INFLUENCE

Leadership is the process of guiding a person or group of persons and managing available resources towards achieving a goal. These resources include the material (e.g. buildings, equipment, vehicles, etc.), as well as non-material (e.g. time, financial cost, human effort).

Leadership is not a position; it is a character. It is also a function. There are people who have occupied leadership positions yet do not carry out the effective functions of a leader. The indoctrinated followers of such leaders follow the leader due to their position and status because they only perceive power in the position they hold, and do not acknowledge the level of responsibility in the function. On the other hand, others who aren't in leadership positions are able to guide people and resources to achieve a goal. But before you can guide people, you need to be able to understand them. And to understand them, you need to have excellent social skills. This is the only way you can *influence* people in such a way that it utilises their personality and skills to achieve the set goal.

Influence is the key quality of a leader. It is the ability to inspire others into action, and one of the strongest qualities indoctrinators possess. This is why they can easily motivate their followers into wrong thinking. As a non-indoctrinated person, you also need to also possess this quality in order to counteract the influence of indoctrination, otherwise there is no way you will be able to guide people to abandon indoctrinated behaviours. Influence can be used to disempower or empower people.

It is important to note that influence is not coercion or intimidation. As Roshan Thiran says, 'The heart of strategic influencing is to gain willing cooperation instead of mere compliance. It's about getting others to follow us because they want to and not because they have to. Influencing moves work from being merely transactional to relational. The most effective way to influence others is first to build a relationship of trust.'[21] Does this remind you of a story we saw earlier? The story of Daryl Davis and the KKK?

Influencing is a difficult task. Trying to get people to work together to achieve a goal whilst still retaining their humanity and uniqueness is no walk in the park and takes a great deal of courage.

10. COURAGE

Being courageous means being confident: bold, unafraid, not easily intimidated by people, tasks or events. Goals, no matter how small, are daunting. Once the body is nudged to leave its comfort zone, it fights back. The mind is capable of showing you 1,001 reasons why that goal cannot be achieved. To move past this resistance, you need courage. Harvard Business School Professor Nancy Koehn explains that 'a courageous leader is an individual who's capable of making themselves better and stronger when the stakes are high and circumstances turn against that person. [They] are not cowed or intimidated. They realise that, in the midst of turbulence, there lies an extraordinary opportunity to grow and rise'.[22] When we realise we are no longer products of our environment, and that we are not defined by circumstance, we can begin to employ the keys of courage to move beyond that space of fear to grow and rise above our situation in life. Courage is the key.

11. COMMUNICATION

This is the process of using verbal and/or nonverbal methods to send and receive messages. These methods include speech, writing, graphical representations, signs, body language and behaviour. Richard Nordquist for *ThoughtCo* writes that communication can be said to be 'the creation and exchange of meaning'.[23]

Nordquist's definition establishes that communication is completed at the point of exchange. The definition is a summary of the processes involved in indoctrination and overcoming indoctrination. An indoctrinator creates a chaotic meaning out of the world and exchanges this meaning with others who then go ahead to exchange this meaning with other people. The implication here, of course, is that without communication, indoctrination is dead. And yet without communication, we cannot rid the world of indoctrination.

In overcoming indoctrination, it is not enough to create a rational meaning out of the world. You need to exchange and propagate this meaning as you stifle the plans of indoctrinators to exchange and propagate theirs.

12. DELIBERATE PRACTICE

This is where many are found wanting. We humans learn but refuse practice. Sometimes, this refusal is not intentional; we are just too engrossed in the status quo that we forget to cement the knowledge we've gained. James Clear describes deliberate practice as 'a special type of practice that is purposeful and systematic. While regular practice might include mindless repetitions, deliberate practice requires focused attention and is conducted with the specific goal of improving performance'.[24]

Deliberate practice is the key to relearning. The individual must constantly remind themselves of the new knowledge they've gained and why this new knowledge is important. The racist has to practice relating with people of colour differently. The religious fanatic has to practice relating with the so-called infidels differently.

13. ASSERTIVENESS SKILLS

Being assertive is a communication strategy where you pass your information in a clear and direct way while maintaining respect for those you are communicating with. Some people confuse assertiveness with being blunt and rude. They call it 'speaking their truth'. But this is not speaking one's truth; it is simply a lack of assertiveness. You can always speak the truth or air your opinion without hurting or disrespecting the next person.

Being assertive is important in overcoming indoctrination. Many people fail to assert their perspectives because they are indoctrinated to believe that speaking up is the same as being disrespectful – and this has become even more challenging in view of the current wave of political correctness, an ideology that shuns assertiveness as it simultaneously encourages one to curb opinions and behaviours to that which is deemed 'socially acceptable' under the new umbrella of 'appropriateness'.

14. PURPOSE AND PASSION IDENTIFICATION

Purpose and passion are somewhat tied together. One is a destination; the other is the vehicle to the destination. Purpose is the reason why you are in the world. University of California, Berkeley, states that to psychologists, purpose is 'an abiding intention to achieve a long-term goal that is both personally meaningful and makes a positive mark on the world'.[25]

Life is a conundrum. Science and religions have put forward a number of theories of *how* the world came to be, but none has stated *why* the world exists. It can get confusing and frustrating trying to understand your place in a world you never asked to be in. This is the reason, I think, why many question the meaning of life. However, the answer to this lies in purpose. Purpose gives life meaning.

When you identify your purpose, you begin to gain clarity about life. Your purpose might be eradicating poverty in developing countries, restoring peace to warring nations, giving the underprivileged access to good education or leading your company. When you identify your purpose, you begin to figure out the medium(s) for achieving your purpose. And when you do this, you channel your entire energy towards achieving your purpose through that medium. The medium – and the energy you associate with it – is what we call *passion*.

When you are passionate about a cause, you feel joyful doing it, even if it may be demanding. This is one way to identify your passion, which most often aligns with your purpose. For instance, let's say you have a passion for public speaking; if you search your heart, you will discover that you have a desire to impact, influence and inspire people positively in order to positively transform your community and the world around you. Effecting positive change in your world is your purpose; public speaking is your passion. As a public speaker, you are able to bring the problems of the world to the fore and inspire people to take action towards solving these problems.

Purpose is the destination; passion is the vehicle to the destination.

15. KNOWING YOUR STRENGTHS AND WEAKNESSES

As you journey towards fulfilling purpose, the ability to know your strengths and weaknesses is an important skill to have. Your strengths are areas that come naturally to you or areas you have developed over time. Your strengths can be your passion or be a part of your passion.

Everyone has a zone of incompetence (things they suck at) and a zone of genius (things they shine at). Part of the self-discovery of education that is missing in the conventional education system is enabling people to discover their natural strengths. Imagine what would happen if young people had a strategic plan that would help them nurture their natural strengths and align their choice of occupation with those strengths, instead of spending disproportionate amounts of time working on their weaknesses – something that schools that practice indoctrinated thought are notorious for.

16. CLARITY OF VALUES

When choosing influencers or ambassadors, companies go for people whose values align with the image of the company. Your value system is a testament to who you are and what you represent. Your values guide your walk through life. This is why you should be clear on them.

Clarity of values is a vital skill. People who aren't clear on their values and beliefs can be easily influenced to deviate from them. Their lack of clarity indicates a lack of conviction in what they believe. These are the kinds of people indoctrinators target.

As a non-indoctrinated person, your ability to present your values to the indoctrinated mind determines whether you are capable of releasing yourself from the dangerous clutches of indoctrination.

*

These are the skills people should imbibe when they go to school. From elementary school onwards, teachers can inculcate these skills into pupils. They should instead create exercises and activities to develop the child's leadership skills, intuition, problem-solving skills and all-round intelligence.

All-round intelligence? Isn't that what they are doing already by training mentally robust individuals?

But do conventional educational systems train students to be 'intelligent' – or do they train them to be intellectual?

My personal observations here are that when individuals identify with their external identity (occupation, religion, culture, nationality) excessively without first establishing a deep-rooted connection to their inner identity (purpose, passion, personal values, strengths, mission), they become less conscious of the choices they are making, less independent in their decisions and more vulnerable to groupthink.

INTELLECTUAL OR INTELLIGENT?

For decades, if not centuries, we have confused being intellectual with intelligence. What we celebrate in child prodigies is their brilliance that shines forth in an aspect of their intellect, but we continuously refer to them as intelligent kids.

Being intellectual is different from being intelligent. When we say someone is intellectual, we mean that such a person has a good reasoning and analysis capability. This capacity may be innate or developed. Intelligence, on the other hand, is a big word and one with many facets. Intelligence is not limited to a person's intellectual or mental capacity; it expands to their social and emotional capacities. It extends to awareness, adaptability and the ability to determine what knowledge is necessary and how a skill corresponding to that knowledge can be acquired.

Society, through conventional education, has normalised filling the world with intellectual (and many times indoctrinated) people instead of intelligent people, and that is why we have many knowledgeable people in the world; yet our problems, despite having simple solutions, are unending.

Some very creative, independent and brilliant minds end up underperforming in schools, universities and even corporations (due to their need for conformity over creativity), because at the deepest level, such students intuitively sense (and reject) the subtle attempts made at indoctrination.

True intelligence has several different facets – in fact, there are four main facets that stand out – however, in my personal opinion, there are many more. These include spiritual intelligence, money intelligence, moral intelligence, body intelligence, cultural intelligence and commercial intelligence. How many educated professionals have you encountered who demonstrate mastery of spiritual awareness and understanding; cultural awareness and understanding; financial awareness and understanding; physical awareness and understanding; business awareness and understanding, and moral/ethical awareness and understanding? The worst part of this is that the majority of educated professionals are aware that these areas of development exist.

Let us discuss the main ones that have been the subject of formal research.

They are: intelligence quotient (IQ), emotional quotient (EQ), social quotient (SQ) and adversity quotient (AQ).

Intelligence quotient (IQ)

IQ is the measurement of one's ability to reason or think analytically when addressing issues or solving problems. It also refers to a gauge or measurement of how well an individual easily answers questions, using logic, memory recall and information to predict certain events and outcomes. The conventional education system focuses on this type of ability.

Emotional quotient (EQ)

People have different ways of handling happiness, success, anger, pain and other emotions. While certain situations can cause some people to break down, others will forge ahead, regardless of how dire the situation may be. Managing emotions varies from person to person, just as people have different IQ levels. When it comes to handling pressure, relationships or goals, everyone needs to know how well they manage emotions, and this is called the emotional quotient.

Emotional quotient (EQ) refers to the management, use and understanding of an individual's emotions in a positive way to relieve stress and enhance communication. EQ also refers to the positive way an individual empathises with others, their ability to overcome challenges, and their ability to manage and settle crises. EQ may be a greater predictor of commercial and career success than IQ alone.

Society generally considers those with a high IQ as the smartest amongst us. However, to the discerning observer, it becomes clear that a high IQ is not a substitute for common sense, objectivity or self-awareness (one of the main tenets of emotional intelligence). Simply because an individual can process information or data, doesn't mean they can process their own and others' emotions, biases and perspectives. People with dominant left-brain thinking can be particularly susceptible to propaganda or 'expert' opinion. This is probably because their educational conditioning makes them place a higher value on intellectual data (which is prone to intentional distortions and hence can contribute to the practices of indoctrination). Professionals with deep expertise acquired through institutional conditioning tend to place less value on intuitive insights, because at the end of the day, intuitive insights often bypass intellectual analysis. I won't go into detail here regarding intuitive intelligence and its function in solving complex problems (there are many books and white papers published on the subject); suffice to say, there are many studies that demonstrate that excessive reliance on data without common sense 'risk benefit analysis' or 'unintended consequence analysis' can result in inferior decision-making, sometimes with disastrous consequences.

Social quotient (SQ)

It is difficult for someone who has a low or no social quotient to sense other people's feelings. However, one with a high social quotient can easily make friends and thrive in a social setting. A person with a high social quotient intuitively knows what to say when they find themselves in a social situation. Some of the attributes of a person with a high social quotient include human behaviour observation, sense of humour and judgement in social situations.

Research carried out by the Carnegie Institute of Technology shows that 85% of one's financial success is owing to personality and the ability to communicate, negotiate and lead. Shockingly, only 15% is due to technical knowledge. Additionally, Nobel-Prize-winning Israeli-American psychologist Daniel Kahneman correctly observes that people would rather do business with a person they connect with and trust, over someone they don't. With this in mind, instead of exclusively focusing on intelligence quotient, conventional education should invest in strengthening a student's intelligence in other areas as well – with a view towards holistic development as the overall goal. Such concepts may be elusive and more difficult to measure, but their significance is far greater than IQ. Information and data can be researched; school and university curriculums need to focus more on developing the student's ability to identify what information they need, what information remains unknown, why the information is useful in the first place and which information connects to paint a picture. *How* to think is infinitely more important than *what* to think.

Adverse quotient (AQ)

The word adversity carries with it a very hostile meaning. Everyone in the world will face a critical situation at some point in time and have to navigate their way through life's adversities; yet it is precisely in the face of such adversity that one is able to determine how well they respond to challenging situations. Just as IQ, EQ and SQ measure certain things about humans, so too does the adversity quotient. Adversity quotient helps determine winnings in people's lives, including how they succeed and how well they brace, face and solve troubles.

Adversity quotient refers to a score that helps an individual measure how they can handle or deal with adversities in life. When adversities arise, one of the most important tools we can use to combat them is resilience. Many educated professionals make 'certainty-based' and 'safe' choices due to their incessant need to pre-empt and know how to act before committing to that action. This can be a blessing in some situations and a curse in others. Risk-averse professionals may not make great entrepreneurs because in entrepreneurship, many times, problem-solving can be messy, reactive and perpetual. The need for certainty often drives a compulsive tendency to connect the dots by looking forward, instead of connecting the dots looking back. This inspires problem-avoidance behaviours instead of problem-solving behaviours, which are more connected to grit and agility.

CHAPTER THIRTEEN
A New Kind of Education

All that we've discussed throughout this book points to one fundamental fact: conventional education is not doing enough to develop human beings in terms of knowing who they are or what they want enough to confidently make autonomous decisions for their life, free of heavy cultural, educational, media or religious-based indoctrination. The knowledge received solely from conventional education is not holistic, and the current generation of students are sensing this. They want more. They are questioning why the education system is not teaching them the path to life through mindset, health, relationships, career and money mastery.

The fact that the institutions (schools, universities and corporations) continue to ignore the need for humans to develop holistically is fuelling people's apathy towards education and work.

This apathy should not be ignored. Education is a wonderful pursuit to undertake, so the time is now for educational and work systems to focus on making education more appealing. The current methods of education need modification – we need a new kind of education – one that teaches students to develop themselves, their business acumen and their spirituality. The emergence of coaches, consultants, trainers, influencers, speakers and mentors is perhaps a sign that the most basic needs of people to become well-rounded, accomplished, balanced and confident humans is not being met by the current conventional systems in place.

MASTERY OF SELF

'Who am I?' This is a profound and important question every thinking person asks themselves. Understanding who you are is the rudder that governs your course through life. Maybe this is why Aristotle's words resonate: 'Man, know thyself.'

Self-mastery is one's ability to recognise, understand and control their physical, mental, emotional and spiritual components. It is knowing *what* you are, who you are, what you stand for and your place in this world. It is *cultivating* your character, skills and relationships to align with your life's purpose.

Lacking self-mastery means lacking inner understanding. The path to self-mastery includes:

- Understanding your purpose and passion.
- Maintaining your autonomy of thought.
- Developing emotional intelligence (with particular focus on self-awareness).
- Developing your adversity quotient.
- Developing desirable skills like intuition, original thinking, creativity, courage, etc.
- Knowing your strengths and weaknesses.
- Being clear on your values and strengths.
- Understanding how your mind works.

Self-mastery is a lifelong process that never ends. As long as you live, life uses events to reveal emotions, behaviours and characters you never knew existed. These discoveries aren't to be discarded – the more you understand yourself, the better decisions you will make and the more fulfilled you will become.

MASTERY OF BUSINESS AND FINANCIAL FUNDAMENTALS

Anyone who has an income, has expenses and has to pay tax, is in the money game. But how many understand the rules of money? How many know how to read the scoreboard of money?

Can you imagine how a tennis player or cricketer or soccer player ever wins a game, regardless of their talent, if they don't understand the rules of the game/or if they don't know how to interpret the scoreboard?

How many professional graduates understand the concept of risk mitigation? And no – risk avoidance is not risk mitigation.

How many understand how to calculate their net worth, or how much money they will need at retirement? Or how to factor inflation into their future plans? Or the difference between good and bad debt? Or the difference between investing and speculation?

If you believe that the above concepts are not relevant to you because you are not in the field of finance, congratulations. You have been successfully indoctrinated.

If you believe that employees do not need to learn business, again, congratulations. You have been successfully indoctrinated. A typical employee mindset thinks only in solos. An emphasis on specialisation (a by-product of the industrial revolution) has made many employees myopic and unconcerned about the role they play in an organisation's growth. Most employees are concerned only with job security, salary packages, holiday entitlements and promotions based on tenure. They rarely think in terms of business unit profitability, high performance, productivity, outcomes and contribution. Most have never been trained to read or analyse personal or business financial statements. This myopic and entitlement-based mindset is more detrimental to an employee's prospects than to the employer's success because, by not thinking in business terms, most employees never rise to executive positions, never secure enough equity to build their own asset base and never hold key decision-making positions in the organisations in which they are employed. The ability to think in these terms requires an entrepreneurial and commercial mindset – which most employees (due to their indoctrinated conditioning through the education system), subconsciously believe is not necessary to career success. Trials and errors along with multi-dimensional experiential analysis, is how one builds business acumen over time. Unfortunately, school curriculums and university degrees prefer theoretical learning, and trial and error is therefore discouraged. Even most corporate managers perpetuate one-dimensional work experiences, not realising that employees who have gained multidimensional experiences tend to be better problem-solvers, more innovative thinkers and less prone to groupthink.

Specialisation implies knowing more about less and less. It promotes silo thinking. Unfortunately, our world does not work in silos. For example, politics has a connection to history, geography has a connection to biology, financial management has a connection to wellbeing and so forth. Specialist workers who have spent many years in structured and linear learning, struggle to adapt to new ideas, change and innovation.

To a great extent, specialisation of both education and work life results in not only stifling the individual of creativity but also results in fostering critical attitudes towards those who do engage in any type of individual expression or new idea generation. Ask most corporate employees how they are treated when they come up with a new idea or initiative and most will tell you that they prefer not to speak up, even when they identify systemic inefficiencies in operation and management. The constant pressure that society and parents alike place on young people towards academic excellence, and the pressure to opt for traditional occupations such as medicine, law, engineering, management, accounting etc., causes young people to form the subconscious belief that creativity does not pay, where the vast majority of young people subconsciously seek security instead of diversity and growth. According to Gallup Engagement Polls 2020, only 20% of employees feel engaged at work globally. And who can blame them! Not having the ability to create, express or experiment naturally results in a dull, uninspiring and limited career. The question is: can somebody who does not find meaning and engagement at work, ever produce anything significant or legendary?

It needs to be understood that any business is ultimately an extension of a person's value addition, problem-solving, contribution and vision. Business mindset and skills can be learned. The aim of a business is to offer value while making money. These two aims are people centred. You offer value to people, and in return, they offer you money. To offer value and earn from it, you need to work with people who understand your vision and purpose for the business. Therefore, mastery of business entails cultivating people and financial skills in order to offer value and create wealth. These skills include:

- Leadership and influencing.
- Original thinking.
- High emotional, social and adversity quotients.
- Communication.
- Creativity.
- Negotiation.

I believe these skills create the foundation for what renowned business coach, Tony Robbins, calls the 7 Forces of Business Mastery.[1] Below are the seven forces and their explanations according to Robbins. I have italicised my comments on each point.

1. Knowing where you really are and creating an effective map. Robbins states that the biggest challenge of business leaders is that they are not honest about where their business really is. They see the business as better than it is, and this causes them to have blind spots that eventually affect the business. *As I mentioned earlier, self-mastery leads to mastery in other areas. One of the cardinal features of self-mastery is self-awareness; the ability to understand your emotions and behaviours, and develop or improve upon them. Business leaders who lack honesty about the state of their business are probably also those who lack self-awareness. The aim of self-awareness or, in this case, 'business awareness' is to be conscious of what your business is and where it is, using the truth to design where you want it to be. Being dishonest about this blinds you to areas that need improvement – because a business built on faulty foundations will crumble in the end.*

2. Strategic innovation. Robbins says this is finding a way to meet the needs of your clients better than anyone else. *This is where out-of-the-box thinking, original thinking and lateral thinking come into play.*

3. World-class, strategic marketing. Robbins defines this as the process of getting a large number to want to do business with you. He also calls it 'value-added marketing'. *You cannot do this if you lack emotional and social intelligence. You cannot present your offering to people if you don't understand how they feel, what their needs and wants are, and their emotional state. Good communication skills are also necessary here.*

4. Sales mastery systems. This means creating systems that convert your clients to growth and sales.

5. Financial and legal analysis. Robbins says: 'If you aren't able to understand and analyse the financial condition of your business on an ongoing basis, you're like the pilot of a plane who doesn't know how to read the gauges in front of him. It's easy to fly when there are clear skies (i.e. a good economy), but when you find yourself surrounded by storms and fog, if you can't read the gauges, you're going to crash. It's only a matter of time.' *As a businessperson, it will not always be financially rosy. So how high is your adversity quotient?*

6. Optimisation and maximisation. Robbins states that creating explosive growth in your company is not about making big changes; it is in optimising and maximising people and processes. *This relates to the first-principles approach of problem-solving. Optimising and maximising the basic components cause large changes to the overall system.*

7. Create raving fan customers and culture. This is the ultimate outcome for any business. 'Satisfied customers leave you when somebody gives them a better deal. Raving fan customers are loyal; they know who you really are and they stick around even when you screw up because you've consistently added value to them in a way that nobody else can.' *Business is more about offering value than it is about offering products. You offer value when your clients can connect and resonate with your offerings at an emotional level.*

MASTERY OF SPIRITUALITY

Because of so much religious indoctrination, many have turned away from spirituality. Our spirituality is not meant to dilute or suppress our true selves; rather, it is there to make us more robust as human beings. Spiritual mastery adds to our knowledge – it does not subtract from it. Connecting to your spiritual self improves your self-awareness, guides your relationship with others and helps you add value to your world. It is not a gateway to display sanctimoniousness and become judgemental. If you do this, then you have already scored low in both your emotional and social quotients.

Your spiritual self must align with your physical, mental and emotional states. This is what many do not realise, and this is why they are so easily indoctrinated – because in a bid to connect with their spiritual selves, they forget what it means to be human. If your spirituality does not add value to you (and consequently to others), then you may need to re-evaluate it.

CONCLUSION

Our world is suffering from a lack of creative and independent change-makers. People continue to seek and gain admission into institutions of learning, yet for all our collective academic excellence, we are still buried knee-deep in problems that have plagued us for generations. Problems like crime, hate, discrimination, corruption, environmental degradation, oppression and exploitation continue to exist at every turn, where the only improvements we see worldwide are primarily technological, rather than psychological in nature.

Despite the level of knowledge in the world, we've not been able to solve our problems, and it seems to me as though the current educational systems are too focused on having a world rapidly advancing economically and technologically, and at the cost of our collective holistic intelligence.

Education has failed us. Here is why: we have never truly been educated. Rather, what we pass through as education is in fact systematic processes of indoctrination, a system that has made many robots out of brains.

Hegel says that 'the true is the whole'. This is such a simple yet powerful statement, because in order for truth to be realised, we need to understand that we must all participate in it. Truth does not exist in a vacuum; therefore we must actively and willingly seek it out, for this is also part of the story of our evolution.

However, we are not without hope. The beauty in overcoming indoctrination is that mastery in one aspect of our lives translates into mastery in other aspects. Therefore, we become masters of ourselves, our business and our spirituality. Let this book be our first initial and tentative diagnosis of the problem, and a panacea for the world's ills. Overcoming indoctrination is the first step to reclaiming ourselves and solving our problems. It unfurls in us the totality of our intelligence, where we will become not just book smart but emotionally smart, equipped to understand our emotions and behaviours and how they affect the people around us in heightened and ever-present ways. We shall become people-conscious beings, present and courageous enough to face our challenges because we know the world depends on us for the sake of our continued evolution.

> *'To be independent of public opinion is the first formal condition of achieving anything great.'*
> *– Georg Hegel*

APPENDIX

Conventional education may have fallen short in many ways but there are some cases, albeit few, where it has tried to function optimally. I have decided to share these cases in two bonus chapters to show that all hope is not lost. These true stories drawn from different examples prove that if we can become intentional about redefining what education means to us, we would be able to change the course of humanity and our world for the better in no time.

Cases Where Conventional Education Gets It Right

Deep in the Nilgiris Biosphere Reserve in southern India lies the small village of Kadichanokolli in which the Betta Kurumba people of Tamil Nadu live. If you travelled to this village two decades ago, you would see a small town of tea and coffee plantations; a small town with no hospitals or schools, and where night-time was nothing more than a darkness punctuated by the flickering golden flames of oil lamps. But all of that changed when Prathibha Balakrishnan came into the village.

In 2008, Prathibha, a teacher, went to Kadichanokolli on a mission to teach the Betta Kurumba people. She was assisted by Badichi, a matriarch who had seven children and a grandchild. Badichi had little education but understood its power. With the help of Badichi, Prathibha was able to persuade the locals to allow her to teach them. Both women forged ahead to *successfully* petition the local government to install a primary school, electricity and roads in the village. Prathibha taught the natives in their own language, while one of Badichi's daughters, Vasanthi, trained to become a nurse in a hospital and spoke three languages.

With their simple yet important mission to liberate a village,

Prathibha used the power of education to transform the Betta Kurumba people. Her work was so remarkable that it was featured in an exhibition at the UN headquarters in 2019.[1]

Reading Prathibha's story, I decided to research the current state of the Betta Kurumba people. I wanted to find out how had they sustained Prathibha's impact in the now. Although much is not known about the current educational standards of the people, from several reports I was able to glean that the average literacy rate of the tribe in 2017 was 80.33%.[2] This is a highly impressive result, especially given that it was once a community without schools, roads or health care nine years before.

The story of Prathibha and the people of Betta Kurumba sets the golden standard and begs us to answer the question: Why education?

*

Education represents that place in which a person or a community needs to know that the world is more, and that, as human beings, they deserve more. The human mind, upon entering the world, is a tabula rasa. A blank slate. The mind is aware of its environment; yet it cannot comprehend it. Its reaction to the environment is unguarded and innately motivated, which is why a child is fascinated by a bright, beautiful flame without understanding the inherent danger that lies within its beauty. It takes education – either by experiencing pain or by continuous caution from an adult – for the child to understand what fire is and what it can do.

This simple illustration sums up the basic duty of education: to make us understand what the world is, what it can do and our role in it. The truth is, humankind wouldn't have thrived without education. (Now, education in this sense is not restricted to the formal setting, but rather to any process that inculcates and cultivates intelligence in a person.) In Chapter One, we explored the histories of education in different societies – how they used education to transmit their traditions and values from one generation to the other. However, these histories do not tell us why these societies thought it was important to educate and transmit knowledge. What would have happened if the older generation had just kept what they knew to themselves?

The impracticality of such a decision makes it difficult to imagine. Humans are simply not wired this way; they are wired to teach and be taught. There lies within us an intrinsic apparatus that sparks curiosity, spurs us to seek answers and stirs the desire to transmit what we know to others for the sake of continuity and preservation. It is this apparatus and its cascade of desires that led to the development of education.

We have seen the trajectory of education turn from ancient societies like Mesopotamia to present-day communities like the Betta Kurumba tribe of southern India. However, we need to look more specifically now at the importance of education to the individual (the smallest, most important unit of a society) as it pertains to society at large.

EDUCATION AND THE INDIVIDUAL
The power to dream
Children are often asked the popular question: What do you want to be when you grow up? Beneath these simple, banal words lies the power to dream. First, the child sees other children going to school and wants to be part of it. Once they get into school, they start to dream of being the best. Perhaps, they dream of getting into high school, dream of going to college. As one dream becomes a reality, they dream even higher. As each new educational level or status is attained, they may realise that their dreams are achievable.

Often, we underestimate this power to dream that education births in us. Education enlightens the mind. It unwraps the world before us, showing us its merits and flaws – and our place in it. Education creates a hunger in us to add value to the world; and as long as this ambition is sustained, we continue to work to satisfy it.

As I write about the power to dream, Martin Luther King comes to mind. Martin Luther King was so intelligent, yet he never completed high school, skipping his first and last year at Booker T Washington High School and entering Morehouse College at the age of fifteen. We remember him most for his civil rights activism and popular speech, *I Have A Dream*. But what many may not know is that this dream was inspired by Henry David Thoreau's writings, specifically Thoreau's essay on civil disobedience.[3] In his essay penned in 1849, Thoreau argued that citizens must disobey the law of the state if such law is an unjust one.[4]

That essay injected a boldness into Martin Luther King. MLK understood his rights as a human being and refused to allow such rights to be taken away from him purely on the basis of skin colour. As I stated earlier, we have an intrinsic apparatus in us, and it was this apparatus that stirred King to transmit his knowledge and boldness to other black Americans. Martin Luther King dreamt of a better America where people wouldn't be judged by the colour of their skins but by the content of their character. His dream was contagious. Because of him and others like him, black people like Barack Obama dared to dream and turn their dreams into reality.

In an alternate reality, Martin Luther King might just have been an intelligent boy trying to navigate life and escape the oppressive clutches of racism. Maybe he would never have known that he could push back against the unjust laws of his nation. Maybe he would have become another docile black American whose name would never have been heard. Not only does education give us the power to dream – it also gives us the power to turn our dreams into reality.

When he was fourteen, William Kamkwamba, a young Malawian boy, dreamed about building a windmill for his village. After reading about windmills, he wanted his village to enjoy electricity and running water – luxuries only elite Malawians enjoyed. Undeterred by the fact that the villagers called him crazy, William went ahead to build the windmill using and modifying plans he found in a library book titled *Using Energy*.[5] In his book, *The Boy Who Harnessed the Wind*, William writes: 'With a small pile of once-forgotten science textbooks; some scrap metal, tractor parts and bicycle halves; and an armoury of curiosity and determination, [I] embarked on a daring plan to forge an unlikely contraption and small miracle that would change the lives around [me].'[6]

A library book birthed a dream in William's mind and showed him how to bring his dream to life. A library book awakened William to the world. His story was covered by *The Daily Times* and *The Wall Street Journal*, and this fame exposed him to more educational opportunities – and even more ways to actualise his dreams. He got a scholarship to the African Leadership Academy and graduated from Dartmouth College in New Hampshire with a degree in environmental studies. By 2013, *TIME* had named William as one of the '30 People Under 30 Changing The World'.

In 2010, *The Boy Who Harnessed the Wind* became selected reading for all incoming students at the University of Florida and Boise State University. In 2014, Auburn University and University of Michigan College of Engineering followed suit as the book became listed as required reading. Through William's fame, we can only imagine the number of young boys and girls in Malawi and abroad who would read his story and become so impacted by it that they would dare to dream, too.

Stories like William's and others validate Elizabeth King's statement in a World Bank article: 'The human mind makes possible all developmental achievements, from health advances and agricultural innovations to efficient public administration and private sector growth. For countries to reap these benefits fully, they need to unleash the potential of the human mind. And there is no better tool for doing this than through education.'[7]

SKILLS FOR LIVING

In January 2020, hilarious footage of Taylor Garcia – a little girl of about eight – went viral. In the nearly two-minute long video (which later caught the attention of popular TV host and comedian, Ellen DeGeneres), Taylor ranted to her mother about her stolen Perfect Attendance pencil, a pencil she had earned for not missing any days of school. She had left it in the pencil sharpener box and upon returning to school the next day, the pencil was gone. According to her, it was stolen by a girl named Lizzy. Her mom tried to pacify her, telling her it was just a pencil, but little Taylor kept harping on the fact that it was not just a pencil but her *Perfect Attendance* pencil. What struck me most about Taylor's tirade was when she said that Lizzy didn't *earn* the pencil because she went on a vacation to Canada.

At such a tender age, Taylor already understood the concept of earning, in that we have to work for what we want. Such understanding is vital because it strips the individual of any sense of entitlement. A wrong or misplaced sense of entitlement will make the armed robber believe they can steal from others since life has been unfair to them. The same wrong sense of entitlement allows a rapist to justify his right to a woman's body. Sense of entitlement inflates the autocrat's ego, believing the presidential seat is their birthright. Yet proper education that promotes self-reflection strips the individual of entitlement, and instead implants in us a culture of hardwork, helping us to desire only what we deserve *and* earn. This is the lesson Taylor thankfully imbibed at an early age.

Education builds a set of qualities and skills in us. These life skills are the life jackets with which we swim through the vast ocean called life. It is not that an uneducated person cannot attain these skills, but the fact is that the educational system is a microcosm of the world – a rehearsal for the individual to interact successfully with their environment as it prepares them for the real world. Some of these skills include self-motivation, time management, organisation, resourcefulness and out-of-the-box thinking.

SELF-MOTIVATION

The education system we find ourselves in sets us up for challenges throughout the length of study. The hurdles never end. From elementary school, one looks forward to high school; from high school, the aim is to get into college or university. There is always another level to desire and attain. And self-motivation is the critical life skill needed to attain these heights.

Although psychologists state that there are children who need extra external sources of motivation to learn, for most students, motivation is intrinsic. Beata Souders mirrors my thoughts when she states that curiosity and motivation to learn is the force that drives students to seek 'intellectual and experiential novelty'. It also encourages them to approach peculiar, challenging circumstances as they anticipate growth and expect success.[8]

Students who are intrinsically motivated need no external push or reward. The thought of passing an exam or contributing to a group task is enough motivation, where the fulfilment derived from such pursuits towards success is motivation enough. After decades of research, the National Research Council reports that those who are intrinsically motivated to learn are more likely to set goals for themselves, and regard increasing their competence as a goal in itself.[9] Similarly, in an article for *Harvard Business Review*, Deborah Grayson Riegel quotes Daniel Pink, who says: 'When we make progress and get better at something, it is inherently motivating. In order for people to make progress, they have to get feedback and information on how they're doing.'[10]

The right pathways in education enable a student to set meaningful and relevant goals for themselves and offers a system that monitors and provides feedback. Education not only ignites inspiration in us, but also comes with a built-in mechanism that *sustains* this inspiration.

TIME MANAGEMENT

There is a popular Brazilian story of a fisherman and a businessman. (Renowned author, Paulo Coelho, states that the story may be present in other cultures, but it is a classic Brazilian story.[11]) Many lessons have been extracted from this story, and I want to use this same story to buttress the need for time management and how education plays a role.

A businessman sat by the beach in a small Brazilian village watching a Brazilian fisherman row his boat to the shore after catching some big fish. Impressed by the fisherman, the businessman decided to strike up a conversation.

Businessman (*impressed*): How long does it take you to catch so many fish?

Fisherman: Oh, just a short while.

Businessman (*surprised*): Then why don't you stay longer at sea to catch more?

Fisherman: This is enough to feed my family.

Businessman: So, what do you do for the rest of the day?

Fisherman: Well, my day always starts with me waking up early in the morning to go to sea and catch some fish. When I return, I play with my kids. In the afternoon, I take a nap with my wife. In the evening, I join my friends in the village for a drink – we play the guitar, sing and dance all through the night.

Businessman: I have a PhD in business management. I can help you become successful. From now on, spend more time at sea trying to catch as many fish as you can. Save some money, and when you have saved enough, you can buy a bigger boat and catch even more fish. In no time, you will be able to buy more boats, set up a company, and own a production plant for canned food and distribution networks. By then, you will have moved out of this village to Sao Paulo where you can set up your headquarters to oversee and manage other branches.

Fisherman: After that, what next?

Businessman (*laughs*): After that, you can live like a king! When the time is right, you can go public and float your shares in the stock exchange. You will be rich!

Fisherman: After that, what next?

Businessman: After that, you can retire. You can move to a house by the fishing village, wake up early in the morning, catch some fish, return home to play with kids, have an afternoon nap with your wife, and in the evening, you can drink with your friends, play the guitar, sing and dance throughout the night.

Fisherman (*puzzled*): Isn't that what I am doing now?

As I stated earlier, the uniqueness of this story lies in its multi-faceted lessons. The story teaches that happiness and success take up different meanings. It also teaches the dangers of mediocrity. Whatever lesson we extract from this story is valid, but for the sake of argument within the context of this book, we can clearly see that the fisherman wasn't a good time manager.

The beauty of education is that it shows us that life has many sides, and each side is important. It teaches us to allocate our time efficiently and to each area of our life so that none lacks attention. This is why a key feature of any educational system is compartmentalisation.

There is time for each lesson, a break time and time for extracurricular activities – all geared towards creating a balanced, well-rounded individual.

For the fisherman, his priorities lay in the connection he had with his family, friends and community. He treasured these connections above his job as a fisherman and reduced his fishing to being a means to an end, as long as it provided enough sustenance for himself and his family. Now, treasuring the bond of family and friendship is not a bad thing – but humans have the ability and potential to aspire to be more in other aspects of their life, but this can only happen when one allocates time and resources to the other aspects. The right education furnishes the individual with the skills of time management early in life.

When we talk about time management, we often understand it as how we allocate our time to the many important activities competing for our attention *daily*. But time management goes beyond daily allocations of time; it also involves yearly or *future* allocations. Are you like the fisherman – enjoying a life of retirement now when you should be working and building wealth for yourself?

Proper education enabled students to understand the value of time. It helps them understand the compounding value of time and teaches one how to prioritise what is important over what is urgent or not urgent. It teaches the difference between busy and productive and how to make the best use of time.

Maybe if the fisherman were educated, he would have focused on building a big business in the now and choose to live a life of retirement later. I guess he was living a carefree life, albeit one without guidance. When the guidance did come in the form of the businessman offering his knowledge, the thought of building anything became strange to the fisherman's ears. His ability to effectively manage his time for greater success exposed other qualities he lacked:

creative thinking and resourcefulness. The fisherman's ignorance in these matters is understandable. But what about the educated professional? Should we expect them to have a better understanding of prioritising, managing and allocating time? If they are already trained in these areas, why is that so many struggle to make time for the truly important things in life, and why is it that hundreds of millions of people walking this earth have so little to show for themselves after decades of hard work? It is estimated that less than fifty million people have a net worth of more than $1 million USD worldwide. If seen as a percentage of the global working population (when you consider the number of graduates and professionals), this represents a very tiny minority. And if you think a million dollars is a lot of money, think again. With increases in life expectancy in both the developed world and emerging economies, a million dollars in net worth by retirement age can no longer be considered sufficient when you consider longevity, rising medical expenses and inflation over a fifteen-to-thirty-year period. How many educated professionals are even aware of these new challenges in the face of a changing world – and do any of them have a preparation plan in place? I will safely bet here that most do not, perhaps because they haven't bothered to think about how their own financial dependency weighs long-term upon the government or family, or even whether this will be a feasible option in the future.

RESOURCEFULNESS AND CREATIVE THINKING

In 2001, renowned Australian cook and food writer, Stephanie Alexander, partnered with an inner-Melbourne school community to establish a program called the Kitchen Garden Program at Collingwood College. The program aimed to deliver kitchen and garden classes to students, enabling for skills-based learning in these areas as part of the school curriculum. The program ensured that the students, aged eight to twelve years old, would spend time in a productive vegetable garden and home-style kitchen as part of their daily school experience. By doing this, they would become resourceful, learn how to prepare for contingencies and bounce back from challenges. As of 2015, 561 schools across Australia, comprising of over sixty thousand students, all participated in the program. The program trained students to grow, harvest, prepare and share fresh, seasonal food.[12]

I can imagine the students being excited as they got their hands dirty tilling the soil. I can also imagine teachers deliberately withholding certain requirements needed for optimal growth of the crops so that the students had to problem-solve and come up with alternative methods for growing their garden. Even if the teachers didn't deliberately limit their requirements, the students would have still encountered other challenges during the planting period, forcing them to have to think of new solutions in order to navigate their way around it. For me, however, the question is: would these students have imbibed this same set of skills if they weren't in school? Maybe not.

Recall earlier my stating that the skills education offers an individual can be attained without education, but education provides a primordial and preparatory platform for such skills to be imbibed, tested and utilised. For example, the Accel Innovation Scholars (AIS) program at Stanford University introduces doctoral students of engineering to the entrepreneurial ecosystem of Silicon Valley. It was reported that many of the students ended up taking the skills they learned in the program and applied them in other fields.[13] This is what education does – it takes the skills one receives from education and applies them to other areas of human life.

Resourcefulness is a valuable life skill one acquires through education. It is a such a vital quality every human being can and must consciously develop and is directly linked to our survival. Resourceful people do not get stuck because they find and use different methods to achieve their goals. Resourceful people do not see obstacles as stop signs, because they understand that those who demonstrate the most resourcefulness, end up with the most *resources.*

Apart from extracurricular activities like gardening and cooking, educational systems are structured to make students achieve their goals amid certain constraints. For instance, tests and exams are usually timed; thus, students are expected to use the time available at their disposal to show what they know. Resourcefulness goes hand in hand with creative thinking too, which is why teachers set class works, assignments and projects: students are required to use what they've learned to produce creative solutions to problems.

One way of building resourcefulness is by relating concepts from analogous fields. This was how Joseph Skhlovsky, an astronomer, proposed the current theory of dinosaur extinction, and Ben Silbermann, the co-founder of the image-sharing platform, Pinterest, modelled the platform's visual approach on the way he had collected insects as a youth.[14] *Harvard Business Review* notes that it was this same approach that 3M, the multinational conglomerate corporation, used to develop a breakthrough concept for preventing surgery-associated infections – an idea they in turn had stumbled upon from a theatrical make-up specialist knowledgeable about facial skin infections.[15]

Proper education exposes the individual to a variety of fields, from sciences to arts to business management. Thus, the individual has an array of analogous fields to draw connections from, enhancing their overall development.

But back to the fisherman for a moment: he never used his faculty of thought to ask himself: *How do I become a better fisherman? How do I catch more fish?* Let us forget for a moment all the businessman told him. Why was the fisherman comfortable providing fish only for himself and his family? Certainly, not everyone in the village knew how to fish. Some would have relied on the fishermen to provide fish for them. Why didn't the fisherman think of meeting his needs (and that of the village) and make some more money while he was at it?

Within minutes of sitting by the river, the businessman's interest piqued in the fisherman, which saw him start a conversation with the man, which then presented a gap in knowledge, and the businessman offered up measures to fill that gap based on his own knowledge and expertise. Would the businessman have done this if he wasn't educated? Would he have been able to do this if his education had not taught him how to allocate time, connect with new people and broaden his thoughts to gain insights for better opportunities?

THE REFINERY OF EDUCATION

To refine crude oil, three basic processes must come into play: distillation, cracking and reformation. Distillation involves separating the crude oil constituents based on their degree of volatility. This is followed by cracking, which is breaking up heavy molecules into lighter, more valuable molecules. Then reformation occurs: the changing of the chemical nature of the lighter molecules to achieve the desired physical properties and also increase their market value.

Like a crude oil refinery, we can think of education refining the individual through a similar process. In elementary school, pupils are observed for intelligence, character and interactions with other children. Before they move into high or secondary school, the teachers already know the students' strong/positive and weak/negative traits. Once in high school, discipline is enforced to mould the child – by breaking down the negative traits and reinforcing the best and most desirable traits. At tertiary level, the individual receives formal training for a selected profession, all of which improves and raises their social status.

Every human being is a body of thoughts and ideas. These thoughts and ideas often exist in crude form. As mentioned earlier, a child is fascinated by fire. Initially, the child has only a crude idea about fire and can only interpret it as a bright, beautiful flame. Education provides the child with knowledge to understand that fire is not only beautiful but dangerous.

Just as educated thoughts enhance one's thinking, thoughts harboured by the uneducated mind can hurt not just the individual but those around them. This was a lesson learned when, in 2017, a group of researchers conducted a study in Karachi, Pakistan, to compare the knowledge and attitudes of educated and uneducated individuals towards HIV/AIDS. The study showed that while educated participants knew about HIV/AIDS and its symptoms, the uneducated believed that the infection could be transmitted through water and that those suffering from the disease had to be isolated.[16]

Somewhat surprisingly, the study revealed that the uneducated people in Karachi were a risk to themselves, as the irony of their logic backfired; while believing that not drinking the contaminated water protected them from becoming infected with the HIV strain, they then proceeded to have unprotected sex. They also became a risk to others – because if they couldn't protect themselves due to ignorance, then others (both the uneducated and promiscuously educated) were also at risk. This risk continued to be extended to already infected members of the community, and discrimination against them jeopardised the mental and emotional health of those with the virus.

Education refines the human mind; and because this is true, we therefore cannot totally blame the uneducated folks of Karachi, Pakistan, for their predicament. Without education, man can only churn out crude, unrefined thoughts; but with education, a man becomes enabled to detect unrefined thoughts and turn them into something more. Science, through education, has taught us that HIV/AIDS cannot be transmitted through food or water. It has taught us that HIV/AIDS patients should not be discriminated against because being HIV positive doesn't make them less human. As education refines our thoughts it allows for us to effectively interact with biotic and abiotic components of our environment. As educated beings, we can screen our thoughts and ideas through different sieves, ensuring that we produce the best decisions for ourselves, others and our environment. One may even argue that civilisation is a product of education. Indeed, cultural education became the chief means of transmitting societal values only after organised religion ceased to fill this need. So was the case made by the pre-eminent contemporary English philosopher of the twenty-first century, Sir Roger Scruton, in his book, *Culture Counts*. In it, Scruton says that: 'The decline of religion had not bereft mankind of intrinsic values; through aesthetic education – in other words, culture – we could reconnect to those primordial experiences of wonder and awe, which show us the lasting meaning of our life on earth.'

In essence, education makes us recognise *and* fit into what it means to be human. Without education, would we have ever known what it means to be humane? Would we have ever understood kindness, empathy, sympathy, sacrifice? Would we have known boundless creativity?

LITERACY AND SOCIETY

John Akec, the vice-chancellor of the University of Juba, South Sudan, wrote a brief article in 2020 in which he highlighted the need for literacy in a society.[17] In this article, Akec refers to the words of Alfred North Whitehead, a twentieth-century English mathematician and philosopher, who claimed that: 'The society that does not value trained intelligence is doomed.' Akec also quotes Clark Kerr, former chancellor and president of the University of California, Berkeley, in his book, *The Uses of University.* In it, Kerr writes that: 'It will be a sad situation if, over the long run, public investments in prisons continue to take a higher relative priority than investments in universities; and if internally, within the universities, preservation of the status quo takes priority over an aggressive commitment to access, to quality and to autonomy.'

Akec reflects on the views of these two men because their observations mirror the happenings in his own society in South Sudan. Akec reveals that his is a society that prioritises purchasing arms, funding unending military and security apparatuses, and enriching the privileged and the connected at the expense of providing and investing in schools and health care. Furthermore, he believes that the South Sudanese society exists in a paradox, a way of life contrary to what is obtained elsewhere: too much education is seen as a disadvantage and a threat to the status quo. Therefore, highly educated and intelligent people are not employed and engaged to provide solutions to the nation's existential socioeconomic, security and development challenges.

And since every (in)action has consequences, South Sudan is currently on the brink of social and political chaos, based upon the disorder of its neighbouring and politically volatile nations of Libya, Somalia, Yemen and others.

One may wish to fault Akec's sentiment with the argument that even educated societies are not immune to breakdowns of social and political order. While this may be true, we cannot ignore the fact that war-torn countries generally have lower literacy rates. Data from the World Bank shows that Afghanistan has a literacy level of 43%; Yemen, 54%; Ethiopia, 52% and Burkina Faso, 41%.

Illiterate societies are time bombs. Lawson Luke rightly notes that countries with low literacy rates are more prone to armed conflicts. More often than not, illiterates make up the population of armed bandits or rebels.[18] This can stem from two reasons: first, the uneducated often have a limited scope of information, knowledge and choice. Thus, it is easy to capitalise on these deficiencies and delude them with the idea that resorting to conflict is a better approach for making demands. Second, the illiterate may subscribe to banditry and rebellion as a way of expressing their grievances to the government (and elites) for not creating an environment for mass literacy. Whichever the case, it is the nation that ultimately suffers.

In a white paper by the World Literacy Foundation,[19] it is reported that about 85% of juvenile delinquents are functionally illiterate. This means that their reading and writing skills are inadequate for daily living and employment activities that require literacy beyond the basic level. Luke Lawson states that inmates who are still illiterate upon their prison release have a higher probability of being reoffenders.[20] Lawson's assertion is confirmed by a case study reported in the World Literacy Foundation's white paper. A pilot scheme called the Dyspel Project was initiated to re-educate fifty out of 150 prisoners in London prisons. Out of the fifty prisoners, only five reoffended. Thirteen returned to college, while four got a job.[21] The results of the study further support Lawson's words, 'Education therefore enlarges one's choices and capabilities to lead better lives ...'

Choices are not only limited to decisions of which the individual is the sole recipient of the rewards; it also involves decisions that affect other people. An example of such a decision is electoral franchise. The illiterate can easily be misguided by the empty promises of politicians because they lack knowledge and information to analyse if a particular candidate has prospects. It is pertinent to state that, in a society, the uneducated are also steeped in poverty. Thus, illiteracy *plus* poverty can be seen as the corrupt politician's tool to bend the uneducated and do his bidding for him. This is why Van Anderson, a retired public school teacher, titled his one-minute opinion piece, *Letters: Uneducated people, a dream for politicians.*[22] In the article, Van

Anderson declares: 'An illiterate populace is a politician's dream. They don't read newspapers or "computer" news, don't watch news or news specials on TV, don't discuss current events and mainly rely on what they hear from friends and family. And most importantly, they don't know the difference between fact and opinion.'

The words of William Reich, I think, sum it up best. 'We have no right to tell our children how to build their future since we have proved unfit to build our own; we cannot hope to build independent human characters if education is in the hands of politicians.'

Anderson further claims that politicians are aware of this knowledge gap; hence they milk the opportunity to fill the ears of the uneducated populace with what they want to hear. Through skilful presentations, they have them believe things that are 'untrue, unrealistic or impossible' – things educated folks won't fall for.[23]

If you think Anderson's sentiment is impractical, then let Isaac Mohr's article on *CBS News*[24] reorient your thoughts. In the 2008 article, which appeared as Americans awaited the election results, Mohr reveals how ignorance and superficiality had a stronghold over America's voting system. He asks a student how the student voted on a few of the propositions. Mohr recounts how the student passionately recited his 'yes' and 'no' votes; but when asked to explain what the propositions meant, the student didn't know. It was even more frustrating to Mohr when the student admitted that he had only voted because a friend had told him to. Mohr proceeded to ask a close family member about their choice of candidate. This family member – like the student – similarly expressed their choice with passion. However, when Mohr tried to speak in favour of the opposing party, the family member could only counter Mohr's points by reciting, word-for-word, a commercial in favour of their candidate. This troubled Mohr because the points their candidate had raised had already been addressed and discredited in at least one of the three *televised* presidential debates. So, either the family member hadn't watched any of the debates, or didn't know anything about their candidate, save for what they saw in TV commercials. Whichever the case, the family member failed to provide any convincing or credible reason for their choice.

Mohr states that elections in America were no longer about the candidate or appealing propositions but about the best commercial and most memorable slogan. 'People, more than ever before, are voting without knowing what they're voting for.' Young citizens, especially student voters, no longer carried out extensive research on economic plans and propositions – and the resultant reckless casting of votes occurred through sheer ignorance.

This is a serious issue because uneducated voters can and do greatly influence the results of any election. *The Economist*, in light of the 2016 US election, blatantly stated that: 'Poorly educated voters hold the keys to the White House.' Proof of this came in the form of statistics from the 2016 election that saw the Republicans ousting the Democrats from the White House.[25]

This is the case of America, the most powerful country in the world. God's own country. A country with a current literacy rate of roughly 86%. The statistics do not lie. **This clearly demonstrates that literacy, by itself, does not produce critical thinkers either**. Now, imagine societies where illiteracy thrives. What becomes of these societies? What kinds of leaders do they elect?

In Thailand, the middle class and elite understood the dangers of illiteracy and clamoured, in 2013, that the uneducated and the poor be denied the right to vote.[26] It was – and still is – an extreme demand, and one which I do not support. However, their concerns were valid: the uneducated and those in the lower rung of the economic ladder are often gullible and prone to selling their votes. (This does not mean that the educated cannot negatively influence an election.)

Middle-class and elite Thais were not only bothered about how the educational status of the populace could affect elections; they were also concerned about their economic or financial status. Interestingly, a correlation does exist between education and economic wellbeing (albeit at a basic level in most cases).

Horace Mann, often called the Father of the Common School, was the Secretary of Education in 1837. During his time in this position, he published annual reports – twelve of them, in fact – and in the *Fifth Annual Report*, he emphasised that education is the most productive venture – in terms of economic development – an individual or community can undertake. Mann stated that: '… education is not only a moral renovator, and a multiplier of intellectual power, but … is also the most prolific parent of material riches. It has a right, therefore, not only to be included in the grand inventory of a nation's resources, but to be placed at the very head of the inventory. It is not only the most honest and honourable, but the surest means of amassing property.'[27]

This means that any society that fails to educate itself effectively cheats itself out of wealth. The World Literacy Foundation notes that illiteracy comes at an economic cost. Their white paper (presented at the 2018 World Literacy Summit in Oxford, United Kingdom), states that the annual costs of illiteracy to the UK and global economies are about £80 billion and £800 billion, respectively, and to detail this breakdown: about £24.8 billion goes to welfare, unemployment and social programs to help the uneducated and the poor, while a further £55.2 billion is lost through lower personal income and productivity.[28]

While the economic cost of illiteracy varies from nation to nation, all share a common problem: limited earning potential. The uneducated earn 30–42% less than their educated compatriots. The uneducated also lack the skills required for further vocational training.

Thus, they most likely do not have the skills to advance their careers and/or earn a higher salary.[29]

According to the World Literacy Foundation, lack of income is just one aspect of the economic cost of illiteracy. There is also the opportunity cost of wealth creation lost due to the inability of the uneducated to understand mortgages or loans or make sound financial decisions. The World Literacy Foundation states that in Egyptian communities, where the illiterate population is about 28% of the entire country, adults don't even know how to use a credit card or ATM. (Just like in Thailand, some elite folks[30] in Egypt called for the removal of voting rights from illiterate communities.) The correlation between illiteracy and poverty makes it imperative for a nation to bridge the education gap. If this is not done, then the poor will continue to keep looking for any way out of poverty, even when that escape route can harm them emotionally or physically. Take Uganda for example; in the last fifteen years, the country has fallen to over eighteen Ponzi and pyramid schemes, where over 200,000 Ugandans have lost a total of over $1 billion dollars to these scams – almost 4% of the country's GDP.[31]

Aside from economic and political development, education and its structures provide the first veritable platform for individuals to interact with one another. If basic education and literacy can have this impact, just imagine the level of progress humanity could make if literate people with academic education were also trained in the areas of self-education, money/business education and spiritual education. Not only would we progress technologically and economically, we would also see vast progress being made in terms of being a more conscious society. Currently, however, we only see basic incremental improvements in terms of global standards of living, where wealth disparity (the difference in the net worth of the poor/middle class and the elite rich) is at an all-time high.

A New Kind of Education and the Tripartite Nature of Humankind

Human beings exist in a trichotomy: the body, the mind, the spirit. Some may argue it is a dichotomy, considering the mind and the spirit to be one entity. Personally, I believe the tripartite view is more accurate. A human being has a connection to two worlds at the same time – the physical world and the metaphysical world. The body is in constant contact with the physical, corporeal world; meanwhile the spirit is in constant contact with the metaphysical, ethereal world.

If the human being were to exist in a dichotomy then this would be a constant source of conflict, because these two worlds are so dissimilar. To avoid this conflict, we have the mind, and the mind is the bridge linking these two worlds. This is why it is also called the sixth sense. It is not tangible like other sense organs, yet it plays a vital role in our activities in the physical world. It is the seat of our emotions, feelings and intellect – qualities that cannot be seen or touched, yet control the most integral aspects of our lives.

It is important to lay this foundation for this chapter, so that we can appreciate how proper education is meant to influence the three aspects of the human condition. The right education is fundamental to human existence, because through it, humans understand the totality of their existence. The right education helps us preserve the body, enlighten the mind and direct the spirit.

PRESERVING THE BODY

In 2016, James Hamblin, a doctor and a lecturer at Yale School of Public Health wrote an article in *The Atlantic* that went viral. In the article titled 'I Quit Showering, and Life Continued',[1] James advocated for less frequent showering, stating that if one lived for one hundred years and bathed for twenty minutes each day, they would have spent over 12,167 hours (or two years) showering. 'How much of that time (and money and water) is wasted?'

For James, it was not just about the waste of valuable resources, it was also about the danger the skin is exposed to through continuous showering. He noted that bathing, especially with soaps and other skin products, disrupts the skin microbiome – an ecosystem of microbes which are healthy for the skin.

When I read James' article and similar ideas expressed by other medical experts, I was both surprised and thrilled. Surprised: because a key aspect of cleanliness and hygiene is being questioned (and rightly so, because not questioning conventional wisdom can and does lead to indoctrination). Thrilled: because science and all aspects of education undergo what I call an 'amusing evolution' in an attempt to teach us 'what is best' for us – which is amusing because medicine once frowned on bathing, believing it was harmful and dangerous. Later, doctors would begin to encourage bathing following the advent of the germ theory.[2] Now, this same science advocates for infrequent showering again because showering is potentially harmful. Think of how this applies to vaccination or smoking (there was also a period of time where doctors recommended smoking, believe it or not). Any narrative that comes from people of authority in any area, whether it be medicine, education or politics, will be quickly imbibed and accepted as gospel by the unthinking masses. An indoctrinated mind has a tendency to latch onto information coming from an authority and form beliefs around it without ever questioning its validity, while the enlightened mind delays in forming a belief and can remain in that zone of 'not knowing' quite comfortably for extended periods.

This vacillating quality of education is what makes it interesting and a pillar for human existence. Proper education will keep testing and retesting theories, while indoctrination will attempt to preserve status quo.

Among all living things, human beings remain the major guardians and custodians of the universe. We would be unable to care for our world if our bodies (that are in constant contact with this world) are not protected from harm. Therefore, it is likely that we wouldn't know the best ways for caring for ourselves without proper education. Through education, we make conscious and constant effort to protect ourselves from diseases and other ills that threaten our existence. To fully understand the impact of education on the preservation of the human body, it is necessary to highlight before-after scenarios and compare our lives to that of our progenitors.

Diseases: how education is the bridge between ancient guesswork and modern accuracy

One may wonder why, if education plus civilisation have made living better, we continue to suffer deadly diseases we find too difficult to treat, diseases that were probably even alien to our ancestors?

To compare medicine now to earlier forms of medicine, I thought it best to travel back to an age where there was no trace of (formal) education. Enter: The Prehistoric Age or The Stone Age.

Before we answer this question, it is necessary to state that the optimum health enjoyed by our ancestors was not due to intentional healthy eating and living; it was just a mixture of luck and the natural forces of preservation. Their knowledge was limited, and their only aim was survival through any means possible. They depended on animal skins to keep warm during the cold. They killed animals for food, not minding if the animals were vectors for diseases. They lived and slept in caves. In today's world, we know that such a lifestyle would not be sustainable or be any guarantee of good health. Our ancestors only survived because it was in the nature of living creatures to adapt to their environment.

The earliest humans were afflicted with illnesses they didn't know how to treat unless they accidentally stumbled upon some therapy serendipitously. Without facts, their medical discoveries happened purely by chance, and if the medicine did something to relieve discomfort, they relied on it. Never was there any need to question side effects; it was enough of a miracle to discover the medicine itself, therefore there was no question of the possibility of harm that could come as a result.

Medical experts believe that trial and error played a role in prehistoric medicine, especially in the area of herbs. People in prehistoric sometimes attempted to heal their wounds and set broken bones, but from fossils analysed by archaeologists, these bones, although healthy, were very badly set.[3] Furthermore, experts have revealed that prehistoric humans did not bother about disease prevention. Prioritising public health (like the prevention of the spread of diseases, good hygiene and clean water) probably didn't occur to our forebears because they were nomadic in nature. Apart from cuts and bone fractures, they came down with bacterial, viral, fungal and other forms of pathogenic diseases. Yvette Brazier notes that these infections might have become serious, life-threatening epidemics even, since they knew very little if at all about infections and their complications.[4] As a matter of fact, researchers state that there is a high probability that an epidemic wiped out the Neanderthals, probably caused by

Helicobacter pylori (a bacterium that causes stomach ulcers) or *Herpes simplex 2* (the virus that causes genital herpes).[5,6]

These and other research indicates that people in historic times lacked sufficient knowledge to protect themselves from disease. They relied on guesses to know which herbs to use for their ailments. One may tentatively argue the possibility that the herbs they considered effective were only 'effective' because the people *believed* it could cure them, and not because the herbs were actually therapeutic in themselves.

But things today are different for us. Education eliminates the burden of guessing and leaves us with a wealth of information, from tested guides and resultant remedies (proven after repeated testing). We can now prevent and cure diseases with greater precision than at any other time in history. Pathogens like *Helicobacter pylori* are now incapable of wiping out an entire species, and we know what/and what not to do to preserve our bodies. This is not to say that at certain times the hostilities between us humans and microbes have not escalated into a full-blown war (think: the bubonic plague, Spanish flu, HIV/AIDS, and the more recent wave of COVID-19) – but microbes have never won, thanks to advancement in science. And thanks to education.

The influence of education on our health is not only restricted to the prevention and treatment of diseases; it spills into our nutrition. Many have said that our grandparents ate better than us, but is this really true?

Nutrition: how education transformed us from unselective omnivores to choosy eaters

If a child is asked to choose between a plate of cake and a plate of salad, there is a 99% chance that the child will go for cake. If the same options are placed before an adult, which do you think the adult would go for? The adult's choice today is most certainly based on their knowledge of the palatability of the foods *and* how the foods affect body function, enabling adults to make far more educated decisions based on what they now *know* about cake and salad.

When we contemplate two or more options, our contemplation births from the advanced knowledge we now have about the options available to us. We know what they are and what they can do to us. We do not choose things superficially, anymore, primarily because we now *know* there is much more to it. The cake may be more aesthetically appealing than the salad, but we are now so informed, so *knowledgeable* that we contemplate, we weigh our options – this is what education gives to us. The same cannot be said for our grandparents.

Our grandparents, we can safely say, were probably closer to the hypothetical child who would have chosen cake instead of salad. In the absence of education and knowledge, their food choices were most likely based on availability, palatability and cost. They didn't have enough information back then to consider the health impact of foods consumed. In his article for *ABC News*, Tegan Taylor queried if our grandparents were really healthier than us. Extracting ideas from Jan O'Connell's book, *A Timeline of Australian Food: From Mutton to Masterchef*, Taylor explores how people in the 1920s and 1930s probably had vegetable gardens and raised their own meat but also ate a fair amount of unhealthy food – from heaps of sugar, to meat, to tea with sugar, to bread and butter. We know they ingested a lot of saturated fat. They ate a lot of meat. Before meat rationing took place during the Depression and World War II, low-income families commonly had sausages for breakfast, meat sandwiches for lunch and meat for dinner. By the 1950s, a lot of people were dying from heart diseases.[7]

Despite being better educated than our grandparents, we still have a high evidence of heart disease and other diseases, though today the cause is more likely linked to poor nutritional choices than to lack of knowledge. Our forebears died of heart diseases because of ignorance, while we die of heart diseases because of carelessness. Education and information serve as our guides for healthy living; *choosing* to follow these guides is another matter entirely. As Dr Peter Hobbins, a medical historian and head of knowledge at the Australian National Maritime Museum and an honorary affiliate in the Department of History at the University of Sydney, notes: 'These days we have a lot more information about eating well, even if we don't eat well.'[8]

Education has taught us the importance of preserving our bodies through food and medicines. Our forebears never enjoyed this privilege – little wonder then that their life expectancy was so much lower than ours. A timeline of the average life expectancy of humans reveals that life expectancy increased with the advent and development of education. People who lived in the 1200s had a life expectancy of just thirty-five years due to poor hygiene and scarce health care, resulting in high rates of infant mortality. By the 1800s, life expectancy had increased to forty years. Currently, many industrialised nations have a life expectancy of seventy-five years.[9] Experts now assert that in a world where disease stems from lifestyle choices (e.g. diabetes) the major threats to our lifespan will ultimately be determined through education, not wealth; education will increase longevity.[10] And it will be education, not wealth, that will teach our *minds* to ignore the delicious cravings and stick to healthy options, no matter how unpalatable.

ENLIGHTENING THE MIND

Hiero, an ancient Greek tyrant, suspected fraud in the manufacturing of his golden crown. He suspected that the goldsmith left out a measure of gold and replaced it instead with silver. Yet Hiero couldn't punish the goldsmith based on mere suspicion; he needed proof. So, he contracted a *polymath*, a math whiz, to detect the fraud. One day, as the polymath went for his evening bath, it occurred to him that the more his body sank into the water, the more water became displaced. The displaced water, he soon realised, gave an exact measure of his volume, and this realisation brought him to answer the tyrant's problem: if the crown were a mixture of gold and silver, then it would be heavier than a crown made of pure gold; thus, if the crown were truly a mix of both metals it would displace more water than if it was pure gold. The polymath jumped out of the bathtub and ran home naked, screaming, 'Eureka! Eureka!'

Although many have questioned the authenticity of this story, it is a story often told about the famous mathematician, Archimedes, who stated the principle of flotation, or the Archimedes' principle. In this story, we see the influence of education on the human mind. Recall that I stated earlier that our mind can produce its own thoughts. Crude thoughts. But not only does education refine human thought, it also broadens our thought processes.

Education exposes us to an array of information, and our minds leverage this information to come up with solutions to life's problems. Would an uneducated mind be able to solve Hiero's mystery? Maybe. Maybe not. The chance of this happening is slim, because inspirations do not just spring up; they come from a place of stored knowledge. We consume information through our five senses, but then our mind incubates the information, where it sits, until one day it comes up as inspiration.

This is why every professional is advised to read and study professionals who came before them in their designated field. The logic behind this is simply that the more information you expose the mind to, the more raw material it has to draw upon for inspiration. Education enhances our insights and thoughts to the point where we birth groundbreaking inventions with ever greater speed and accuracy; it also increases our ability to set up more humane social systems.

Education as a catalyst for modern technology

I once stumbled on an article online that listed five people who changed the world without formal education. The list included greats like Thomas Edison, the Wright Brothers, Bill Gates, Larry Ellison and Michael Dell. Apart from Edison (who was homeschooled and self-taught), all the others had a stint with education. The Wright Brothers finished high school, Bill Gates dropped out of Harvard University, Larry Ellison attended the University of Chicago and University of Illinois at Urbana-Champaign, and Michael Dell attended the University of Texas at Austin.

The lack of educational backgrounds of these men supports the inherent idea being developed in the article; yet it also raises the question of whether these men would have become such technological giants had they had no formal education. Intuition may not require education for it to form, but it surely needs education for it to flourish. Edison had to read books (just like Kakwamba earlier) to understand how technology worked. Yet would we say that Edison wasn't educated? Would his mind have been able to harness the concept of making of the light bulb if he hadn't read books? Can we say that, without education, the human mind would have been less able to conceive and birth the Boeings and Teslas and smartphones of today? Would humans have been able to conceptualise space travel? Or invent the internet? Would we have been able to create the rise of artificial intelligence? I doubt it.

Looking at the evolution of technology in terms of timelines shows that it took two thousand years for humans to invent the first sailing ships, just after another major invention, the development of irrigation systems two thousand years earlier. It took almost another three thousand years for the production of iron to become widespread.[11] Interestingly enough, these inventions emerged at the burgeoning first stages of education. Would it have been the same today? Would it take the modern world thousands of years to invent irrigation systems or sailing ships or iron? I think we do not need to search too far for the answer, and here is why: education shifted from Calvinism (a strict curriculum on moral values) and became standardised in the 1800s (thanks to Horace Mann).[12] The rate of innovation increased rapidly around the same period. It took three years to move from railways to steamboats, thirty-two years to shift from the telegraph to the telephone, and nine years to move from the internal combustion engine to automobiles.[13] Thus, one may safely posit that there is a direct correlation between education and the dramatic and rapid rise of technology. Education has also given rise to some of the wittier inventions of the twenty-first century – from augmented reality to artificial intelligence, blockchain and many more. With the right education we have the potential to stretch our minds – not only in science and technology – but also in restructuring social systems. The possibilities are endless. Education continues to affirm the truth of the motivational platitude: *If you can think it, you can achieve it.*

Education as a tool for restructuring societal norms and practices

Imagine that the first time you gained an understanding of the world, you were working with your mother on a small plantation. Now, this plantation did not belong to your mother; neither did it belong to any other member of your family. This plantation was the property of another person not related to you by blood. Now imagine that one day, you realised that there was no difference between you and the plantation you worked on, because both you and the plantation were referred to by the same noun: property. Yes, you were a slave.

As a slave, you tried to learn how to read from your master's son, while your mother taught you how to read and write – especially how to read the Bible. She passed on to you her passionate love for your creator and hatred for slavery. As you began to read, your mind became free, and soon after that it became restless: your mind struggled, because it wanted to release your body from captivity. And not just your body – but the minds and bodies of all the other slaves like you.

Then, just as you were toying with this idea, you were sold again. This time, to a craftsman. One day in August, you thought there was an eclipse of the sun, and you took it as a sign to break free. That night, with seven other slaves you trusted, you murdered your new master and his family in their sleep. Across two days and two nights, you and your fellow slaves killed about sixty slave masters. The slave masters fought with the state militia, a force of three thousand men. A lot of slaves were killed. You escaped, eluding your pursuers for six weeks. However, you were finally captured, tried and hanged. You died, but your rebellion sparked a desire like no other in the hearts of other slaves. Your rebellion taught them that they could choose and fight for their freedom, especially if they became learned.

The story you just read is not a short work of fiction; it's the true-life story of Nat Turner, a slave who, according to *Encyclopaedia Britannica*, 'led the only effective, sustained slave rebellion in US history'.[14] What makes Turner's story interesting and memorable was not only the rebellion but what inspired the rebellion. Because of Turner's rebellion in August 1831, legislation became intensified to limit the access of black people to education. Turner's ability to inspire a revolt was clearly rooted in his ability to read. He read the Bible and found stories that supported fights against justice, and he educated himself in ways his forebears had not been able to. Before this, the enslavers had twisted and controlled Biblical narratives to support their acts of slavery. However, educated black Americans like Turner could read and comprehend the Bible for themselves – and knew what was right and true.[15]

Turner's insurrection wasn't the first time the literacy of black slaves threatened the white enslavers. Between 1829 and 1830, David Walker, a black writer and abolitionist, had distributed a pamphlet titled *Appeal*, which called for uprisings to end slavery.[16] White abolitionists – those who didn't support this culture of slavery – also posed a problem to the enslavers. One such person was William Lloyd Garrison, who began publishing his abolitionist newspaper, *The Liberator*. This paper, although written by a white abolitionist, was seen as a 'black newspaper' because majority of its readers were African Americans.[17]

Enslavers were bothered about the literacy of African Americans, and here's why: the justification for slavery of black people was because they were 'less than human, permanently illiterate and dumb'. Thus, the literacy of the black American and his ability to read threatened these justifications for slavery, for its ultimately flawed logic.[18] The literacy of African Americans proved that they were educated, smart, and most of all, *human*.

Oppressors never want to relinquish control; as such, the states began to enact and tighten laws against literacy. In April 1831, the state of Virginia declared illegal any meeting to teach free African Americans to read or write. New laws also proscribed teaching slaves. In 1833, Alabama declared that 'any person or persons who shall attempt to teach any free person of colour or slave, to spell, read or write, shall upon conviction thereof of this indictment be fined in a sum not less than $250'.[19] (A sum equivalent to about $8,000 in today's dollars.)

But these laws did not deter the slaves. They continued to learn to read, and the kind of work many enslavers gave to their slaves only reinforced the need for black literacy. Slaves were entrusted with sophisticated jobs, including operations management.[20] This meant that the enslavers *needed* their slaves to be literate, thus, outlawing black literacy became impractical in the end.

Literacy, through the written word, became the torch that illuminated the path to black emancipation. Sarah Roth, a professor of history, describes an interesting truth: 'Literacy promotes thought and raises consciousness. It helps you to get outside of your own cultural constraints and think about things from a totally different angle.'[21] In other words, education enlightens the mind. As more written texts against slavery surfaced, enslavers became weakened. And in 1862 came the Emancipation Proclamation, which declared 'that all persons held as slaves [within the rebellious states] are, and henceforward shall be free'.

Slavery in America was not the only time in history oppressors have tried to prevent the oppressed from gaining access to books. More than six decades after the rebellion of Nat Turner, the Nazi book burning of 1933 took place in Germany. This event had been predicted more than a hundred years earlier by the German poet, essayist and journalist Christian Johann Henrich Heine, who in his 1821 play *Almansor* wrote: *'Dort, wo man Bücher verbrennt, verbrennt man am Ende auch Menschen,'* which, translated means, 'The place where books are burnt, people will be burned at the end.'

In May 1933, Nazi students publicly burnt books they considered 'un-German'. More than twenty-five thousand books from Jewish, liberal and leftist authors like Bertolt Brecht, August Babel, Karl Marx, Arthur Schnitzler, Ernest Hemingway, Thomas Mann, Erich Maria Remarque, Helen Keller and others were affected. The affected books criticised fascism and championed pacifism and causes for social justice like women's voting rights and improved conditions for industrial workers and the disabled.[22]

The Nazis understood the power of and in books. They understood that they could only bind the hands and feet of their victims, but not their minds – especially minds liberated by books. Thus, they resorted to censoring reading as a way to wield and sustain control over their people.

The United States Holocaust Memorial Museum produced a short film reflecting on the book burning. The film featured the commentators Azar Nafisi, the author of *Reading Lolita in Tehran*; Ruth Franklin, a literary critic and contributing editor in *The New Republic*; and Robert Behr, a Holocaust survivor. Nafisi opined that books represent the best and worst of humanity. Thus, the primal desire of a totalitarian regime is not just to confiscate and mutilate reality – but to confiscate history and culture. Ruth Franklin similarly believes totalitarian regimes are afraid of literature because it forges human connections and promotes the free flow of ideas. Corroborating Franklin, Azar Nafisi adds that this fear is triggered by the unpredictability of knowledge, the risk of it – and that tyrants fear this unpredictability because it deprives them of control. They understand that with books, citizens can connect to 'the unknown parts of themselves, of their past [and the world]'. Oppressors do not want this. They want their citizens to, as Franklin states, 'resign themselves to thinking that this is all there is [and] that there aren't any other options'.[23]

It is noteworthy to see how Nafisi and Franklin's ideas shed even more light on the story of Nat Turner and his journey to rebellion. White enslavers prevented African Americans from learning how to read and write in order to present a false reality to them. The enslavers knew that through reading, the average African American would know the truth about his obscured and mutilated reality. Then, with Nat Turner, everything changed. Through reading, he forged connections with fellow slaves and shared his ideas of freedom with them. Through reading, Turner and his fellow slaves came to understand that there was a reality different from the one they had always known, and it opened their minds, for they started to be realise they had options. They had the *power* to choose and to change their lives. And just like that, the winds changed. Nafisi states that knowledge is unpredictable.

Who knew that Nat Turner would damn every consequence and lead a rebellion as a direct result of coming into contact with the knowledge of his reality?

Holistic education helps us come into contact with our reality, existence and humanity. It reveals the essence of our lives and how we should preserve this essence by forging *human* connections. Not racial connections, not tribal connections, not religious connections, not sexual connections, but human connections. Good education erases the dividing *lines* that separate us and forces us to question our humanity.

In 2020, in the heat of the COVID-19 pandemic, African Americans came out in numbers to protest the unjust murder of George Floyd, a forty-six-year-old African American who was killed by a white cop. The protest was not just against police brutality, but against racism and white supremacy. The protests spread rapidly to different parts of the country as Americans defied the stay-at-home orders and within days of Floyd's death, the white officer, Derek Chauvin, was charged with second-degree murder. But let's now rewind the clock seventy-six years earlier to when another George was killed.

George Stinney, a fourteen-year-old African-American boy from South Carolina was arrested for the murder of two white girls back in 1944. Stinney did not receive a fair trial. During his interrogation, he was kept away from his parents and any legal counsel. He was not allowed to prove his innocence. Within three short months, George had been investigated by white officers, prosecuted by white counsels and convicted in just ten minutes by an all-white jury, based solely on the testimony of two white cops who declared that George had admitted to the killings. In 2014, some seventy years later, the family of George insisted again on his innocence and another trial was conducted. After considering the accounts from Stinney's surviving family and questioning autopsy findings along with Stinney's original confession, the judge overturned the conviction.[24]

Let's examine the two stories of George Floyd and George Stinney. It took just four days to arrest and charge the white officer because of the protests. But in 1944, even though African Americans protested the unfair arrest of George Stinney, the state, governed and controlled by the whites, proceeded to execute an innocent fourteen-year-old kid. So, what changed in seventy years? Why did one government refuse to bend to the will of the people, while another government ruled in his favour after just four days? The fact is, the first government knew that only a handful of African Americans at the time were enlightened enough to understand the goings on; therefore only a handful of African Americans understood their rights and that they shouldn't cower to the bullying of another human just because of skin colour. But seventy years later, with the application of education and knowledge, the second government knew they couldn't take African Americans for a ride. Unlike the African Americans seven decades earlier, this new wave of African Americans knew their rights, and they knew and understood the law. They didn't surrender to the law being manipulated against them. Did you know that initially the courts only charged Derek Chauvin with third-degree murder? This was a deliberate attempt to twist the law so that Chauvin would either be exonerated or serve a lighter sentence. It was only because of further agitations that Chauvin's case was upgraded to the charge of second-degree murder. (At the time of writing this, the Minnesota Court of Appeals has reinstated the third-degree charge, resulting in three charges against Chauvin: second-degree murder, third-degree murder and second-degree manslaughter.[25])

George Floyd's case ended in justice because our current world now consists of many educated, enlightened people; people who have freed themselves from fear, people who have recognised their own voice. Unfortunately, this was not the case for George Stinney, because justice for him came seventy years too late, because he lived in a time when the black race was made to believe they were less human.

The contrasting tales of Floyd and Stinney validate Rebecca Winthrop's idea on how education can help fight systemic racism.[26] Winthrop, a senior fellow and co-director of the Center for Universal Education at the Brookings Institution, notes that education 'plays a powerful role in shaping worldviews, connecting members of a community who might have never met before, and imagining the world we want'. Citing what is known in education circles as the 'De Lors Report', she states that the four purposes of education are: learning to know, learning to do, learning to be and learning to live together.

Although the lines of racism have not been completely erased, we see these purposes manifest every day and provide a semblance of unity to the world.

DIRECTING THE SPIRIT

It's said that Nat Turner came into contact with his spirituality when he learned to read and write. Although his religiousness developed into fanaticism, it was the tool he used to influence and inspire other slaves to action. They even called him 'the Prophet'.[27]

An interesting relationship exists between spirituality/religion and education. Every religion used some form of education to propagate its tenets. Even the founders of the different religions we have today first taught their followers orally. But oral teachings are often problematic because they are short lived and the message can be distorted during transmission. Written texts came onboard to solve this problem. In fact, the original meanings of some holy books are rooted in educational terms like 'read' or 'book'. For instance, the 'Bible' is derived from the Latin word, *Biblia,* meaning 'book' or 'books'. *Biblia* is traced to the Greek phrase, *Ta Biblia*, which means 'the books'.[28] The 'Quran' is derived from the Arabic word, 'Qara', meaning 'to read or recite',[29] and the word 'Sutra' in Buddhism is a Sanskrit word meaning 'thread' or 'string' and refers to a collection of aphorisms in the form of a *text* or *manual*. Similarly, in Hinduism, a Veda refers to any of the four collections of hymns and prayers used as a sacred text. 'Veda' is a Sanskrit term meaning 'knowledge, insight, sacred writings'.[30]

The original meanings of the words – these sacred texts – show the role of education in the spiritual realm. Adherents of these religions cannot understand and develop a connection with their deity if they cannot read and write. In recent times, education has gone past being a tool for propagating doctrines to being one that waters our spiritual belief – or unbelief.

For those who have *chosen* to believe in a supernatural force, education enables them to achieve insights into this force. And for those who have taken the path of unbelief, they credit their acclaimed enlightenment to education. In the 1971 Canadian census, 4% of respondents reported that they didn't belong to any religion. By 2001, that number had increased to 16%[31] and by 2011, it was 23.9%.[32] A similar scenario played out in the United States: the proportion of citizens not affiliated to any religion was 5% in 1972, 14% in 2000,[33] 17% in 2009 and 26% in 2019.[34] This increase in the proportion of religiously unaffiliated citizens coincided with the educational gains in the population.[35]

Whether you share a belief or unbelief, education connects us all to our spirituality – or it disconnects us from it. Education essentially directs and aligns our spirit and relationship with the world we cannot see or touch. Parker Palmer, the author of *The Courage to Teach*, defines our spirituality as the different ways we answer the heart's yearning to be connected with the largeness of life. And what better way to connect with the largeness of life, if not through education. Education expands the mind. It provides insights for us to understand and connect with the natural world and then transcend into the supernatural.

We discover our life's purpose through education, and through education we understand that our lives go beyond merely existing in the natural world. By connecting with the supernatural force, we live not just for ourselves, but for others.

This book is meant to educate and inform the world about indoctrination and its dangers. I expect at least a mini educational revolution to take place in my lifetime, as people open their minds and start asking more questions. However, because these indoctrinations have been ingrained firmly into global systems over the last four decades (and another ninety years since the advent of organised Marxism in the West), the change I hope for will not come about without staunch resistance against those who are indoctrinated to preserve the status quo.

NOTES

CHAPTER ONE
Is Education Enough?

1. 'Difference Between Education and Learning'. https://pediaa. com/difference-between-education-and-learning/ 9 November 2015. Accessed 15 March 2021.

2. Mads Holmen. 'Education vs. Learning – What Exactly is the Difference?' EdTechReview, 6 August 2014. https://edtechreview. in/trends-insights/insights/1417-education-vs-learning-what-exactly-is-the-difference/ Accessed 15 March 2021.

3. Samrat Kundal. 'In why did Mark Zuckerberg drop out?' Online posting. 18 January 2017. https://www.quora.com/Why-did-Mark-Zuckerburg-drop-out?no_redirect=1

4. Ibid.

5. Alan Singer and Michael Pezone. 'Education for Social Change: From Theory to Practice'. https://louisville.edu/journal/ workplace/issue5p2/singerpezone.html Accessed 15 March 2021.

6. Kathleen Elkins. 'Billionaire Bill Gates shares his "one big regret"'. CNBC, 17 May 2017.

CHAPTER TWO
Learned or Just Literate?

1. 'What is literacy? An investigation into definitions of English as a subject and the relationship between English, literacy and "being literate"'." A research report commissioned by Cambridge assessment. January 2013.

2. Erin Blakemore. 'What is colonialism?' National Geographic, 19 February 2019.

3. Thomas, R Murray; Chambliss, JJ; Riché, Pierre; Arnove, Robert Cert F; Graham, Hugh F; Swink, Roland Lee; Anweiler, Oskar; Meyer, Adolphe Erich; Marrou, Henri-Irénée; Naka, Arata; Mukerji, SN; Lawson, Robert Frederic; Huq, Muhammad Shamsul; Shimahara, Nobuo; Ipfling, Heinz-Jürgen; Browning, Robert; Bowen, James; Chen, Theodore Hsi-en; Vázquez, Josefina Zoraida; Nakosteen, Mehdi K; Szyliowicz, Joseph S; Gelpi, Ettore; Scanlon, David G; Lauwerys, Joseph Albert; and Moumouni, Abdou. 'Education'. Encyclopedia Britannica, 9 November 2020. https://www.britannica.com/topic/education Accessed 27 March 2021.

4. Satish C Aikant. 'From Colonialism to Indigenism: The Loss and Recovery of Language and Literature'. 2000. 31. 337 – 345.

5. 'What is Numerical Literacy?' https://saraparker.weebly.com/definition.html#:~:text=Numerical%20literacy%2C%20also%20known%20as,complex%2C%20in%20real%20world%20situations Accessed 30 March 2021.

6. Diana Coben. Numeracy, mathematics and adult learning. In I. Gal (Ed.), Adult numeracy development: Theory, research, practice. 2000. Cresskill, NJ: Hampton Press. pp. 33-50.

7. MathWorks Math Modeling Challenge. https://m3challenge.siam.org/

8. Kevin Anderton. 'We Now Know How To Inspire Kids To

Study Math [Infographic]'. Forbes, 1 May 2020.

9. Ibid.

10. David Tuten. 'The Importance of Numerical Literacy'. York Country Day School, 8 May 2017. https://ycdslife.com/2017/05/08/the-importance-of-numerical-literacy/ Accessed 1 April 2021.

11. Karen Patten. 'Stories About Math That Will Inspire Kids to Love Numbers (Proven By Science)'. Intentional Family Life, https://intentionalfamilylife.com/stories-about-math/ Accessed 2 April 2021.

12. Ibid.

13. Gies, Frances Carney. 'Fibonacci'. Encyclopedia Britannica, 22 January 2021, https://www.britannica.com/biography/Fibonacci Accessed 2 April 2021.

14. Tia Ghose. 'What is the Fibonacci Sequence?' Live Science, 24 October 2018, https://www.livescience.com/37470-fibonacci-sequence.html Accessed 2 April 2021.

15. Ut supra, 13.

16. Parmanand Singh. 'The So-called Fibonacci Numbers in Ancient and Medieval India'. Historica Mathematica, 1985. Volume 12. 229-244.

17. The Better India. How Nasim Ali Used the Computer to Transform the Lives in his Village [Video File], 16 December 2016. Retrieved from https://web.facebook.com/watch/?v=10154847267834594 Accessed 3 April 2021.

18. David Bawden. 'Origins and Concepts of Digital Literacy'. In Lankshear Colin and Michele Knobel (Eds.), Digital Literacies: Concepts, Policies and Practices. 2008.

19. Clifford Delle. 'What Is Digital Literacy and Why Does It Matter'. World Literacy Foundation, https://worldliteracyfoundation.org/digital-literacy-importance-for-studentswhy-does-it-matter/

Accessed 3 April 2021.

20. Ibid.

21. Estela M Kennen, Linda Martin and Terry C Davis. 'Stories of Women, Words, and Well-Being: The Effect of Literacy on Women's Health'. Women's Studies Quarterly 32, no. 1/2 (2004): 90-99. http://www.jstor.org/stable/40004393 Accessed 4 April 2021.

22. Avanthika Panchapakesan. 'The Importance of Health Literacy'. World Literacy Foundation, https://worldliteracyfoundation.org/importance-of-health-literacy/ Accessed 4 April 2021.

23. 'The Definition of Physical Literacy'. The International Physical Literacy Association, May 2014.

24. Claude Steiner. Emotional Literacy; Intelligence with a Heart. Personhood Press. 2003.

25. 'Cryptoqueen: How this woman scammed the world, then vanished'. BBC, 24 November 2019.

26. Jason Fernando. 'Financial Literacy'. Investopedia, 1 April 2021.

27. Some Ugandans blamed President Yoweri Museveni for the scams. Actually, Museveni meant well for all Ugandans. He had learned of cryptocurrency and wanted his people to be part of the movement. However, he failed to set up institutions that could distinguish fake from genuine cryptocurrency investments, and this could likely be because he couldn't tell the difference himself. This ignorance made government regulatory institutions porous and careless as many of these scams were registered by the government as legitimate businesses. Source: Godfrey Olukya. 'The Billion-Dollar Cryptocurrency Scams You've Never Heard About'. OZY, 24 February 2020. https://www.ozy.com/around-the-world/the-billion-dollar-crypto-currency-scams-youve-never-heard-about/266860/ Accessed 5 April 2021.

28. Laurel Bloomfield. 'The Illiterate Billionaire'. LinkedIn, 3 August 2019. https://www.linkedin.com/pulse/illiterate-billionaire-laurel-bloomfield/ Accessed 6 April 2021.

29. Peter Daisyme. '9 Billionaires Who Didn't Graduate High School'. Entrepreneur, 9 December 2015.

30. 'Mark Duggan death: Timeline of events' BBC, 27 October 2015.

31. 'The Killing of Mark Duggan'. Investigation Report and Methodology, Forensic Architecture, Centre for Research Architecture, Department of Visual Cultures, Goldsmiths University of London, United Kingdom. January 2020.

32. Roy Greenslade. 'What the media did wrong in the riots – and how to put it right'. The Guardian, 31 July 2012.

33. According to the Information Competence Project at California Polytechnic State University, other qualities possessed by the media literate person include sensitivity towards verbal and visual arguments, and the ability to recognise the use of metaphors and symbols in entertainment, advertising and political commentary. Source: Teresa S Welsh, Melissa S Wright. 'Media literacy and visual literacy'. In Teresa S Welsh, Melissa S Wright (Eds.), Information Literacy in the Digital Age. Chandos Information Professional Series, Chandos Publishing. 2010. pp 107 – 121.

34. Gisselli Rodriguez. 'The Power of Media Literacy'. National Eating Disorders Association, https://www.nationaleatingdisorders.org/blog/power-media-literacy Accessed 7 April 2021.

35. Peter Dizikes. 'Study: On Twitter, false news travels faster than true stories'. MIT News, 8 March 2018. https://news.mit.edu/2018/study-twitter-false-news-travels-faster-true-stories-0308 Accessed 7 April 2021.

36. 'What is cultural literacy?'. Western Sydney University, https://www.westernsydney.edu.au/studysmart/home/cultural_literacy/

what_is_cultural_literacy Accessed 7 April 2021.

37. ED Hirsch Jr 'Cultural Literacy'. The American Scholar, Vol. 52, No.2 (Spring 1983). pp 159 – 169.

38. Ut supra, 36.

CHAPTER THREE

How Conventional Education Falls Short

1. 'The Education Crisis: Being in School Is Not the Same as Learning'. The World Bank, 22 January 2019.

2. Sally Weale. 'St Olave's teacher; "Weak students are treated as collateral damage"'. The Guardian, 29 August 2017.

3. Sally Weale. 'Grammar school "unlawfully threw out" students failed to get top trades'. The Guardian, 29 August 2017.

4. Ibid.

5. Ut supra, 2.

6. Ibid.

7. Other schools adopted this practice to maintain top positions in the league table. In the words of Dave Thomson, the chief statistician at Education Datalab, these schools were 'more concerned with league table standings than the interests of their students. [They offer] a perverse incentive to encourage students to leave, in the race to improve indicators of attainment'. Source: Ut supra, 2.

8. Ibid.

9. According to Steven Gerrard, he could pick up his phone and call past managers of the club, but not Benitez. There was no bond between them. Gerrard said that at press conferences, Benitez might call other players by their first name, but always referred to him as 'Gerrard'. Gerrard referred to their working relationship as 'ultra-professional'. He also pointed out that it was Benitez's frostiness that drove him to become a better player; he hungered

to earn a compliment from the manager – to let him know he really needed him as a player. Source: Tom Webber. 'Gerrard: I don't think Rafael Benitez liked me'. Goal, https://www.goal.com/en-us/news/85/england/2015/09/13/15313782/gerrard-i-dont-think-rafael-benitez-liked-me Accessed 9 April 2021.

10. Before becoming Liverpool's manager, Rafael Benitez coached Valencia FC. It was reported that he was hated and despised by the players. It may seem as though this discordance with his players became a characteristic feature of Benitez because some Liverpool players left the club on his account. Javier Mascherano left because he was maltreated by Benitez, while Fernando Torres took his exit after being frustrated by many failed promises during and after Benitez's time as manager. Source: David Hendrick. 'Liverpool FC: The 5 Worst Transfers of the Rafa Benitez Era'. Bleacher Report, 1 August 2011. https://bleacherreport.com/articles/786388-liverpool-fc-the-5-worst-transfers-of-the-rafa-benitez-era Accessed 9 April 2021.

11. It's said that Rodgers often used players out of position. It was for this reason players like Raheem Sterling, Emre Can, Jordan Ibe, Lazar Markovic and Mario Balotelli left the club. Source: Jack Lusby. 'Breakdown in Brendan Rodgers relationship motivating Raheem Sterling move'. This Is Anfield, 8 July 2015. https://www.thisisanfield.com/2015/07/breakdown-in-brendan-rodgers-relationship-motivating-raheem-sterling-move/ Accessed 9 April 2021.

12. Alex Oxlade-Chamberlain revealed that he left Arsenal for Liverpool because of Klopp's relationship with the players. His words were: 'The thing that stood out for me was his relationship with the players, how close he seems to bond with the players on and off the field. That's massive and it's definitely a big plus when you're looking to progress, having that relationship

with the manager, that definitely helps.' Source: 'Animated Klopp's relationship with players key to Oxlade-Chamberlain's Liverpool move'. FourFourTwo, 6 September 2017. https://www.fourfourtwo.com/news/animated-klopps-relationship-players-key-oxlade-chamberlains-liverpool-move Accessed 9 April 2021.

13. Andy Hunter. 'Trust, patience and hard work: how Jürgen Klopp transformed Liverpool'. The Guardian, 26 June 2020.

14. 'Jurgen Klopp explains how he cultivates his incredible relationship with players'. This Is Anfield, 19 March 2020. https://www.thisisanfield.com/2020/03/jurgen-klopp-explains-how-he-cultivates-his-incredible-relationship-with-players/ Accessed 10 April 2021.

15. 'The Education Crisis: Being in School Is Not the Same as Learning'. The World Bank, 22 January 2019.

16. Alison Gopnik. 'In Defense of Play'. The Atlantic, 12 August 2016.

17. Ibid.

18. Ibid.

19. Hershey H Friedman, Linda W Friedman and Taiwo Amoo (2002). 'Using Humor in the Introductory Statistics Course'. Journal of Statistics Education, 10:3.

20. David L Neumann, Michelle Hood and Michelle M Neumann (2009). 'Statistics? You Must be Joking: The Application and Evaluation of Humor when Teaching Statistics'. Journal of Statistics Education, 17:2.

21. Rolighetsteorin. Piano stairs - TheFunTheory.com - Rolighetsteorin.se [Video]. YouTube, 7 October 2009. https://www.youtube.com/watch?v=2lXh2n0aPyw

22. Alice Truong. 'The Company With The Best Culture? Twitter, According to Glassdoor'. Fast Company, 22 August 2014.

23. Sujan Patel. '10 Examples of Companies With Fantastic

Cultures'. Entrepreneur, 6 August 2015.

24. Andy Greenberg. 'The Confessions of Marcus Hutchins, the Hacker Who Saved the Internet'. Wired, 5 December 2020.

25. At fourteen, Hutchins had created a simple password stealer that could retrieve passwords from web accounts stored on Internet Explorer. Although the passwords were encrypted, Hutchins figured out where the browser hid the decryption key. At fifteen, he ran a botnet of over eight thousand computers. He later sold web hosting services that allowed illegal sites. Users of his service could host phishing sites for impersonating login pages to steal passwords. By the time he clocked sixteen, Hutchins had created a rootkit for a client, and when he was seventeen, the client got him to build a new version of the kit. This new version had a keylogger – that recorded victims' keystrokes and their entire screen; and a web inject – a feature designed for bank fraud. Source: Ibid.

26. 'Rote'. Merriam-Webster.com Dictionary, Merriam-Webster, https://www.merriam-webster.com/dictionary/rote Accessed 19 April 2021.

27. Laura McGuinn. 'Should My Child Repeat a Grade?' healthychildren.org, 23 September 2019. https://www.healthychildren.org/English/ages-stages/gradeschool/school/Pages/Repeating-a-Grade.aspx Accessed 20 April 2021.

28. Ibid.

29. 'Are multi-age classes the future of learning?' International Baccalaureate, 5 March 2018. https://blogs.ibo.org/blog/2018/03/05/are-multi-age-classes-the-future-of-learning/ Accessed 21 April 2021.

30. Soundview School in Lynwood, Washington, USA employed multi-age grouping for their Primary Years Program where they cluster K-2 (five-to-eight-year-olds) and grades 3–5 (eight-to-eleven-year-olds). They also employ this learning method in their

Middle Years Programme (MYP) to teach grades 6–8 (eleven-to-fourteen-year-olds) design, physical health education and music. Xi'an Hi tech International School used multi-age grouping in its MYP and Diploma Programme (DP) to teach music to MYP students aged twelve to sixteen. Source: Ibid.

31. Pictures of the suicide notes were downloaded from Orange County Register. They ran a story on how Patrick Turner's suicide was a call for change. Source: David Whiting. 'This 16-year-old's suicide letters are a cry for help and a national call for change'. The Orange County Register, 19 March 2018.

32. Ibid.

33. Jasmine Paul and Felicia Jefferson. 'A Comparative Analysis of Student Performance in an Online vs. Face-to-Face Environmental Science Course From 2009 to 2016'. Front. Comput. Sci., 12 November 2019.

34. Samuel Ayele Bekalo, Michael Brophy and Geoff Welford. 'Post-Conflict Education Development in Somaliland'. Somaliland CyberSpace, 2015.

CHAPTER FOUR
The History of Education

1. Former 2 1. Thomas, R Murray; Chambliss, JJ; Riché, Pierre; Arnove, RoberCert F; Graham, Hugh F; Swink, Roland Lee; Anweiler, Oskar; Meyer, Adolphe Erich; Marrou, Henri-Irénée; Naka, Arata; Mukerji, SN; Lawson, Robert Frederic; Huq, Muhammad Shamsul; Shimahara, Nobuo; Ipfling, Heinz-Jürgen; Browning, Robert; Bowen, James; Chen, Theodore Hsi-en; Vázquez, Josefina Zoraida; Nakosteen, Mehdi K; Szyliowicz, Joseph S; Gelpi, Ettore; Scanlon, David G; Lauwerys, Joseph Albert; and Moumouni, Abdou. 'Education'. Encyclopedia Britannica, 9 November 2020. https://www.britannica.com/

topic/education Accessed 18 February 2021.

2. Former 4 2. 'Education in pre-historic times: Informal yet lasting'. Lepole. https://lepole.education/en/pedagogical-culture/22-history-of-education.html?start=1 Accessed 18 February 2021.

3. Ibid.

4. Ut supra, 1.

5. 'Key Components of Civilization'. National Geographic, 6 February 2018.

6. Ancient History Encyclopedia. 'Culture and Society in Ancient Mesopotamia'. Newsela, 25 July 2017.

7. Judith Cochran. Education in Egypt (RLE Egypt). Routledge, 2013.

8. Ut supra, 1.

9. Ibid.

10. Former 12 10. Shihkuan Hsu. Education as Cultivation in Chinese Culture. Shihkuan Hsu and Yuh-Yin Wu (Eds.) Education in the Asia-Pacific Region: Issues, Concerns and Prospects, 26. 2015. p 10.

11. Ut supra, 1.

12. Ut supra, 10.

13. Ut supra, 1.

14. AS Altekar. Education in Ancient India. Isha Books, 2009. pp 1, 8.

15. Ut supra, 1.

16. Ibid.

17. Harmut Scharfe. Education in Ancient India. Volume 16 of Handbook of Oriental Studies. Section 2 South Asia, 18/2 Series. Brill, 2002. p 6.

18. Ibid.

19. Ut supra, 1.

20. Ibid.

21. James L Crenshaw. Education in Ancient Israel: Across the Deadening Silence. Yale University Press, 1998.

22. Ut supra, 1.

23. Ibid.

24. Habib Elahi Sahibzada, Shakirullah and Sadaf Naz. 'Education in the Ancient Greek Civilization – Lessons from the Past'. Ancient Pakistan, Vol XXVI. 2015.

25. Ut supra, 1.

26. Ibid.

27. Ibid.

28. Mark Griffith. 'Public and Private in Early Greek Institutions of Education'. In Lee Too, Education in Greek and Roman Antiquity. Brill, 2001.

29. Ut supra, 1.

30. Ibid.

31. Ibid.

32. Ibid.

33. Ibid.

34. Ibid.

35. Ibid.

36. Ibid.

37. Ibid.

38. Ibid.

39. Ibid.

40. Effie Sherwood Goozee. 'Roman education under the early Empire'. Boston University, College of Liberal Arts. 1923. 41 Ibid

41. Ibid.

42. Ibid.

43. Ut supra, 1.

44. Ibid.

45. Ibid.

46. New industries emerged, while old industries saw the continuous introduction of new methods, processes and machines; thus, old skills became irrelevant. Also, agricultural workers were no longer needed since farmers adopted new methods of food production.

47. Source: Ibid.

CHAPTER FIVE

The Abundance-Scarcity Paradox

1. Merriam-Webster (n.d.). Knowledge. In Merriam-Webster Dictionary. https://www.merriam-webster.com/dictionary/knowledge Accessed 11 April 2021.

2. 'The 6 Types Of Knowledge: From A Priori To Procedural'. Udemy, February 2020. https://blog.udemy.com/types-of-knowledge/ Accessed 11 April 2021.

3. Ibid.

4. Ibid.

5. Chris Drew. 'The 14 Types of Knowledge'. https://helpfulprofessor.com/types-of-knowledge/ Accessed 23 April 2021.

6. Ut supra, 2.

7. Ut supra, 5.

8. Ut supra, 2.

9. Ibid.

10. Ibid.

CHAPTER SIX

The Gaping Hole and Blind Spots

1. Elizabeth Culotta. 'Roots of Racism'. Science, 18 May 2012. Vol. 336, Issue 6083, pp. 825–827.

2. Ibid.

3. Kubota, J, Banaji, M and Phelps, E 'The neuroscience of race' Nat Neurosci 15, 940–948 (2012).

4. William Wan and Sarah Kaplan. 'Why are people still racist? What science says about America's race problem'. Washington Post, 14 August 2017.

5. National Museum of African American History & Culture. 'Historical Foundations Of Race'. https://nmaahc.si.edu/learn/talking-about-race/topics/historical-foundations-race Accessed 8 July 2021.

6. Ibid.

7. Ibid.

8. Ron Malhotra. How To Speak Like the World's Top Public Speakers. KMD Books, October 2020.

9. Jeffery Robinson. 'Five Truths About Black History'. ACLU, https://www.aclu.org/issues/racial-justice/five-truths-about-black-history Accessed 13 July 2021.

10. 'A history of Apartheid in South Africa'. South African History Online, https://www.sahistory.org.za/article/history-apartheid-south-africa#:~:text=Across%20the%20world%2C%20racism%20is,their%20jobs%2C%20culture%20and%20language 6 May 2016. Accessed 15 July 2021.

11. Alistair Boddy-Evans. 'The Origins of Apartheid in South Africa'. ThoughtCo, 5 December 2019. https://www.thoughtco.com/when-did-apartheid-start-south-africa-43460 Accessed 15 July 2021.

12. Britannica, The Editors of Encyclopaedia. 'John Wilkes Booth'. Encyclopedia Britannica, 6 May 2021, https://www.britannica.com/biography/John-Wilkes-Booth Accessed 18 July 2021.

13. Peter Morrall. 'Murder and society: why commit murder?' Crime and Justice, 2007.

14. Ann O'Neill. 'Stolen kids turned into terrifying killers'. CNN, 12 February 2007.

15. John Hall. 'ISIS is brainwashing children to murder their own parents, child soldier who escaped from Raqqa reveals'. Independent, 18 January 2016.

16. 'Patriarchy'. Merriam-Webster.com Dictionary, Merriam-Webster, https://www.merriam-webster.com/dictionary/patriarchy Accessed 19 July 2021.

17. Zack Sharf. 'Heather Graham Says Harvey Weinstein Implied She Had to Have Sex With Him to Be Cast in His Film'. IndieWire, https://www.indiewire.com/2017/10/heather-graham-harvey-weinstein-sexual-harrasment-movie-role-1201885876/ 10 October 2017. Accessed 20 July 2021.

18. Vladimir Hernandez. "Jose Mujica: The world's 'poorest' president" BBC, 15 November 2012.

19. Lorraine Murray. "José Mujica" Encyclopedia Britannica, 16 May 2021, https://www.britannica.com/biography/Jose-Mujica Accessed 26 July 2021.

20. Giles Tremlett. 'José Mujica: is this the world's most radical president?' The Guardian, 18 September 2014.

21. Victor Oluwole. 'Mapped: The 25 Poorest Countries in the World'. Business Insider Africa, 21 May 2021.

22. 'Pierre Nkurunziza: Burundi leader to get $530,000 and luxury villa'. BBC, 22 January 2020.

23. Ibid.

24. Ut supra, 20.

25. Federica Durante and Susan T Fiske. 'How Social-Class Stereotypes Maintain Inequality'. Curr Opin Psychol., December 2017. 18: 43–48.

26. Katherine M Gehl. 'US politics isn't broken. It's fixed'. TED, December 2020, https://www.ted.com/talks/katherine_m_gehl_

us_politics_isn_t_broken_it_s_fixed?language=en

27. Ibid.

28. Jonathan Rauch. 'How American Politics Went Insane'. The Atlantic, July/August 2016 Issue.

29. Chris Stedman. 'The 'atheist Pope Francis'? Uruguay's president draws comparisons'. Religion News Service, 22 May 2014. https://religionnews.com/2014/05/22/atheist-pope-francis-uruguays-president-draws-comparisons/ Accessed 28 July 2021.

30. The Associated Press. 'Obama sets record straight on his religion'. NBC News, 21 January 2008.

31. Prerna Kundu. 'Indians vote on caste, religion because they lack information on MP, MLA performance: Study'. ThePrint, 12 April 2020. https://theprint.in/opinion/indians-vote-on-caste-religion-because-they-lack-information-on-mp-mla-performance-study/400141/ Accessed 29 July 2021.

32. Alison Saldanha. 'How caste and religion influence selection of political leaders in India'. Business Standard, 18 July 2018. https://www.business-standard.com/article/politics/how-caste-and-religion-influence-selection-of-political-leaders-in-india-118071800122_1.html Accessed 29 July 2021.

33. Anil Ananthaswamy and Kate Douglas. 'The origins of sexism: How men came to rule 12,000 years ago'. NewScientist, 18 April 2018. https://www.newscientist.com/article/mg23831740-400-the-origins-of-sexism-how-men-came-to-rule-12000-years-ago/ Accessed 29 July 2021.

34. Kate Tuttle. 'Tracing the roots of misogyny to ancient Greece and Rome with Mary Beard'. Los Angeles Times, 28 December 2017.

35. Cydney Grannan. 'Has Pink Always Been a 'Girly' Color?' Britannica, https://www.britannica.com/story/has-pink-always-been-a-girly-color Accessed 29 July 2021.

36. Ibid.

37. 'Voting Rights for Women'. Library of Congress, https://www.loc.gov/classroom-materials/elections/right-to-vote/voting-rights-for-women/#:~:text=Since%201878%2C%20a%20women's%20suffrage,proposed%20each%20year%20in%20Congress.&text=With%20these%20words%2C%20-Congress%20at,state%20on%20account%20of%20sex Accessed 30 July 2021.

38. Constance Grady. 'The waves of feminism, and why people keep fighting over them, explained'. Vox, 20 July 2018.

39. Ibid.

40. Brandon Ambrosino. 'How and why did religion evolve?' BBC Future, 19 April 2019.

41. Pew Research Center. 'Religion in India: Tolerance and Segregation'. Pew Research Center, 29 June 2021. https://www.pewforum.org/2021/06/29/religion-in-india-tolerance-and-segregation/Accessed 31 July 2021.

42. Ibid.

43. Ibid.

44. Ibid.

45. Jalal Baig. 'Opinion: Muslim doctor: My patient refused to let me treat her because of my religion'. The Washington Post, 10 August 2016.

46. Britannica, The Editors of Encyclopaedia. 'Al-Qaeda'. Encyclopedia Britannica, 6 February 2019, https://www.britannica.com/topic/al-Qaeda Accessed 1 August 2021.

47. Ibid.

48. On 11 September 2001, the hijackers boarded four domestic flights all bound for the West Coast from the East Coast. Immediately after take-off, they disabled the crews and seized control of the airplane. The first plane, which took off from

Boston, was piloted into the north tower of the World Trade Center, New York City. Many thought this to be an accident. But when the second plane, also from Boston, crashed into the south tower seventeen minutes later, it was obvious that the nation was under attack. The third plane struck the west side of the Pentagon, while the fourth plane's attack was foiled because the passengers had already been informed of the attack, however, the plane crashed, killing forty people. Source: Bergen, Peter L. 'September 11 attacks'. Encyclopedia Britannica, 10 September 2020, https://www.britannica.com/event/September-11-attacks Accessed 1 August 2021.

49. Miriam Cooke. 'Near Middle East/North Africa Studies: Culture'. In: International Encyclopedia of the Social & Behavioral Sciences (Second Edition). Edited by James D Wright, Elsevier, 2015.

50. Henry McDonald. 'Jesus wept … oh, it's bad plumbing. Indian rationalist targets "miracles"'. The Guardian, 23 November 2012.

51. Ibid.

52. Kif Leswing. 'Here's how big tech companies like Google and Facebook set salaries for software engineers'. CNBC, 15 June 2019.

53. Quora. 'They Say You'll Never Get Rich Working as an Employee … but They Are Wrong'. Inc., 14 April 2017.

CHAPTER SEVEN

Indoctrination: Education's imperceptible aberration

1. Cambridge Dictionary. 'Indoctrination'. Cambridge Dictionary, https://dictionary.cambridge.org/dictionary/english/indoctrination Accessed 2 August 2021.

2. Sarah Harris. 'Left-handed children 'still penalised' because teachers fail to spot signs they are struggling and do not know

how to help them'. The Daily Mail, 14 August 2017.

3. Scott Korb. 'The Soul-Crushing Student Essay' The New York Times, 21 April 2018. https://www.nytimes.com/2018/04/21/opinion/the-soul-crushing-student-essay.html Accessed 3 August 2021.

CHAPTER NINE

Consequences of indoctrination: The centre cannot hold

1. The murder rate of Los Cabos in Mexico was 138.26 for every 100,000 people living in the city. Source: Statista. 'Ranking of the most dangerous cities in the world in 2020, by murder rate per 100,000 inhabitants'. April 2020.

2. South Sudan and Somalia ranks first and second for the most unstable countries in the world. They rank low for refugees, factionalised elites, and human rights, among other indices. Source: 'These are the 25 most unstable countries in the world'. Business Insider, 26 July 2021.

CHAPTER TEN

Overcoming Indoctrination: Unlearning, Learning, Relearning

1. Mark Bonchek. 'Why the Problem with Learning Is Unlearning'. Harvard Business Review, 3 November 2016.

2. Morena Duwe. 'Daryl Davis: the black musician who converts Ku Klux Klan members'. The Guardian, 18 March 2020.

3. Daryl befriended more Klansmen and as they quit the organisation, they gave him their robes. Source: Ibid.

4. Ibid.

5. By allowing their employees to work from home, FlexJobs were able to save money that could have been channelled to overhead, real estate costs, transit subsidies and continuity of operations. Source: Emily Courtney. 'The Benefits of Working From Home:

Why The Pandemic Isn't the Only Reason to Work Remotely'. FlexJobs, https://www.flexjobs.com/blog/post/benefits-of-remote-work/ Accessed 21 August 2021.

6. Kim Parker, Juliana Menasce Horowitz and Rachel Minkin. 'How the COVID-19 Outbreak Has – and Hasn't – Changed the Way Americans Work'. Pew Research Center, 9 December 2020. https://www.pewresearch.org/social-trends/2020/12/09/how-the-coronavirus-outbreak-has-and-hasnt-changed-the-way-americans-work/ Accessed 22 August 2021.

7. Gad Levanon. 'Remote Work: The Biggest Legacy Of Covid-19'. Forbes, 23 November 2020.

8. Jennifer Liu. 'How companies are preparing employees for long-term work-from-home'. CNBC, 25 August 2020.

CHAPTER ELEVEN

The Autonomy of Thought

1. Simon McCarthy-Jones. 'The Autonomous Mind: The Right to Freedom of Thought in the Twenty-First Century'. Frontiers in Artificial Intelligence, 26 September 2019.

2. Berlyne, DE, Vinacke, W Edgar and Sternberg, Robert J. 'Thought'. Encyclopedia Britannica, 14 May 2008, https://www.britannica.com/topic/thought Accessed 27 August 2021.

3. Erica Goode. 'How Culture Molds Habits Of Thought'. New York Times, 8 August 2000.

4. Lindsey Smith. 'American Plantation Slave Culture'.

5. Viktor Frankl. Man's Search For Meaning. Beacon Press, 2006.

6. During the trial, the defence attorney relied on racial stereotypes to make his argument for Derek Chauvin. He insisted that George Floyd had died as a result of drug addiction and not because Chauvin restrained him. About the trial, Fern L Johnson and Marlene G Fine wrote: 'From the beginning of the trial,

the defence relied on a narrative rife with racist stereotypes that have been recycled over and over about black people, especially black men: that they are drug addicts, criminals, loud and angry, and therefore, dangerous ... The defence's argument relied on stereotypes of black men: George Floyd was big. He was strong. He was on drugs. He had underlying health conditions that black people have because of the way they live. He had adrenalin pumping through him to amplify his strength.' Source: Fern L Johnson and Marlene G Fine. 'Derek Chauvin Was Convicted. But The Racist Story Of His Defense Remains'. WBUR, 23 April 2021.

7. Staff members at the facility where Derek Chauvin was held after the murder said that only white officers were allowed to guard him. Eight officers filed complaints stating that they were prevented from bringing Chauvin to his cell or being on the same floor with him. All of the officers were people of colour while half were black. In response to the complaint, the superintendent, Mr Steve Lydon said that 'he had segregated employees because he believed having people of colour interact with Chauvin could have "heightened ongoing trauma".' He further stated that he made the decision on short notice and that it only lasted for forty-five minutes before he realised that he had made a mistake, after which he reversed the order and apologised. The aggrieved officers pointed out that Mr Lydon's statement was inaccurate as the order lasted longer and even affected a shift two days later. Source: Nicholas Bogel-Burroughs. 'Jail that held officer who knelt on George Floyd accused of racial bias after only allowing white staff to guard him.' Independent, 22 June 2020.

8. Bullock, Alan, Bullock, Baron, Lukacs, John and Knapp, Wilfrid F. 'Adolf Hitler'. Encyclopedia Britannica, 26 April 2021, https://www.britannica.com/biography/Adolf-Hitler Accessed 15

September 2021.

9. 'Adolf Hitler'. History, 29 October 2009, https://www.history.com/topics/world-war-ii/adolf-hitler-1#:~:text=After%20his%20father%2C%20Alois%2C%20retired,school%20and%20eventually%20dropped%20out Accessed 15 September 2021.

10. Ira Katznelson. 'What America Taught the Nazis'. The Atlantic, November 2017 Issue.

11. Christina Skreiberg. 'Here's Why Norway Is Consistently Rated The Best Place In The World To Live'. HuffPost, 19 January 2018.

12. Eric Wargo. 'The Mechanics of Choice'. Association for Psychological Science, 28 December 2011.

13. Dr Daniel Hale Williams was the first cardiologist to successfully perform a complex open-heart surgery – the repair of the pericardium. Charles Drew developed new storage methods for preserving blood for transfusions and created the first blood bank. Benjamin Banneker was known for his skill in mathematics and astronomy. He contradicted the forecasts of prominent mathematicians and astronomers of his time when he successfully predicted the solar eclipse of 14 April 1789. Mae Jemison was a NASA astronaut and the first African-American woman to reach space.

CHAPTER TWELVE

Sixteen Desirable Skill Elements

1. Chuck Swoboda. 'Why "Thinking Outside The Box" Is The Wrong Way To Approach Innovation'. Forbes, 3 August 2020.

2. Helmut Schuster. 'ORIGINAL THINKING: How to think like an entrepreneur'. LinkedIn, 1 October 2019. https://www.linkedin.com/pulse/original-thinking-how-think-like-entrepreneur-helmut-schuster/ Accessed 23 September 2021.

3. Ibid.

4. Ibid.

5. Ibid.

6. Ibid.

7. Sahil Bloom. 'First Principles Thinking'. LinkedIn, 1 January 2021. https://www.linkedin.com/pulse/first-principles-thinking-sahil-bloom/ Accessed 27 September 2021.

8. Ibid.

9. Ibid.

10. Ibid.

11. Britannica, The Editors of Encyclopaedia. 'Intuition'. Encyclopedia Britannica, 4 March 2012, https://www.britannica.com/topic/intuition Accessed 28 September 2021.

12. Francesca McCartney. 'Intuitive Children'. Academy of Intuition Medicine, https://intuitionmedicine.org/intuitive-children/#:~:text=All%20children%20are%20born%20with,than%20the%20other%20five%20senses.&text=This%20intuitive%20skill%20is%20clairvoyance,perceiving%20energy%20patterns%20and%20information Accessed 28 September 2021.

13. Ibid.

14. Ibid.

15. Ibid.

16. Sunny Bonnell. '4 Leaders Who Won by Following Their Instincts (Despite Being Told They Were Crazy)'. Inc., 22 January 2018.

17. Ibid.

18. Phil Lewis. 'The Most Valuable Skill In Difficult Times Is Lateral Thinking – Here's How To Do It'. Forbes, 20 March 2020.

19. In a time when science hadn't evolved to the point it is now, Solomon could actually tell the parentage of a child without a

DNA test. Two women living together had given birth around the same period. One night, the first woman rolled over her baby as she slept and the child died, so she exchanged her dead child with the child of the second woman. When the second woman got up in the morning and noticed the dead child, she said it wasn't hers. However, the first woman insisted that the living child was hers while the dead one was that of the other woman. The matter was brought before King Solomon. As the women continued to argue in his palace, Solomon asked for a sword. He said he would divide the living child into two so each woman would have a part. The first woman agreed with the judgement, saying it's best none of them got the child. However, the second woman cried for the child not to be killed; for her, it was better that the child be handed to the woman. With this action that proved motherly love, Solomon knew that the second woman was the actual mother of the child, and he commanded that the child be handed to her. Source: 1 Kings 3:16-28

20. Saga Briggs. 'How to Cultivate Lateral Thinking'. Open Colleges, 21 June 2020. https://www.opencolleges.edu.au/informed/features/cultivate-lateral-thinking/#:~:text=Edward%20de%20Bono%20proposed%20four,stimulation%2C%20alternatives%2C%20and%20alteration.&text=De%20Bono%20thought%20we%20should,first%20step%20toward%20greater%20innovation Accessed 1 October 2021.

21. Roshan Thiran. 'Leadership Is Influence'. Leaderonomics.com, 15 August 2018. https://www.leaderonomics.com/articles/leadership/leadership-is-influence Accessed 2 October 2021.

22. Matt Gavin. '5 Characteristics Of A Courageous Leader'. Harvard Business School Online, 3 March 2020.

23. Richard Nordquist. 'What is Communication?' ThoughtCo, 19 September 2019.

24. James Clear. 'Deliberate Practice: What It Is and How to Use It'. James Clear, https://jamesclear.com/deliberate-practice-theory#:~:text=Deliberate%20practice%20refers%20to%20a,specific%20goal%20of%20improving%20performance Accessed 2 October 2021.

25. 'What Is Purpose?' Greater Good Magazine, https://greatergood.berkeley.edu/topic/purpose/definition Accessed 2 October 2021.

CHAPTER THIRTEEN

A New Kind of Education

1. Jason Fell. 'Tony Robbins on the 7 "Forces" of Business Mastery'. Entrepreneur, 23 December 2013.

BONUS CHAPTER ONE

Cases Where Conventional Education Has Gotten It Right

1. 'The power of education: Inspiring stories from four continents'. UNESCO, 10 July 2019. https://en.unesco.org/news/power-education-inspiring-stories-four-continents Accessed 25 February 2021.

2. Tamil Nadu Rural Transformation Project. Tribal Development Plan. Final Report. April 2017.

3. 'Dr Martin Luther King Education: The Schooling of Martin Luther King Jr'. http://drmartinlutherking.net/martin-luther-king-education. Accessed 26 February 2021.

4. 'Civil Disobedience by Henry David Thoreau'. https://www.enotes.com/topics/civil-disobedience#:~:text=%E2%80%9CCivil%20Disobedience%E2%80%9D%20by%20Henry%20David,slavery%20and%20the%20Mexican%20War Accessed 26 February 2021.

5. 'William Kamkwamba (Inventor)'. TED, https://www.ted.com/speakers/william_kamkwamba#:~:text=To%20power%20his%20family's%20home,Boy%20Who%20Harnessed%20the%20Wind.%22 Accessed 26 February 2021.

6. William Kamkwamba and Bryan Mealer. The Boy Who Harnessed the Wind: Creating Currents of Electricity and Hope. Amazon, 29 September 2009. https://www.amazon.com/Boy-Who-Harnessed-Wind-Electricity/dp/0061730327?tag=tedspeakers-20&geniuslink=true Accessed 26 February 2021.

7. Elizabeth King. 'Education is Fundamental to Development and Growth'. World Bank Blogs, 28 January 2011.

8. Beata Souders. 'Motivation in Education: What it Takes to Motivate Our Kids'. Positive Psychology, 11 December 2020.

9. National Academies of Sciences, Engineering, and Medicine. How People Learn II: Learners, Contexts, and Cultures. Washington, DC: The National Academies Press, 2018. p 110.

10. Deborah Grayson Riegel. 'Stay Motivated When Feedback Is Scarce'. Harvard Business Review, 2 June 2020.

11. Paulo Coelho. '1 MIN READING: The fisherman and the businessman'. Paulo Coelho Writer Official Site, 4 September 2015.

12. Saga Briggs. 'The Ultimate Lesson: Teaching Your Students to Be Resourceful'. Open Colleges, 18 July 2015. https://www.opencolleges.edu.au/informed/features/the-ultimate-lesson-teaching-your-students-to-be-resourceful/ Accessed 28 February 2021.

13. Ibid.

14. Kevon Saber. '3 Ideas For Cultivating Creativity At Work'. Fast Company, 13 December 2012.

15. Marion Poetz, Nikolaus Franke, Martin Schreier. 'Sometimes the Best Ideas Come from Outside Your Industry'. Harvard

Business Review, 21 November 2014.

16. Ahmad Z, Sadiq S, Asghar M, Khan AR, Arif O, Shah SH, Nadeem S, Waseem Y, Aibani R, Syed AS, Mustafa RM, Abdulrahman Z, Fatima K. 'Comparison of Knowledge, Attitudes, and Practices of Educated and Uneducated Adults Regarding Human Immunodeficiency Virus in Karachi, Pakistan'. Cureus, 9(6). 2017.

17. John Akec. 'Reflection On The Role of Education In Society'. Somaliland Sun, 29 August 2020. https://www.somalilandsun.com/reflection-on-the-role-of-education-in-society/ Accessed 9 March 2021.

18. Lawson Luke. 'The Role of Illiteracy in Conflict and Development'. Booksie, 3 March 2015. https://www.booksie.com/posting/lawson-luke/the-role-of-illiteracy-in-conflict-and-development-422874 Accessed 9 March 2021.

19. World Literacy Foundation. 'The Economic & Social Cost of Illiteracy'. A white paper presented at World Literacy Summit, Oxford, United Kingdom. March 2018.

20. Ut supra, 18.

21. Ut supra, 19.

22. Van Anderson. 'Letters: Uneducated people, a dream for politicians'. The Advocate, 9 December 2016. https://www.theadvocate.com/baton_rouge/opinion/letters/article_9c861d84-bcc8-11e6-8e5c-efcb4ada5bac.html Accessed 9 March 2021.

23. Ibid.

24. Isaac Mohr. 'Uneducated Voters Have Disturbing Effect On Elections'. CBS News, 6 November 2008.

25. In the 2016 election, Hillary Clinton won 66% of the votes in better-educated counties in Iowa, but had only 27% in less-educated ones. Michael Sances, an assistant professor in the Department of Political Science at Temple University, noted

that the shift in the educational divide was decisive to Trump's victory. If the counties in the bottom 10% of America's education distribution had stuck to the past voting behaviour, Clinton would have tied with Trump. And if 20% of the education distribution had maintained the same behaviour, she would have won. One reason for the Democrats' loss was that left-leaning programs like Medicare for all were only popular with well-educated liberals. Source: 'Poorly educated workers hold the keys to the White House'. The Economist, 11 November 2019.

26. Pravit Rojanaphruk. 'Taking voting rights away from poor and uneducated not the answer: election commissioner'. The Nation Thailand, 20 December 2013. https://www.nationthailand.com/politics/30222629 Accessed 9 March 2021.

27. Maris A. Vinovskis. 'Horace Mann on the Economic Productivity of Education'. The New England Quarterly, Vol. 43, No. 4 (Dec., 1970), pp. 550-571.

28. Ut supra, 19.

29. Ibid.

30. The cause was championed by the Egyptian author Alaa al Aswany and former Egyptian vice-president and Nobel Laureate for Peace Mohamed ElBaradei. Source: Ibid.

31. Godfrey Olukya. 'The Billion-Dollar Cryptocurrency Scams You've Never Heard About'. OZY, 24 February 2020. https://www.ozy.com/around-the-world/the-billion-dollar-crypto-currency-scams-youve-never-heard-about/266860/ Accessed 10 March 2021.

BONUS CHAPTER TWO

The New Kind of Education and the Tripartite Nature of Humankind

1. James Hamblin. 'I Quit Showering, and Life Continued'. The Atlantic, 9 June 2016.

2. AC Grimes. 'The Untold Truth Of The World's Dirtiest Man'. The Grunge, 26 November 2019. https://www.grunge.com/176687/the-untold-truth-of-the-worlds-dirtiest-man/ Accessed 1 March 2021.

3. Yvette Brazier. 'What was medicine like in prehistoric times?' Medical News Today, 2 November 2018. https://www.medicalnewstoday.com/articles/323556 Accessed 2 March 2021.

4. Ibid.

5. Stanford University – School of Humanities and Sciences. 'Neanderthal extinction linked to human diseases'. ScienceDaily, 7 November 2019. https://www.sciencedaily.com/releases/2019/11/191107160610.htm Accessed 2 March 2021.

6. Maev Kennedy. 'Neanderthals may have died of diseases carried by humans in Africa'. The Guardian, 10 April 2016.

7. Tegan Taylor. 'Were our grandparents really healthier than us?' ABC News, 5 July 2018.

8. Ibid.

9. Sharon Basaraba. 'A Guide To Longevity Throughout History: Increases in Life Span From Prehistory Through the Modern Era'. VeryWellHealth, 24 April 2020.

10. Deborah Mackenzie. 'More education is what makes people live longer, not more money'. NewScientist, 18 April 2018.

11. The first irrigation systems arose in 6000BC in the Tigris-Euphrates River valley in Mesopotamia and the Nile River valley in Egypt. Sailing ships were first used on the Nile River in 4000BC, while iron was produced in 1200BC. Source: Erik Gregersen. 'History of Technology Timeline'. Encyclopaedia Britannica. https://www.britannica.com/story/history-of-technology-timeline Accessed 3 March 2021.

12. 'Educational Reforms'. Lumen Learning, https://courses.lumenlearning.com/boundless-ushistory/chapter/educational-

reforms/ Accessed 3 March 2021.

13. The first railway locomotive was built in Wales by Richard Trevithick in 1804, while Robert Fulton built the steamboat in 1807. Samuel Morse sent the first message over a telegraph line in 1844, while Alexander Graham Bell made the first telephone call in 1876, same year Nikolaus Otto built the internal combustion engine, which was used to power automobiles in 1885. Source: Ut supra, 11.

14. The Editors of Encyclopaedia Britannica. 'Nat Turner'. Encyclopaedia Britannica, 7 November 2020. https://www.britannica.com/biography/Nat-Turner Accessed 11 March 2021.

15. Colette Coleman. 'How Literacy Became a Powerful Weapon in the Fight to End Slavery'. History, 17 June 2020. https://www.history.com/news/nat-turner-rebellion-literacy-slavery Accessed 11 March 2021.

16. Ibid.

17. Ibid.

18. Ibid.

19. Ibid.

20. Ibid.

21. Ibid.

22. Holocaust Encyclopedia. 'Book Burning'. United States Holocaust Memorial Museum.

23. United States Holocaust Memorial Museum. 'Nazi Book Burning'. YouTube. https://youtu.be/yHzM1gXaiVo

24. Loulla-Mae Eleftheriou-Smith. 'George Stinney Jr: Black 14-year-old boy exonerated 70 years after he was executed'. Independent, 18 December 2014.

25. If convicted, Chauvin may face up to forty years in prison for second-degree murder, twenty-five years for third-degree murder and ten years for second-degree manslaughter. Source: Brad Parks,

Aaron Cooper and Eric Levenson. 'Judge reinstates third-degree murder charge against Derek Chauvin in George Floyd's death'. CNN, 12 March 2021.

26. Rebecca Winthrop. 'Learning to live together: How education can help fight systemic racism'. Brookings, 5 June 2020. https://www.brookings.edu/blog/education-plus-development/2020/06/05/learning-to-live-together-how-education-can-help-fight-systemic-racism/ Accessed 12 March 2021.

27. Ut supra, 14.

28. Joshua J Mark. 'Bible'. World History Encyclopedia, 2 September 2009. https://www.ancient.eu/bible/ Accessed 14 March 2021.

29. 'What is the Meaning of the Word "Quran"?' Ask the Sheik, 1 February 2012. http://www.askthesheikh.com/what-is-the-meaning-of-the-word-quran/ Accessed 14 March 2021.

30. Merriam-Webster (n.d.). Veda. In Merriam-Webster Dictionary. https://www.merriam-webster.com/dictionary/Veda. Accessed 14 March 2021.

31. Daniel M Hungerman. 'The Effect of Education on Religion: Evidence from Compulsory Schooling Laws'. University of Notre Dame and NBER, 2013.

32. 'Canada: Religious affiliation in 2011'. Statista.

33. Ut supra, 31.

34. 'In US, Decline of Christianity Continues at Rapid Race'. Pew Research Center, 17 October 2019. https://www.pewforum.org/2019/10/17/in-u-s-decline-of-christianity-continues-at-rapid-pace/Accessed 14 March 2021.

35. Ibid.

36. Ann M McGreevy and Susan H Copley. 'Spirituality and Education: Nurturing Connections in Schools and Classrooms'. The Spirit of Education. Vol 2, No. 4. 1999.